SELF-EMPLOYED WORKERS ORGANIZE

Self-Employed Workers Organize

Law, Policy, and Unions

Cynthia J. Cranford
Judy Fudge
Eric Tucker
Leah F. Vosko

McGill-Queen's University Press
Montreal & Kingston · London · Ithaca

© McGill-Queen's University Press 2005
ISBN 0-7735-2872-5 (cloth)
ISBN 0-7765-2901-2 (paperback)

Legal deposit first quarter 2005
Bibliothèque nationale du Québec

Printed in Canada on acid-free paper that is 100% ancient forest free (100% post-consumer recycled), processed chlorine free.

This book has been published with the help of a grant from the Social Sciences and Humanities Research Council of Canada.

McGill-Queen's University Press acknowledges the support of the Canada Council for the Arts for our publishing program. We also acknowledge the financial support of the Government of Canada through the Book Publishing Industry Development Program (BPIDP) for our publishing activities.

Library and Archives Canada Cataloguing in Publication

Self-employed workers organize: law, policy, and unions / Cynthia J. Cranford ... [et al.].

Includes bibliographical references and index
ISBN 0-7735-2872-5 (bound)
ISBN 0-7735-2901-2 (pbk.)

1. Self-employed – Legal status, laws, etc. – Canada – Case studies. 2. Labor unions – Canada – Case studies. I. Cranford, Cynthia J., 1971-

HD8037.C3S44 2005   331.88   C2004-904880-5

This book was typeset by Interscript Inc. in 10/13 Sabon.

Contents

Figures and Tables   vii
Acronyms   ix
Acknowledgments   xi
Introduction   3

1   *Star* Wars: Newspaper Distribution Workers and the Possibilities and Limits of Collective Bargaining   29
    ERIC TUCKER

2   Deemed to be Entrepreneurs: Rural Route Mail Couriers and Canada Post   56
    JUDY FUDGE

3   From Precarious Workers to Unionized Employees and Back Again?: The Challenges of Organizing Personal-Care Workers in Ontario   96
    CYNTHIA J. CRANFORD

4   The Precarious Status of the Artist: Freelance Editors' Struggle for Collective Bargaining Rights   136
    LEAH F. VOSKO

Conclusion: What Have We Learned?   171
Notes   193
References   233
Index   249

Figures and Tables

FIGURES

1 Self-Employment as a Share of Total Employment, Own-Account (OASE), and Employers (SEE), 1976–2000   10

2 Class of Worker by Immigrant Status and Sex, and Visible Minority Status and Sex, 2000   11

TABLE

1 Type of Self-Employment by Immigrant Status, Visible Minority Status, and Sex, 2000   28

Acronyms

ARRMC	Association of Rural Route Mail Couriers
CAPPRT	Canadian Artists and Producers Professional Relations Tribunal
CAW	Canadian Auto Workers
CCAC	Community Care Access Centre
CEP	Communications, Energy and Paperworkers Union of Canada
CILT	Centre for Independent Living in Toronto
CIRB	Canadian Industrial Relations Board
CLC	Canadian Labour Congress
CMA	Census Metropolitan Area
CNA	Canadian Newspaper Association
CPAA	Canadian Postmasters and Assistants' Association
CPP	Canada Pension Plan
CSIS	Canadian Security Intelligence Service
CTCU	Canadian Textile and Chemical Union
CUPE	Canadian Union of Public Employees
CUPW	Canadian Union of Postal Workers
CWA	Communication Workers of America
DGC	Directors' Guild of Canada
EAC/ACR	Editors' Association of Canada
EI	Employment Insurance
ESA	*Employment Standards Act*
GIS	Guaranteed Income Support
GST	Goods and Services Tax

ICMA	International Circulation Managers Association
ILO	International Labour Organization
ILRCs	Independent Living Resource Centres
LCUC	Letter Carriers' Union of Canada
NAALC	North American Accord on Labour Cooperation
NAFTA	North American Free Trade Agreement
NAO	National Administrative Office
NDP	New Democratic Party
NLRA	*National Labor Relations Act* (USA)
NLRB	National Labor Relations Board (USA)
OASE	Own-Account Self-Employment
OECD	Organization for Economic Development
OHSA	*Occupational Health and Safety Act*
OLRA	*Ontario Labour Relations Act*
OLRB	Ontario Labour Relations Board
OMA	Ontario Medical Association
OPSEU	Ontario Public Service Employees Union
ORRMC	Organization of Rural Route Mail Couriers
PWAC	Periodical Writers Association of Canada
QPP	Quebec Pension Plan
PUC	Playwrights' Union of Canada
RSMC	Rural and Suburban Mail Couriers
RWDSU	Retail, Wholesale, and Department Store Union
SAA	*Status of the Artist Act*
SartEc	Société des auteurs de radio, télévision et cinéma
SEIU	Service Employees International Union
SEE	Self-Employed Employers
SLID	Survey of Labour and Income Dynamics
SSLU	Social Support Living Units
TWUC	The Writers' Union of Canada
TTA	Temporary Technical Assistant
UNEQ	Union des écrivaines et des écrivains québécois
UPS	United Parcel Service
WFP	*Winnipeg Free Press*
WGC	Writers' Guild of Canada
WSIB	Workplace Safety and Insurance Board (Ontario)

Acknowledgments

Self-Employed Workers Organize: Law, Policy, and Unions is a collaborative endeavour. Its introduction and conclusion are jointly authored. Eric Tucker is principal author of chapter 1, Judy Fudge of chapter 2, Cynthia Cranford of chapter 3, and Leah Vosko of chapter 4. Each of the sole-authored chapters benefited from the comments and input of the other collaborators.

This book grew out of a five-year Community University Research Alliance (CURA) on Contingent Work funded by the Social Sciences and Humanities Research Council, and it was supported by the Law Commission of Canada for a related project on the legal definition of employment.

Jackie Esmonde, Beth Jackson, Kate Laxer, and Albert Wallrap served as research assistants for the project – we thank them for their diligence and their careful work. For his able and meticulous assistance in editing and formatting the manuscript, we thank Brent Arnold. We also benefited from the comments of two anonymous manuscript reviewers, the editorial assistance of Mary Williams for McGill-Queen's University Press, and the careful work of Barbara Schon, who prepared the index.

We are especially grateful to all of our community and university colleagues in the CURA, particularly researchers in its legal stream: Stephanie Bernstein, Mary Gellatly, Katherine Lippel, Chris Schenk, and Lynn Spink. Each provided vital feedback at key moments in the preparation of the manuscript, as did Abigail Bakan, who chaired a session on the case studies in the book. Cynthia Cranford also thanks Jenny Anh, president of Local 40 of the Canadian Auto Workers; the workers who agreed to be interviewed for her study; and Robert Wilton, for his love and support. For their contributions to her chapter, Judy Fudge thanks Sue Eybel, the Canadian Union of Postal Workers, and the Organization of Rural Route Mail Couriers for sharing time and documents regarding the campaigns to organize rural and suburban mail couriers, and Osgoode Hall Law School, York University, for a research fellowship that supported her initial research on this topic. Eric Tucker extends his thanks to Howard Law from CEP for his comments on an earlier draft and to Lisa Brand for her love and support through a difficult time. Finally, Leah Vosko thanks the executive director of the Editors' Association of Canada, Connie John; the editors she interviewed for her study; Josée Dubois, Samantha Maislin-Dickson, and Lorraine Farkas of the Canadian Artists and Producers Professional Relations Tribunal; and Gerald Kernerman for his love and support.

Our hope is that, in some small way, this book contributes to self-employed workers' efforts to better their conditions by telling the stories of their struggles.

C.J.C., J.F., E.T., and L.F.V., summer 2004

SELF-EMPLOYED WORKERS ORGANIZE

Introduction

Early every morning, 2,000 men and women, many of whom have recently immigrated to Canada, deliver the *Toronto Star* to tens of thousands of homes in metropolitan Toronto. This job is their primary source of income. Five days a week, about 6,000 couriers – a significant majority of whom are women – drive across rural and suburban Canada delivering the mail. Every day in Toronto, hundreds of women, many of them members of visible minorities and new to Canada, travel to work in private homes, providing personal care for disabled, ill, and elderly people. Across Canada, professional editors – primarily women – work at home, compiling indexes, making tables, and plying the skills of their trade for a variety of clients. In recent years, each of these groups of workers has tried to use the law to obtain collective bargaining rights. They have faced an uphill battle. In every case, their self-employed status was a contentious legal issue.

Despite differences in the kinds of work they do, their labour markets, and their social situations, *Toronto Star* newspaper carriers, rural route mail couriers, personal-care workers, and freelance editors have a common bond: their employment relations diverge from the employment norm that has been the lynchpin of Canadian labour law since World War II. That norm is best characterized as a continuous, full-time employment relationship in which the worker has one employer and works on the employer's premises or under his or her supervision

(Buechtemann and Quack 1990, 315; Muckenberger 1989, 267; Schellenberg and Clark 1996, 1). In Canada, the standard employment relationship is associated with the rise of mass production and industrial unionism in the 1940s. Because newspaper carriers, rural route mail couriers, personal-care workers, and freelance editors do not conform to this employment norm, they have faced difficulties in availing themselves of the protections offered by collective bargaining law. Moreover, even when they have obtained bargaining rights, the way in which their work is organized has made them vulnerable to other techniques for restructuring the employment relationship – such as contracting out – causing them to lose these rights.

Recent attempts by these four groups of workers to obtain some form of collective representation and bargaining is the subject of this book. We selected these groups because the problems they have faced in accessing labour law reflects those faced by a growing share of the employed population: self-employed workers. Self-employed workers have an ambiguous status. Traditionally, self-employment has been equated with entrepreneurship. Legally, it is considered a form of independent contracting and thus outside the ambit of labour protection and collective bargaining. But the evidence suggests that many of the self-employed, especially those who do not employ other workers, are much more like employees than they are like entrepreneurs. There is controversy over where to draw the line between employees and entrepreneurs when it comes to labour protection for the self-employed. In Canada, collective bargaining legislation specifically extends to dependent contractors – whose status lies between employee and independent contractor – but this has not resolved the difficulty of determining the legal status of self-employed workers.

In this book, we have used case studies, because they allow us to draw comparisons between different jurisdictions (federal and the province of Ontario), different labour markets (rural and urban), different sectors (public and private), different forms of collective bargaining legislation (collective bargaining and producers' legislation), different types of workers (skilled and unskilled, immigrant and native-born, women and men), and different types of organizations (unions and professional associations). Case studies are particularly useful for identifying the ways in which political and economic conditions interact with class, ethnicity, and gender to shape the experiences and strategies of working men and women. They also allow us to consider how organizing campaigns and collective bargaining strategies change over time.

Our case studies are based on policy and legal analysis of documents and legal decisions, as well as informant interviews. We have also analysed Statistics Canada data on self-employment to place the case studies in a broader context. Our goal is not to portray each of these cases as representative of the problems facing self-employed workers who want to organize and engage in collective bargaining; rather, the case studies illustrate the heterogeneity of self-employment and the range of strategies and institutions that people can use to improve their working conditions and standard of living.[1]

Since the 1980s, and especially in the 1990s, there has been what the Organization for Economic Co-operation and Development (OECD) calls a "partial renaissance" in self-employment,[2] which has generated an international and interdisciplinary debate over its significance and its causes. Many commentators emphasize the positive features of self-employment, especially its relationship with entrepreneurship, suggesting that the growth of employer self-employment in particular leads to job growth, greater autonomy, and higher incomes (Loufti 1991). By contrast, other commentators stress the diversity within the ranks of the self-employed, pointing out that, for many, entrepreneurship and self-employment do not coincide (Bögenhold and Staber 1991, 224; Dale 1991; Felstead 1991; Rainbird 1991). A large proportion of the self-employed are in very precarious economic situations, receiving low remuneration and enjoying little in the way of employment security or employment-related benefits (Dale 1991, 44). Not only is there a wide range in self-employment – from the self-employed professional who employs others, to the self-employed child-care provider who works alone out of her home – there is also the problem of disguised self-employment. The OECD noted that several countries, including Canada, "have seen growing numbers of self-employed people who work for just one company, and whose self-employment status may be little more than a device to reduce total taxes paid by the firms and the workers involved."[3]

In this introduction, we locate the case studies in the larger context of self-employment, provide an analytic framework for understanding different types of self-employment, and identify the features of Canadian collective bargaining law that make it difficult for self-employed workers to organize. This discussion is divided into two sections. The first draws upon sociological literature and recent statistics on self-employment in Canada to illustrate the problem of distinguishing between employees and the self-employed for the purpose of labour protection. The second section identifies those features of Canadian labour law that make it difficult for non-standard workers in general and the self-employed in particular to participate in collective bargaining.

1. CONFUSED CATEGORIES: EMPLOYEE, SELF-EMPLOYED, OR ENTREPRENEUR?

A. Sociologically Speaking: Power and Authority

A contemporary sociologist points out that "the meaning and measure of self-employment is somewhat of an enigma" (Robert Aronson 1991, xi). Most frequently, self-employment is simply contrasted with employment, which, in turn, is not precisely defined. The distinction is even more complex because it is drawn in a variety of contexts. Angela Dale (1991) identified three important contexts in which the self-employed may be distinguished from employees: the sociological, legal, and statistical. Not only is there debate in each of these literatures about how to define these terms, but also the predominant definitions in the different contexts are not perfectly congruent, although they do overlap.

Class is a key consideration for many sociologists seeking to describe and understand the structure of societies. Karl Marx and Max Weber regarded ownership of the means of production as crucial to an understanding of the nature of power and authority relationships between labour and capital (Curran and Burrows 1986; Dale 1986, 450; Elias 2000, xii). Different classes are distinguished in terms of ownership of the means of production, autonomy of work, and expropriation of the labour power of others. Classical sociologists such as Marx and Weber have identified three classes in capitalist societies: employers (the bourgeoisie), who buy the labour power of others and thus assume some authority or control over them; the self-employed without employees (petit bourgeoisie), who neither sell their labour nor buy the labour of others; and employees (proletarians), who sell their labour power to employers and thus place themselves under their authority and control (Goldthorpe 1980; Wright et al. 1982).[4]

As an ideal type, self-employment is linked to ownership, autonomy, and control over production, clearly distinguishing craftspeople, independent professionals, and small-business proprietors from waged workers (Eardley and Corden 1996, 13). Historically, self-employment has been associated with independence and contrasted with the dependent status of employees (Bercusson 1996; Fraser and Gordon 1997).

Two defining characteristics of the self-employed are their ownership of the means of their own production and their self-direction or autonomy in their work (Dale 1986).

However, this ideal type is becoming increasingly removed from the reality of self-employment. Researchers in Britain, where self-employment grew remarkably during the 1980s, were among the first to identify the changing nature of self-employment. They recorded an increase in consultants, professionals, and contractors, especially in the service sector, and a decline in small-business owners who employed other workers (Dale 1986; Eardley and Corden 1996; Hakim 1988). They also discovered that a sizeable portion of the self-employed included home workers and labour-only contractors, as well as franchisees, freelancers, and outworkers. In their employment situations, these workers differ dramatically from the ideal type of the self-employed, since they do not own much by way of means of production, exercise little control over production, and do not accumulate capital (Brodie, Stanworth, and Wotruba 2002; Dale 1986, 1991; Eardley and Corden 1996; Felstead 1991, Lorinc 1995; Stanworth and Stanworth 1997). Studies indicate that changes in contractual relationships – specifically, the growth of market-mediated work arrangements and networks of firms – relate directly to the rise in self-employment. The nature of the contracts for the provision of labour are changing such that commercial – as distinct from employment – contracts are becoming commonplace (Abraham 1990, 85; Engblom 2001; Jurik 1998, 7). For many new recruits in the ranks of the self-employed, the link between self-employment and entrepreneurship is no longer obvious.

Moreover, research by Wallace Clement on fishers in Canada demonstrates that even the paradigmatic form of self-employment – that of the petit bourgeoisie – is perfectly compatible with a great deal of subordination. His detailed study of property relations in the fisheries illustrates how large capital can shift considerable risk and the supervision of labour onto direct producers (Clement 1986). Helen Rainbird has also focused on the social relations of production of the self-employed in relation to larger capital, although she examined a range of self-employment and small-business formation in the United Kingdom. Concentrating on self-employed who contribute both labour and capital to the production process, she found that "the majority of the self-employed earn a subsistence living only, although there is some scope for them to appropriate surplus value and accumulate capital of their own by virtue of their ownership of capital, self-exploitation and employment of labour" (Rainbird 1991, 214).

Sociologists now recognize a continuum of self-employment that differs in terms of the quality of, and the rewards from, the work and the chances of economic success and security (Hakim 1988; Leighton and Felstead 1992). Self-employment ranges from disguised employees and franchisees,[5] through skilled craftspeople and independent professionals, to the owners of incorporated businesses. At best, some types of self-employment provide sufficient autonomy to allow people to realize their potential and align rewards with efforts; at worst, self-employed workers are marginal.[6] The range within the ranks of the self-employed is explained by a combination of structure, agency, and practice. The concept of "social location" has been developed to specify the ways in which political and economic conditions interact with class, ethnicity, culture, and sexual orientation to shape the meanings and strategies of working men and women (Jurik 1998; Lamphere et al. 1993). This framework helps to explain not only why self-employment is very different for men and women across countries, but also why the type and proportion of self-employment differs between countries.[7]

To counter overly simplistic arguments about the relationship between self-employment and entrepreneurship on the one hand, and between self-employment, unemployment, and employment protection legislation on the other, it is important to attend to the diversity of forms of self-employment. There is no generic category of self-employment, and this militates against any single, simple explanation of self-employment growth. As Nigel Meager notes, "There is no such thing as a 'typical' self-employed person. The self-employed may include, for example, everyone from highly skilled professional workers such as doctors, lawyers and accountants, to entrepreneurial small business owners, to taxi drivers, and to many low-skilled workers in a variety of trades and occupations. Such people may have little in common other than the fact of their self-employment, and the influences of government policies and of economic and structural forces are likely to be very different between these different 'segments' of self-employment" (1991, 66).

Social location, as we shall see in the following discussion of the Canadian data, helps to explain differences in self-employment.

B. Statistically Speaking: Self-Employment in Canada

For the purpose of official statistics gathering, employment and self-employment are distinguished by their mode of remuneration, employees receiving wages and the self-employed enjoying profits (Elias 2000;

Loufti 1991).[8] In broad terms, self-employment can be considered the residual category of gainful employment not remunerated by a wage or salary.[9] The distinction between employment and self-employment is also supposed to capture the greater risk and autonomy associated with self-employment (Elias 2000, xii). However, this distinction does not capture the difference between entrepreneurship and economic dependence, especially where self-employment is simply a form of disguised employment – as it is in many instances. But, despite the limitations of statistical measures, the official Canadian data demonstrates that the self-employed occupy a broad spectrum of socio-economic positions (Bögenhold and Staber 1991, 225).

In Canada, through the 1980s and 1990s, self-employment grew as a share of employment, reaching 16 per cent in 2000. A crucial distinction among the self-employed is whether or not they hire other employees. Self-employed people can employ other workers, or they can be "own account" – that is, they do not hire others. The majority of the increase in self-employment in the 1990s was in the own-account category, which grew from 6 per cent to 10 per cent of total employment between 1976 and 2000. In contrast, the employer category grew from 5 per cent to 6 per cent of total employment over the same period, yet it declined every year from 1995 to 2000.[10]

Own-account self-employment has grown dramatically for both men and women – from 4 per cent to nearly 9 per cent of total female employment, and from 7 per cent to 12 per cent of total male employment between 1976 and 2000 (figure 1). When men's and women's shares of self-employment relative to their shares of total employment are compared, it is evident that women were still under-represented in self-employment in 2000. Only women in the own-account category are nearing their representation in the employed population. Like their counterparts in wage and salary employment, self-employed women are also confined to a very limited number of industries and occupations, such as sales, service, and clerical occupations.[11]

Immigrants are generally as likely as people born in Canada to be employed, except for the cohort that arrived in Canada between 1991 and 1995 – they were 30 per cent more likely to enter self-employment than those born in Canada (Frenette 2002).[12] One explanation for this shift to self-employment by recent immigrants concerns the declining success of immigrants in the paid workforce. Marc Frenette suggests that immigrants from non-English-speaking countries, a rising portion of immigrants, may face difficulties integrating into paid jobs and thus may

Figure 1:
Self-employment as a share of total employment, own-account (OASE), and employers (SEE), 1976–2000

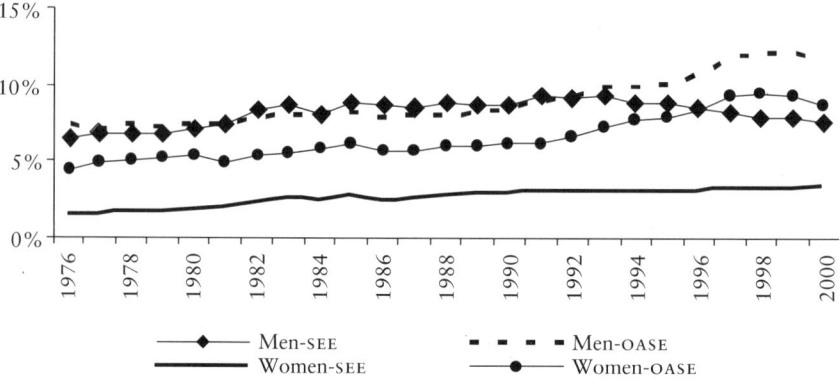

Source: Labour Force Survey, Statistics Canada

choose self-employment (Frenette 2002, 13). Other studies indicate that immigrant workers are, increasingly, people of colour who face systemic discrimination when searching for employment (Galabuzi 2001; Jackson 2002). In 1999, 20 per cent of men in the employer category and 19 per cent of those in the own-account category were born abroad, versus roughly 8 per cent of men in the total population. While data for immigrant women employers are unavailable for that year, 20 per cent of women in the own-account category were born abroad, versus roughly 7 per cent of women in the total population.[13] Moreover, in 1999, 13 per cent of self-employed people were members of "visible-minority groups" (the term used by Statistics Canada) (versus roughly 9 per cent of the whole population), fully 16 per cent of self-employed men, and 9 per cent of self-employed women.[14]

Own-account self-employment is more common among visible-minority and immigrant women than their male counterparts (figure 2). Among visible minorities, 49 per cent of men were own-account self-employed in 2000, in contrast to 62 per cent of women. These gendered patterns also hold for immigrants; 71 per cent of immigrant women were own-account self-employed in 2000, in contrast with 57 per cent of men (figure 1). At the same time, both immigrants and visible minorities are less likely to be in own-account self-employment and more likely to be in employer self-employment than non-visible minorities and non-immigrants, and this pattern holds for men and women (figure 2).

Figure 2:
Class of worker by immigrant status and sex, and visible minority status and sex, 2000

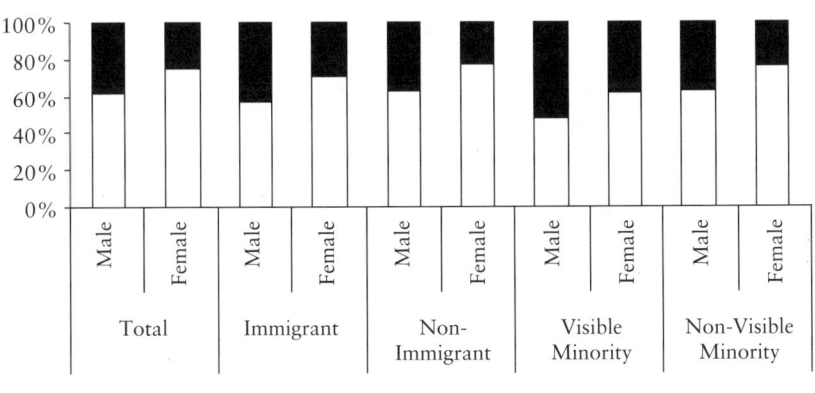

■ Self-employed employer
□ Own-account self-employed

Source: Survey of Labour and Income Dynamics, Statistics Canada

Researchers in the United Kingdom identified an increase in the proportion of relatively poor self-employed in the 1980s. They also found that people had a much higher chance (more than twice as high) of being in a low-income group if they were self-employed than if they were employees, even after allowing for the under-reporting of income by the self-employed. Perhaps even more significantly, the researchers associated self-employment with very low income in later life (Meager, Court, and Moralee 1996, 229–30). This finding is particularly troubling given that it does not reflect the growth of very low-income self-employment in the 1980s or distinguish between self-employed employers and the own-account self-employed.

In Canada, we see the most significant income differences among the self-employed when we look at type of self-employment – in 1999, the average annual incomes of self-employed employers and the own-account self-employed were $46,825 and $16,918, respectively.[15] Income differences are also related to gender – in 1999, female and male employers had average annual incomes of $39,920 and $49,470, respectively, and women and men in the own-account category had average annual incomes of $13,032 and $19,769, respectively. The comparable figures for all female and male wage and salary employees were $26,015 and $40,183, respectively, indicating that the average annual incomes of men and women in wage and salary employment tend to be less than those of their counterparts working as self-employed employers but significantly more than their counterparts in own-account self-employment. When income is examined by immigration status, gender, and type of employment, among the own-account self-employed, where insecurity is greatest, the average annual income of men born in Canada is highest ($20,188), followed by men born abroad ($18,476), women born in Canada ($12,918), and women born abroad ($11,929).

In 2000, fully 55 per cent of all visible minorities in employer self-employment earned less than $20,000 annually, while only 30 per cent of non-visible minorities in employer self-employment earned less than that amount. Moreover, 71 per cent of visible-minority own-account self-employed earned less than $20,000 annually, whereas only 57 per cent of non-visible-minority own-account self-employed earned less than that amount. Immigrant self-employed, whether employers or own-account, also earned less than their Canadian-born counterparts; 46 per cent of all immigrants in employer self-employment earned less than $20,000 annually, versus 30 per cent of non-immigrants, and the equivalent figures for own-account self-employment are 64 per cent and 57 per cent. Regardless of whether they are employer or own-account, visible-minority self-employed, as a group, fare worse in terms of income than their non-visible-minority counterparts, and self-employed visible-minority women earn the least of all groups of self-employed. The same is true for immigrants compared to Canadian-born.[16]

These data suggest that the distinction between types of self-employment, while critical for determining the income of the self-employed population as a whole, is less salient for immigrants and visible minorities. At the same time, the data indicate that race and immigrant status are key axes of differentiation within both categories of self-employment.

The self-employed in Canada give a number of reasons for choosing self-employment that also point to the importance of social location. While independence, freedom, and the ability to be one's own boss are the foremost reasons given by men (42 per cent), women are as likely to cite balancing work and family obligations (23 per cent), as they are to cite independence and freedom (24 per cent) as the reason for choosing self-employment (Delage 2002, 27; see also Arai 2000; Hughes 1999; Vosko 2002). However, recent qualitative research by Karen Hughes demonstrates that survey data is very limited when it comes to identifying the reasons women choose self-employment. Her research suggests that some of the reasons, conventionally characterized as pull factors, such as the desire to be one's own boss, could just as accurately be characterized as push factors, since in follow-up questions, many of the women interviewed cited job stress and an unpleasant work environment as reasons for choosing self-employment (Hughes 2003, 444).

The rewards of self-employment are mixed, and they depend upon the type of self-employment, which, in turn, is influenced by the individual's social location. Own-account self-employment, in which women (from all racial and ethnic groups) are concentrated, is insecure and poorly paid. Moreover, the self-employed are generally less likely to have access to training, earn overtime pay, or receive maternity, parental, or sick leave, and they report longer working hours than paid employees. Indeed, 22 per cent of the self-employed cited uncertainty and insecurity as the most disliked aspect of self-employment, and another 12 per cent cited income fluctuations and cash-flow problems (Akyeampong and Sussman 2003, 13). Although the majority of the self-employed (55 per cent) said they had no interest in subscribing to self-insurance systems, the most common reason given for lack of coverage was affordability (Akyeampong and Sussman 2003; Delage 2002). Not surprisingly, the self-employed, especially those who are own-account, expressed dissatisfaction with self-employment's extrinsic rewards (money, benefits, work time). However, they expressed greater satisfaction with the intrinsic rewards of their work than did employees; the self-employed report greater autonomy than employees in the dimensions of control, pace, and duration of work (Delage 2002, 27).

The statistical problem of blurred categories is not limited to the overlap between paid employees and the own-account self-employed; the distinction between self-employed who are own-account and employers is more porous than is conventionally understood. Statistics Canada classifies those self-employed with paid help in a given reference year as employers, while self-employed who do not hire others are considered own-account. Based on this definition, in 2000, 46 per cent of the self-employed in Canada were employers. Yet, when members of the same group were asked whether they had paid help during a particular reference week, only 38 per cent fell into this category (Delage 2002, 12).

The absence of a clear distinction between wage and salary employees and self-employed individuals is apparent from an examination of the work arrangements of the self-employed. In 2000, a considerable proportion of the self-employed worked in either client locations (20 per cent) or locations supplied by clients (4 per cent); fully 30 per cent of the own-account self-employed worked in such situations (Delage 2002,

B6). Furthermore, 37 per cent of the self-employed (35 per cent of men and 46 per cent of women) received support from their clients; 24 per cent (20 per cent of men and 37 per cent of women) received equipment, tools, or supplies from their clients; and another 21 per cent received support in the form of other office equipment, such as fax and photocopier. Moreover, in 2000, 15 per cent of the self-employed (18 per cent of the own-account self-employed) reported that their last employer was one of their clients. Fifty-one per cent of the self-employed whose last employer was one of their clients obtained more than half of their annual revenue from work done for their last employer (Delage 2002, 27).[17] The day-to-day business operations of many self-employed mirror those of paid employees.

The workers in each of the case studies fall into the broad category of own-account self-employed, at the boundary between employees and self-employed employers. Not surprisingly, given their own-account status, they tend to be poorly paid and precariously employed. The precarious nature of their self-employment is reinforced by their precarious social location; with the exception of freelance editors, the workers in the case studies are considered to be low-skilled. The majority of rural route contractors, freelance editors, and home-care workers are women who are balancing paid work and unpaid family responsibilities. Moreover, many of the home-care workers and the newspaper carriers are recent immigrants who face barriers in their search for wage and salary employment. The economic and social position of these self-employed workers, and others, is significantly shaped by labour law.

2. THE EMPLOYMENT PLATFORM FOR LABOUR LAW PROTECTION

An important dimension of labour protection is its personal scope – the question of who is covered by labour law as opposed to some other body of law, such as commercial and general contract law. This question is difficult precisely because of the diversity of relations of production and the availability of different legal forms to structure them. Recent historical research indicates not only that the legal concept of employment is relatively young, but also that it has never been precise (Deakin 2001). However, by the end of World War II, protective labour legislation was built upon the platform of the contract of employment (Langille 2002). This meant that to claim the benefit of most labour legislation, workers had to establish, at minimum, that they were employees, parties to a contract of employment with an employer, rather than self-employed or independent contractors, parties to a contract for service.

In the context of collective bargaining law, a number of assumptions and public policy considerations made the choice of the contract of employment as the basis for personal scope seem natural. First, competitive markets are a core institution of liberal market economies. They are believed to promote the public good in numerous ways. For example, within these markets, resources are efficiently allocated, innovation is rewarded, and consumer satisfaction is maximized. For this reason, the law promotes competition. Collective and coordinated action by firms or individuals in order to influence the market – "combination," in legal terminology – is viewed with hostility because it exists precisely to reduce competition. Therefore, some special justification is needed before this kind of activity (or combination) can be tolerated, let alone promoted, by law. Both the common law and anti-combinations legislation have historically forbidden entrepreneurs from combining to restrict competition, which is the guiding principle of commercial law and policy (Crysler 1967).

In the context of labour law, numerous justifications for permitting worker collective action have been offered, and, from time to time, they have gained some official acceptance. One justification derives from the recognition that labour is not merely a commodity (*Treaty of Versailles, 1919*, part XIII, section II, article 427), or not a commodity at all, as the International Labour Organization (ILO) famously declared in the 1944 *Declaration of Philadelphia*. A corollary of this understanding of the distinctive nature of labour – its humanity – is, according to the ILO (which is the specialized agency of the United Nations generally considered to be the most authoritative source of labour rights recognized on an international basis), freedom of association, which includes collective bargaining (Creighton 2001; Novitz 2003, chapter 5; Tsogas 2001, chapter 2). Thus, employees should not be subject to anti-combinations law. In line with this general understanding of the distinctive nature of labour, the current Canadian *Competition Act* exempts "combinations or activities of workmen or employees for their own reasonable protection," as well as arrangements pertaining to collective bargaining over terms and conditions of employment.[18] A second justification, which some public policy–makers came to accept during the Great Depression, was that the rise of corporate capitalism had resulted in such a severe imbalance in bargaining power between labour and capital as to produce a crisis of under-consumption, because workers could not afford to purchase the goods and services they produced (Gordon 1994). Collective bargaining was seen as necessary to create a countervailing power sufficient to provide workers with a fair share of productivity increases. For the most part, both justifications required that a sharp distinction be drawn between labour markets, where reduced competition was acceptable, and markets for products and services, where full competition was the norm. Constructing labour law on the platform of the contract of employment was consistent with these normative and economic policy goals.

The justifications for collective bargaining must also be placed in a historical context in which worker combinations were viewed with special horror by elites, including the judiciary. Not only was collective bargaining regarded as anti-competitive behaviour, but also workers' collective action was considered a threat to the very social order that underwrote the privileged positions of the elites (Orth 1991; Tomlins 1985). In that context, the creation of a legal framework that facilitated and regulated collective bargaining did not come about simply because enlightened elites accepted that labour was not a commodity and that workers required more bargaining leverage to sustain a balance between production and consumption. Rather, it was through long and bitter struggle that industrial workers forced the state to accommodate collective bargaining in order to reduce the incidence and severity of labour conflict (Glasbeek 1987).

Collective bargaining law in Canada was designed with a particular setting in mind: the large industrial workplace (Fudge and Tucker 2001). It was also based on the industrial model of unionism, in which unions represented workers on the basis of industry rather than occupation and skill. The centrality of the contract of employment was a given in the context of the large industrial workplace. Industrial workers were hired on the understanding that they would have a long-term relation with a single employer (periodic layoffs notwithstanding), they would be subject to the control of that employer, and they would be paid an hourly wage. Other groups of workers, who did not fit this mould, were largely outside the field of vision of those engaged in the creation of the collective bargaining system, making the construction of labour law on the platform of the contract of employment seem a natural choice.

But the choice of this platform was always problematic, even on its own terms, both because of the diversity of relations of production and because not all employees hired pursuant to contracts of employment worked in the kind of large industrial setting for which collective bargaining law had been designed (Fudge and Glasbeek 1995; O'Grady 1992; Ursel 1992). For example, in the construction industry, employment was organized on a casual and temporary basis relating to a specific job rather than an enduring relationship with a single employer. However, because skilled construction workers had a long history of unionization, collective bargaining legislation was modified specifically to address the unique structure of the industry as well as the organization of employment on a craft basis. Workers who fell outside the narrow model of the industrial worker and did not enjoy the construction workers' power in the labour market were not able to secure collective bargaining legislation tailored to meet their distinctive employment relations. This meant that for a significant group of workers there was ambiguity about the personal scope of collective bargaining law and that collective bargaining law did not work well. The experiences of the workers examined in the four case studies illustrate these problems, but it is useful to explore them more broadly at the outset.

A. *The Personal Scope of Collective Bargaining Legislation*

Two levels of government – the provincial and territorial on the one hand, and the federal on the other – have legislative jurisdiction over labour relations in Canada, and it is divided between them according to the nature of the activity involved. The provinces and territories have general legislative authority over labour relations, which includes manufacturing, mining (except uranium) and natural resources, construction, and service industries, whereas the federal government is limited to specific activities itemized in the constitution, such as interprovincial and international trade, transportation and communications, and banking, as well as the federal public service. In some cases, such as trucking, it is difficult to draw the line between different activities, and the jurisdictional issue is not infrequently a source of dispute and litigation during organizing drives. The issue also adds to the complexity of designing effective Canadian collective bargaining legislation, as the case study on freelance editors illustrates.

Across Canada, labour tribunals administer collective bargaining legislation. This legislation provides a mechanism for unions to obtain the exclusive right to represent groups of workers and bargain terms and conditions of employment on their behalf; it protects workers seeking to exercise their right to join or participate in a trade union; and it regulates the conduct of employers and unions in labour relations disputes.

The question of employment status for collective bargaining is determined in the first instance by an administrative tribunal, typically known as a labour relations board, vested with the authority to apply the law to the facts that it establishes.[19] The applicable law derives from the tribunal's enabling legislation, the labour relations statute. Although, either expressly or by implication, the law applied only to employees, initially there was no statutory definition of the term. As a result, labour relations boards were effectively empowered to select the applicable law governing employee status. Some of the early labour tribunals in Canada, likely influenced by American jurisprudence, emphasized economic dependence for determining employee status (Arthurs 1965, 93). The important question was whether a group of workers would benefit from collective bargaining legislation, not whether they were employees at common law. This approach changed due to a decision of the Nova Scotia Court of Appeal, which overruled a labour tribunal in holding that, in the absence of a statutory definition, the meaning of the term *employee* should be "determined by the general law," by which the court meant the common law. In that particular case, fishers who owned their boats were found to be partners rather than employees for the purposes of collective bargaining law (Arthurs 1965, 92–5).[20]

This choice proved problematic for a number of reasons. First, even by then, the common-law test for employee status, which had centred on control, had become a multiple-factor (known as the four-fold) test that produced little certainty in regard to its probable outcome. Second, and more importantly, even though the four-fold test permitted consideration of the economic realities of the relationship, and thus provided labour boards with a degree of flexibility in determining the scope of employment, certain groups of workers – such as taxicab and truck drivers who owned their vehicles and fishers who owned their boats – were still denied access to collective bargaining because labour boards found them to be independent contractors. The difficulty with this was that many of these workers were participating in the same labour markets as employees, but they constituted a disruptive influence for two reasons. On the one hand, their use of economic force was not constrained by the disciplinary framework of labour law, and on the other, they undermined union strength since they constituted a competing supply of labour power (Arthurs 1965, 115).

In an influential article published in 1965, Harry Arthurs recommended that as part of the solution to this problem, the personal scope of collective bargaining law should be extended to the class of dependent contractors described as persons who, although legally contractors, were economically dependent (Arthurs 1965). This recommendation was endorsed by the influential Task Force on Labour Relations, appointed in 1966 by the federal government to report on industrial relations in the context of rising labour unrest (Woods 1969, 140). Between 1972 and 1977, seven jurisdictions modified their collective bargaining legislation to extend the definition of *employee* to include dependent contractors (Bendel 1982, 376). British Columbia and Ontario adopted a broad definition.[21] By contrast, the definition in the federal *Canada Labour Code* was narrow, limited by industry (joint-venture fishers) and occupation (owner-operators of trucks).[22] However, the actual extent to which the statutory definition of *dependent contractor* expanded the personal scope of collective bargaining law depended on how the labour tribunals interpreted and applied it.[23] Labour tribunals across the country have developed lists of factors to assist them in distinguishing dependent from independent contractors (George Adams 1995, 6–3 – 6–5; Langille and Davidov 1999, 27–8).[24]

Another technique of extending the personal scope of collective bargaining legislation is to give the labour tribunal the authority to designate workers as employees for the purpose of collective bargaining.[25] Although this technique has the advantage of making it clear that the decision to cover a particular group of workers is a policy question and not a matter of adjudicating between competing legal categories, it is not clear that these differences in approach yield significantly different results. Indeed, even in those jurisdictions that did not enact dependent-contractor or deeming provisions, the development of civil and common-law tests of employee status has combined with the increased emphasis on a purposive interpretation of key statutory terms to expand the personal scope of collective bargaining legislation (Bendel 1982).

The expansion of the personal scope of collective bargaining legislation through a variety of techniques has enabled diverse groups of workers – who previously would have been considered self-employed and thus not entitled to the protection offered by collective bargaining legislation – to unionize and establish collective bargaining relationships. Owner-drivers of dump trucks and taxicabs, owner-operators of fishing boats, driver-salespeople, freelance journalists and musicians, couriers, home-care workers, and house parents working for welfare agencies have been recognized as employees for the purpose of collective bargaining legislation (Carter et al. 2002, 252).

The development of a broader conception of employment that emphasizes economic dependence may explain why collective bargaining by dependent contractors has not attracted any attention under competition law. Despite the fact that neither the competition legislation nor the *Criminal Code* were amended to exempt dependent contractors who engaged in collective bargaining, there have been no legal proceedings alleging anti-competitive behaviour on their part (Backhouse 1976; Labour Law Casebook Group 1998, 210).

In general, economic dependence and control are the factors used by labour boards to distinguish workers who are granted access to collective bargaining legislation from workers who are not (Davidov 2002; Langille and Davidov 1999, 28). People who have made a considerable capital investment in the equipment they use to perform their work, who provide services to several different firms, and who hire others on a limited basis have been considered to be either employees or dependent contractors (Carter et al. 2002, 252). However, exactly where a labour tribunal will draw the lines between employees, dependent contractors, and entrepreneurs in a particular case is hard to predict. One important question is whether the degree of economic dependence on a particular employer is enough to keep a dependent contractor in the legal category of employee.[26] Another controversial question is whether contractors who hire other workers should be considered dependent contractors.[27]

Despite the changes in legal definitions and legal tests, which have undoubtedly expanded the personal scope of collective bargaining law, the distinction between employees (including dependent contractors) and independent contractors is as elusive as ever. This problem is illustrated by the *Toronto Star* carrier case study. Moreover, even an expansive definition of *employee* does not address the needs of dependent workers whose legal status remains that of independent contractors, such as freelance editors.

It is important to emphasize that establishing employee status is a necessary, but not a sufficient, condition for gaining access to collective bargaining law. For a variety of reasons, collective bargaining laws also exclude various groups of employees by stipulating that they are not employees or that the legislation does not apply to them. This difficulty manifests itself in two of our case studies. Rural route mail couriers have been deemed by statute not to be employees or dependent contractors for the purposes of the collective bargaining sections of the *Canada Labour Code*[28] and personal-care workers have had to fight being classified as domestic workers employed in a private home – a group to whom the Ontario *Labour Relations Act* does not apply.[29]

Moreover, establishing that statutory collective bargaining law applies is just the first step for workers who wish to unionize and bargain collectively. As Bryan Palmer observed, "The struggle to create and sustain workers' organizations in the face of staunch resistance from capital and the state is, and always has been, an undertaking requiring large commitments and persistent efforts" (Palmer 1995, 39). This is particularly true for contingent or precarious workers, including the self-employed, who, in addition to the problem of employer and state resistance, also have to cope with a statutory scheme that is ill-suited to their circumstances (du Rivage, Carré, and Tilly 1998; Fudge and Vosko 2001b). Here we will touch briefly on a number of issues faced by self-employed workers seeking to use the statutory collective bargaining scheme, including the certification process, bargaining unit structure, contracting out, public sector restructuring, and work organization.

B. Establishing Bargaining Rights: Unfair Labour Practices and Bargaining Unit Determination

In our system of labour law, the starting position is that for every worker, individual contracting is the norm, and workers must actively establish their right to bargain collectively. The starting commitment means that workers must take the initiative and bear the risks of navigating the complex system of labour law. Across Canada, this means that a union that has embarked on an organizing drive must either sign up a majority of the workers it seeks to represent as union members, or, in addition to signing up a sizeable proportion of union members, it must win a majority in a representation vote. This is often more difficult than it sounds, because the organizing drive takes place within the context of unequal power relations that the legal regime does not effectively offset. One problem is that while the law limits employers' property and contract rights when those rights are exercised in ways that interfere with workers' freedom of association, it leaves ample room for employers to play on the justifiable fears of workers that employers will punish them for attempting to unionize. Moreover, when employers resort to unfair labour practices, making it impossible to ascertain the true wishes of the workers, most labour boards in Canada lack the power to certify a union as a remedy for these practices.[30] A second problem is that the law does not give unions the same right of access to workers that employers enjoy. Unions cannot obtain lists of worker names and contact information; union organizers who are not employees cannot enter the employer's property; and organizers who are employees are severely limited in the actions they can engage in during working hours. It is only after an employer is found to have used unfair labour practices that a union is granted any of these organizing opportunities (Macklem 1990).

In Canada, private sector collective bargaining legislation reinforces a specific model of worker representation. That legislation is based on two structural features: a bargaining unit determination process that presumes that collective bargaining will take place at the level of the work site, and a commitment to majority rule in determining collective representation. Labour relations boards determine what constitutes an appropriate bargaining unit within a legal framework that leaves them with a considerable amount of discretion. As a general matter, they take into account a variety of considerations, including the notion of a community of interest between employees and their ability to organize, and an employer's interest in stable industrial relations. This determination process has produced a highly fragmented bargaining structure and a narrow conception of workers' community of interest that, to a large extent, reinforces employer decisions about how to organize production (Forrest 1986; Fudge 1993; Svirsky 1998). With few exceptions, the largest bargaining unit will consist of all non-managerial employees of a particular employer in a defined geographic area within a province. The absence of broader-based bargaining units precludes contractors who have multiple employers from being able to participate meaningfully in the process of collective bargaining unless they can bring themselves within one of the narrow exceptions. Often, however, the unit will be smaller, because particular groups of workers are declared by statute to be appropriate units for collective bargaining. This is the case in Ontario for dependent contractors, who, as a result, will be placed in a separate bargaining unit unless a majority indicate their preference for being assigned to a unit composed of other employees.[31] According to a group of labour law scholars, this may have a negative impact: "Including dependent contractors with other employees for collective bargaining purposes may have the effect of eliminating any economic advantage to the employer of continuing the dependent contractor arrangement whereas the provision of separate bargaining units for dependent contractors may serve to entrench the dependent contractor arrangements. As Canadian firms increasingly contract out many of their core functions, this difference of approach assumes greater significance" (Labour Law Casebook Group 1998, 219).

Not only do Canadian collective bargaining laws require that employees take the initiative to bring collective bargaining into their workplaces (Roy Adams 1991, 147), but they also require that a majority of employees in a designated bargaining unit demonstrate their support for a particular union. These policies stand in marked contrast to collective bargaining regimes in Europe, where employee councils are mandated by law in several countries and where unions that represent a minority of employees at a particular workplace have the right to collectively bargain on their members' behalf (Roy Adams 1991). In Canada, before a legally enforceable collective bargaining relationship can be established, a majority of the relevant group of workers must indicate that this is their preference. Some jurisdictions allow a union to be certified as a bargaining representative solely on the basis of demonstrating evidence of majority union membership among employees. Under collective bargaining legislation in other jurisdictions in Canada, during an organizing drive a union must get at least a substantial proportion (typically 40 per cent) of the workers to sign a membership card and then win a majority in a representation vote. These are particularly challenging obstacles for unions attempting to organize workers, such as those in the case studies that follow, who do not regularly perform their jobs at their employers' premises. As a result, organizers may experience difficulty identifying, let alone meeting, their target audience. Campaigns to organize workers who do not work in a common location are extremely expensive, as the rural route mail contractors' case shows. As well, even though labour law prohibits unfair labour practices such as retaliation against workers for joining a union, contractors have so little security that they may reasonably fear that their employers will easily find an excuse to terminate (or fail to renew) their relationship.

Moreover, Canadian collective bargaining legislation is premised on granting exclusive bargaining rights to one union. But competition between unions over the right to represent specific groups of workers is an enduring feature of the Canadian labour movement. In part, this is because the central trade union organization, the Canadian Labour Congress (CLC) is dependent upon its affiliated unions for funding and institutional support, so it has little power to discipline unions that ignore its jurisdictional rulings. Thus, collective bargaining legislation and labour tribunal policies and practices influence how unions draw jurisdictional lines. Since the union that obtains the support of the majority of employees in an appropriate bargaining unit secures the exclusive right to represent the employees in the bargaining unit, unions that are competing for the right to represent the same group of workers often rely on the labour tribunal to resolve the problem of representation through its authority to determine the appropriate bargaining unit. As we shall see in the case of the rural route mail carriers, certification applications and bargaining unit reviews provide an opportunity for one union to challenge the representational rights asserted by another union. Moreover, because the bargaining unit determines the voting constituency, unions conform to, rather than challenge, the labour tribunal's bargaining unit policies, even if the policies have the effect of disenfranchising a growing proportion of the Canadian workforce (Fudge 1993). Features of Canadian labour law legislation combine with inter-union rivalry over representational jurisdiction to create a serious disincentive for unions to develop broader-based bargaining strategies and institutions, which depend upon union co-operation over matters of jurisdiction.

Even if a union manages to obtain majority support among a group of workers classified by a labour relations tribunal as employees and as an appropriate bargaining unit, it may still fail to establish a collective bargaining relationship. Newly certified bargaining units must negotiate their first collective agreement and, despite the duty to bargain in good faith imposed by labour relations statutes, neither party is under an obligation to accept non-mandatory terms that it finds unacceptable (Langille and Macklem 1988). As a result, a significant number of newly certified units fail to obtain a first collective agreement, and many of those that do must first prove their mettle in industrial conflict.[32] To resolve the recurring problem of intractable first-contract disputes, several jurisdictions in Canada provide for first-contract arbitration. Collective agreements imposed under these procedures, which vary across jurisdictions, last for either one or two years, and subsequent agreements, if any, are reached through negotiation in the normal collective bargaining process (Carter et al. 2002, 294–5).

C. *Contracting Out*

Preserving the right of property owners to deploy their capital as they see fit is another distinctive feature of Canadian collective bargaining legislation. One manifestation of the tilt in favour of property rights over workers' right to associate is that in every jurisdiction in Canada, employers are entitled to contract out work – and lay off and terminate the employment of those who perform the work – unless there is a collective agreement prohibiting it. The law does not impede the subcontracting of bargaining unit work except in very well defined and limited circumstances (such as anti-union animus or the sale of a business) (Carter et al. 2002, 275–7). For the most part, constraints on contracting out for a unionized employer are contained not in legislation but in the collective agreement (Jalette and Warrian 2002). While all employees face the possibility of contracting out, self-employed workers who are treated as contractors are more at risk than most, because their work is often less likely to be integrated into the employers' core business. For example, a production worker on an auto assembly line is less likely to have her or his job contracted out than a truck driver who delivers finished vehicles to dealerships. Moreover, because the terms of the collective agreement only apply to the employer's bargaining unit rather than to all employers in the industry, there may be strong incentives to shift such work to a non-union employer whose labour costs are lower. The attempt of *Toronto Star* carriers to unionize, for example, ran aground when their work was contracted out.

The problem of contracting out also afflicts workers in the broader public sector, especially as governments embrace neo-liberal policies that redefine the core business of government as the facilitation of self-reliance and consumer choice rather than the direct provision of welfare-state services to citizens (Broad and Antony 1999). This policy change has often been accompanied by a contracting out to non-profit agencies or for-profit enterprises of functions that were formerly performed by government. Normally, where an entire operation is transferred, existing bargaining rights are preserved and the new operator is deemed to be a successor employer. In Ontario, however, the government specifically exempted privatization from the successor rights provisions,[33] which means that unions must attempt to reorganize workers who are now likely to be working in decentralized settings and to be much more precariously employed. The case of personal-care workers illustrates these difficulties.

D. The Need for New Forms of Representation

Finally, because the law and practice of collective bargaining was based on the model of the industrial workplace, it often fails to accommodate the different needs of contractors who may have multiple employers and who may work in settings where traditional methods of providing work security are not suitable. For example, the extremely fragmented bargaining structure that requires collective agreements to be established between employees and particular employers precludes the negotiation of sectoral agreements necessary for collective bargaining to be meaningful for workers who contract with multiple employers within an industry. Freelance editors, for example, even if considered employees, would not be able to take advantage of collective bargaining legislation, since this legislation is completely out of sync with the reality of their labour market. These workers sell their services to multiple clients instead of to single firms that can be identified as their employers. Another instance of the mismatch between industrial norms and non-industrial realities occurs in the area of personal-care work, where exclusive reliance on seniority provisions for allocating work fails to address the legitimate demand of people with disabilities to have a voice in selecting the person who provides them services in a way that ensures security for workers.

These difficulties require a fundamental rethinking of the legal framework of collective bargaining and of the kinds of worker collective action that might improve the working conditions and living standards of people who fall outside the norm of standard employment. We will return to this issue at greater length in our conclusion, but for now it suffices to note that broader-based bargaining models and scale agreements such as the *Status of the Artist Act*[34] may be more suitable for a range of self-employed workers than the traditional Canadian collective bargaining regime.

The case studies begin with that of the *Toronto Star* carriers, which reminds us that self-employment is not a new phenomenon, even though its shape and incidence change. Although newspaper publishers have treated carriers as independent entrepreneurs, the case study shows that it is possible to organize and successfully challenge that designation. However, it also demonstrates that employment status alone does not protect workers against precariousness, and that the respect for property rights embedded in labour law provides employers with the opportunity to restructure their operations and contract work out, thereby ridding themselves of these newly minted employees.

Like the newspaper carriers, rural route mail couriers have long been regarded as entrepreneurs by their employer, Canada Post, but they must jump an additional hurdle in order to access collective bargaining legislation: rural route mail couriers are deemed by statute not to be employees. This has not, however, deterred them from organizing first as an independent association, and later as a union. They have pursued a multi-pronged political and legal strategy to gain collective bargaining rights, a strategy involving private members' bills, litigation under the *Charter of Rights and Freedoms*, and complaints under the labour-side accord of the North American Free Trade Agreement. The case study shows the extent to which union strategies can influence the status and power of self-employed workers.

Personal-care workers who provide services to people with disabilities work in a challenging environment because of the nature of the services they provide and because of the restructuring of the service-delivery model. These workers have often been denied employment status, either because they are considered to be domestic workers who are simply excluded from various collective bargaining statutes or because they are considered to be self-employed. As the Ontario government moved to a service-delivery model through contracts with non-profit organizations, many personal-care workers successfully unionized and were able to negotiate decent terms and conditions of employment. Disability activists, however, have found this service-delivery model to be overly bureaucratic and insufficiently flexible to meet the needs of people with disabilities. A number of new service-delivery models are under consideration, some of which could result in workers losing their employment status. Thus, this case illustrates the limits of current collective bargaining law and industrial relations practice and poses the challenge to think about ways of reregulating the labour market to provide both protection and flexibility.

Finally, the study of freelance editors draws our attention to a group of workers who are regarded as self-employed by the purchasers of their services and who would be unable to bring themselves within the definition of *employee*, even under an expansive legal test. Self-employed status, however, has not bestowed many benefits on these workers; as a group, they are low-paid and economically insecure. They formed an association to advance their collective interests, but it was only after the enactment of the innovative *Status of the Artist Act* that it became possible for them to pursue a collective bargaining strategy. The outcome of this enterprise is still uncertain, but this case study provides us with an opportunity to consider the possibilities and the limits of that legislation as well as the need for alternative models of state-facilitated collective bargaining that would meet the needs of contractors who cannot claim status as artists.

The order of the case studies reflects the extent to which each group of self-employed workers challenges the basic norms and institutions of labour law, from the least to the most radical. The studies have a common structure: they describe the socio-economic context in which the workers are located, the history of attempts to organize collective representation at work, the legal framework, and the legal barriers to collective bargaining that the workers have confronted. The book concludes by considering whether self-employed workers like those in the case studies should have access to collective representation and bargaining over the terms and conditions of their work. It argues that there are pressing sociological, normative, and policy reasons for extending collective bargaining rights to these groups of workers, and that there is no single form of workplace representation or collective bargaining that meets the needs of the wide range of types of self-employed workers. Drawing on the case studies, the conclusion emphasizes the need for a plurality of representational forms and mechanisms for achieving collective bargaining, and it suggests a number of different models.

Table 1
Type of self-employment by immigrant status, visible minority status, and sex, 2000

		Self-employed employer	*Own-account self-employed*
Total	Both Sexes	33.3	66.7
	Male	38.7	61.3
	Female	24.2	75.8
Immigrant	Both Sexes	37.8	62.2
	Male	43.2	56.8
	Female	28.9	71.1
Non-immigrant	Both Sexes	32.2	67.8
	Male	37.6	62.4
	Female	23.0	77.0
Visible minority	Both Sexes	44.8	55.2
	Male	51.4	48.6
	Female	38.2	61.8
Non-visible minority	Both Sexes	32.2	67.8
	Male	37.4	62.6
	Female	23.6	76.4

Source: Survey of Labour and Income Dynamics, Statistics Canada.

I

Star Wars: Newspaper Distribution Workers and the Possibilities and Limits of Collective Bargaining

1. STAR WARS

Late in the summer of 1998, the Communications, Energy and Paperworkers Union of Canada (CEP), Local 87-M, Southern Ontario Newspaper Guild,[1] was approached by a newspaper carrier for the *Toronto Star* who was seeking its assistance in organizing a union. The *Star* is Canada's largest newspaper, with a daily paid circulation of approximately 500,000. The CEP had represented the *Star*'s editorial and advertising employees since 1949, and more recently it had begun to represent some distribution workers, including the district representatives in charge of organizing home delivery. The approximately 2,000 carriers who make home deliveries had never been organized. Although for many years the *Star* relied on teenage boys to make home deliveries, in the early 1990s, the paper shifted to an adult, ethnically diverse, and mixed-gender workforce.

The organizing drive started that October and went extremely well. Union staff worked closely with the carriers and hired a Tamil-speaking woman and a male immigrant from Ghana to assist. The union applied to the Ontario Labour Relations Board (OLRB) for certification of the *Star* carriers on 13 November 1998. A representation vote was held a few weeks later, and, after some preliminary legal skirmishing, the ballots were counted. The result was 787 in favour and 250 against.[2]

This did not lead to certification, however, because the OLRB still needed to determine whether these workers were employees for the purposes of the Ontario *Labour Relations Act (OLRA)*.[3] Hearings on the issue dragged on and were not completed until April 2000. The OLRB finally issued its decision, in February 2001. It found that the carriers were employees and certified the union.[4] For a moment it seemed as if the statutory collective bargaining scheme was capable of adapting to the needs of this group of precarious workers.

However, just four days before the OLRB issued its decision, the *Star* announced that it was contracting out its home delivery. The effect would be that the 220 unionized district representatives would lose their jobs and that even if the OLRB found that the carriers were employees they would no longer be employees of the *Star*. CEP filed a complaint with the OLRB, claiming that this was an unfair labour practice because the *Star* had made this decision in order to avoid unionization, but the board refused an expedited hearing. The *Star* made it clear that its decision was unalterable and, following unsuccessful negotiations, the now-unionized carriers began a job action that escalated into a full-blown strike. A short time later, a tentative agreement was reached. It did not stop the contracting out, but rather it provided carriers with compensation and limited guarantees of employment with the new contractors. As well, a deal was reached providing compensation to the district representatives whose jobs were being outsourced. Finally, the union agreed not to seek a declaration that the new contractors were successor employers bound by the collective bargaining rights recently acquired by the carriers.

Drawing on the experience of the *Star* carriers, as well as that of other news distribution workers in Canada, this chapter investigates three areas of Canadian labour law that influence the ability of workers in general, and precarious workers in particular, to gain access to, and benefit from, collective bargaining: employment status; organizing appropriate bargaining units; and employer freedom to restructure operations. The laws regulating each of these areas pose significant difficulties for "standard" workers seeking to unionize; the problems are even greater for workers whose contractual relations are structured to minimize their connection to, and the liability of, the enterprises that benefit from their labour.

Unlike Judy Fudge's study of rural route mail carriers (chapter 2) and Leah Vosko's study of freelance editors (chapter 4), this chapter examines the operation of provincial labour relations statutes. As well, unlike

Fudge's and Cynthia Cranford's studies (Cranford's examination of personal-care workers constitutes chapter 3), it deals with private sector labour relations. Finally, it draws attention to the difficulties that precarious workers face in maintaining collective bargaining rights after their initial acquisition.

The chapter is divided into three parts. The first provides a historical overview of news distribution work to demonstrate that the phenomenon of precarious work is not a recent one. The second part explores the three dimensions of collective bargaining law mentioned earlier. Finally, this chapter considers the possibilities that the current collective bargaining scheme makes available to precarious workers and the challenges that remain.

2. PRECARIOUS NEWSPAPER DISTRIBUTION WORKERS: NOT A NEW PHENOMENON

The newspaper industry depends on a highly fragmented labour force divided between production, editorial, advertising, shipping, and distribution functions. Some of its workers, notably those in the predominantly male production and the now more mixed-gender editorial departments, have enjoyed the benefits of secure, unionized employment, although not without struggle (Burr 1999, chapter 5; Zerker 1982). Indeed, in recent years, employers have intensified their efforts to restructure the labour process and erode many of the previous gains made by these workers (Hardt and Brenen 1995; Hébert 1981; Marjoribanks 2000; Stanger 2000, 2002). For others, most notably those in circulation and distribution, the newspaper industry has always been a bastion of precarious work: part-time, insecure, poorly paid, and largely non-union. As well, many of these workers perform under contracts that purport to deny them, and sometimes succeed in denying them, employment status altogether.

Far from being a recent phenomenon, precarious work has been a standard feature of newspaper distribution for nearly 200 years. From at least the nineteenth century, newspapers were distributed in a variety of ways, including single-copy sales and home delivery (Thorn and Pfeil 1987). Single-copy sales took place through newsstands and other retail outlets, street racks and newspaper boxes, and sidewalk hawking. The last form was quite common in the nineteenth and early twentieth centuries, employing working-class boys and enabling them to make an important economic contribution to their families. Men were more commonly engaged in selling newspapers from newsstands and other fixed locations, and they often played an intermediary role between the publisher or wholesale distributor and the street hawkers. Boys largely undertook home delivery in urban areas, while in rural areas men with access to transportation were often required. The newsboys and the men were usually treated by the newspaper publishers as "little merchants" – independent business people whose earnings consisted of the difference between the price they paid for the paper and the price for which they sold it (Bekken 1995; Bullen 1986, 175–9; Thorn and Pfeil 1987, 45–50).

End-point sales work was not very lucrative, but this was not the principal concern of reform-minded citizens who objected to child labour, particularly when performed on the streets. Rather, contrary to the mythical claims of the newspaper publishers that the boys were learning business skills that would enable them to rise in the world, reformers like W.H. Howland, the mayor of Toronto, asserted: "it was ruinous to become a newsboy, in nine hundred and ninety-nine cases out of a thousand" (the 1889 Royal Commission on Relations Between Labour and Capital, in Bullen 1986, 178). In Toronto and other North American cities, this led to local regulation licensing street vendors under the age of sixteen, but not to the imposition of any obligation on the newspaper publishers to improve working conditions.

Newsboys, however, were not just passive objects of concern for middle-class reformers: they and other news distribution workers were also active agents seeking to advance their individual and collective interests. Individual strategies ranged from more or less benign trickery to violent turf wars, while collective action took many forms, one of which involved the creation of formal unions. For example, there is some record of local newsboy unions being formed in Montreal, Toronto, and London, Ontario, in the nineteenth century, although they appear to have been short-lived organizations (Forsey 1982, 311, 323, 335). In the United States, union organizing seems to have been somewhat more successful in a number of communities, including Seattle, where a newsboys' union was established in 1892 and survived until the 1960s. Despite its name, the union largely represented older boys and men who "owned" corners and often subcontracted with younger boys who hawked the papers. In some cases, newspaper publishers supported this kind of unionization because it helped bring order to what was often a chaotic situation (Bekken 1995, 208–12; Simpson 1992).

Notably, one issue that was not significant in this context was whether the workers who formed these unions were employees. This was because the then-existing labour law regime did not draw a sharp distinction between employees and independent contractors: the state did not compel employers to recognize or bargain with unions, and employers could obtain the benefit of laws protecting private property and freedom of contract regardless of the employment status of the workers in question. As well, the distinction was not yet significant in competition law (Crysler 1967). Thus, business enterprises dealt only with workers' unions when compelled to, or when they perceived it to be to their advantage (Fudge and Tucker 2001; Tomlins 1985, 60–95; Tucker 1994).

The development of mass-circulation newspapers and the continuing efforts of social reformers to more tightly control, if not eliminate, newsboys led to a number of changes in newspaper circulation. In particular, professional circulation managers were hired to bring some of the tools of scientific management to the task of increasing circulation. These new managers formed an association, which became known as the International Circulation Managers Association (ICMA) in 1910, when Canadian newspapers joined. It emerged as a powerful advocate of newspaper industry interests, particularly in the area of labour relations. One of the strategies promoted by the ICMA was the expansion of home delivery and the recruitment and training of a new kind of newsboy: one who came from a middle-class background and who could be more closely controlled and relied upon to solicit new subscribers, deliver the papers on time to the customer's door, and collect payments (Postol 1997; Thorn and Pfeil 1987, 49–57).

Although more research remains to be done, so far, no evidence has been found of union organizing by Canadian newsboys or others involved in the sale and delivery of newspapers during the first three-quarters of the twentieth century. There was much greater activity in the United States, where, in some cities, adult newsstand operators succeeded in establishing reasonably stable collective bargaining relationships. For reasons to be discussed later, the *National Labor Relations Act*[5] facilitated this growth, but it required the exclusion of street hawkers and home carriers from these state-assisted efforts. These American unions, however, were separated from the printing trades, which remained craft-oriented, and from the more recently established Newspaper Guild, which, despite its more industrial outlook, initially focused its organizing campaigns on editorial workers and later on clerical employees (Bekken 1995, 208–12; Leab 1970).

Home delivery by young carriers became the dominant form of distribution by the end of World War II. Most newspapers used district managers to supervise the carriers and various classes of drivers to deliver newspapers to distribution points. Some delivery drivers and district managers subsequently claimed statutory employment status for minimum standards and collective bargaining purposes,[6] but newspapers often responded by contracting out the distribution work, thereby eliminating the possibility of an employment relationship being created (Gyles 1999; Rankin 1986, 11–23; Thorn and Pfeil 1987, 228–55). Another major change in newspaper distribution that is particularly important for this case study was the shift from youth to adult carriers. This happened in the early 1980s at the *Globe and Mail* (out of a belief that adults would be more reliable), and in the late 1980s and early 1990s at the *Toronto Star*, when it was converted from an afternoon to a morning operation (Linder 1997, 73; Seamon 2000). The shift to adult carriers was also accompanied by an increase in the proportion of women doing this work, and in major urban areas like Toronto and Vancouver, new immigrants became disproportionately represented in the workforce.[7] The shift to adult carriers, however, was not accompanied by improved working conditions, thus providing the impetus for a new round of organizing, not only at the *Toronto Star*, but also among carriers in Vancouver and Winnipeg (Gyles 1999; Pearson 2000).[8]

3. THE POSSIBILITIES AND LIMITS OF STATUTORY COLLECTIVE BARGAINING FOR NEWSPAPER DISTRIBUTION WORKERS

From their inception, Canadian statutory collective bargaining schemes have only benefited a limited segment of Canadian workers, principally male workers who possessed key skills or who were employed in mass-production industries that prospered in the post–World War II period (Drache and Glasbeek 1992; Fudge 1993). Precarious workers found it particularly difficult to gain access to collective bargaining, and when they did, they often achieved only limited improvements. As this case study demonstrates, although precarious workers have benefited from some recent developments in various legal regimes, they must still overcome formidable barriers to benefit from collective bargaining.

A. Establishing Employment Status

Newspaper publishers have long opted not to fully integrate distribution into their operations, preferring instead to adopt a variety of arrangements, including full outsourcing to wholesalers, partial subcontracting of some components of the distribution network, and the use of workers who are designated as independent contractors. Although hard data on recent trends in the newspaper industry are not available, a reading of case law and industry trade journals suggests that these forms of vertical disintegration are becoming more prevalent. In general, publishers have been guided by a number of considerations, including the distribution of risk, efficiency, and profitability. Integral to their calculations is the reduction of labour costs, which, in turn, is closely related to the legal consequences of having employees, including liability to pay minimum wages, payroll taxes, and workers' compensation premiums, and the possibility of unionization. As noted in the introduction, however, determining whether a worker is legally classified as an employee or an independent contractor is a dicey business, especially for precarious workers like those in newspaper distribution. We will explore the legal classification of these workers in greater detail, first in the United States and then in Canada, focusing on the OLRB's decision in the *Star* carriers' case.

The American Experience: The Triumph of "Little Merchantism"
Newspaper publishers in the United States have fought tooth and nail to keep various classes of news distribution workers from claiming statutory employment status. One strategy has been to seek statutory amendments that simply exclude classes of workers, despite their employee status. For example, at the behest of the newspaper lobby, the *Social Security Act* was amended in 1939 to exclude minors delivering papers, and in 1949, all news-delivery workers were excluded from the minimum standards contained in the *Fair Labor Standards Act* (Linder 1997, 839–49). More recently, publishers have become concerned about other liabilities. In the words of Mark Anfinson, legal counsel to the Minnesota Newspaper Association, "when carriers are reclassified from independent contractors to employees bad things happen to good papers: Suddenly, publishers have a new, big staff full of people eligible for benefits, who require payroll withholding for taxes and workman's compensation, who can sue the paper on a wide variety of employment

issues and who open the newspaper to numerous other liabilities" (in Fitzgerald 1995, 18).

Recent campaigns have prodded many states to deny workers' compensation coverage to delivery workers, and in 1996, they prompted the federal government to amend the *Small Business Protection Act* to make it much easier for publishers to avoid tax liabilities by classifying newspaper carriers and distributors as independent contractors (Hernandez 1996; Linder 1997).

American newspaper publishers have also engaged in a long campaign to deprive newspaper carriers of access to the *National Labor Relations Act* (NLRA). The issue famously arose in *Hearst Publications Inc. v. National Labor Relations Board*.[9] The Los Angeles Newsboys Local Industrial Union Number 75 successfully petitioned the National Labor Relations Board (NLRB) to be certified for four units of news distribution workers who sold newspapers full time at established spots. Street hawkers and home-delivery carriers were not included in the proposed bargaining unit. The newspaper publishers challenged the NLRB's decision on the ground that the newsboys were independent contractors, not employees. At the time, the act did not define the term *employee*. The case wound its way up to the United States Supreme Court, where eight of the nine judges upheld the NLRB. The majority opinion, written by Mr Justice Rutledge, rejected the employer's contention that the term *employee* should be given its common-law meaning. Rather, it adopted a purposive approach to the interpretation of the term, emphasizing that the act aimed "to encourage collective bargaining and to remedy the individual worker's inequality of bargaining power" by protecting freedom of association for the purposes of negotiating terms and conditions of employment.[10] The court recognized that there were diverse arrangements through which services were provided and reasoned that to advance Congress's purpose it would be necessary to extend access to statutory collective bargaining beyond those who were employees according to a narrow common-law approach. Determining which service providers were to benefit was left to the NLRB, using its expertise to assess the underlying economic facts, including inequality of bargaining power. Using this approach, the court did not find it necessary to define *employee* precisely or to draw a clear distinction between employees and independent contractors.

Needless to say, employers were unhappy with this outcome, and when the political conditions changed, they succeeded in having independent contractors specifically excluded from the *NLRA* by the Taft-

Hartley Amendments of 1947 (Linder 1989, 186–95; Tomlins 1985, 247–317). Clearly, the intended effect was to exclude some service providers who might have been deemed to be statutory employees by the board under the *Hearst* approach, but the actual extent of the exclusion depended upon how and where the NLRB drew the line between employees and independent contractors. To perform this task, the NLRB developed a factor test that focused on control, opportunity for profit, and risk of loss. In the context of newspaper distribution workers, the board held that adult distributors and sellers were employees. However, because the Taft-Hartley Amendments also excluded supervisory employees from the NLRA, it became necessary to determine whether the adult distributors' relation to the child carriers brought them into this excluded category. In addition to finding that the degree of direction exercised by the distributors over the carriers was insufficient to make them supervisory employees, the board also concluded that the carriers were not employees of the newspaper. One consequence of this decision was that unions had little interest in challenging the classification of carriers as independent contractors, since to do so might be to undermine their claim that higher levels of outside adult distribution workers, a group that the union was attempting to organize, were non-supervisory employees who could participate in the collective bargaining regime (Linder 1990, 849–51).[11]

By the 1970s, however, the NLRB had begun to reverse its earlier jurisprudence. While continuing to recognize that adult distribution workers were employees, it expressed the view that carriers were employees and the adults were their supervisors. In support of this conclusion, the board pointed to the extensive control exercised over the carriers' activities, including the publishers' unilateral determination of the buying and selling price of newspapers and the size and location of routes. In these circumstances, it was simply unrealistic to think of the carriers as little merchants in business for themselves. The classification of carriers as employees under the NLRA meant that they could, in principle, unionize and bargain collectively, but all of this was hypothetical because no organizing activity was taking place among the still largely youth carriers. Indeed, carriers were not represented in any of these decisions about their status because they were not parties to the applications being made (Linder 1990, 853–9).

The issue has not received much attention in the last decade because of the paucity of organizing activity. In the *Evening News*, the UAW applied to certify a unit composed of motor-route carriers who delivered to customers in suburban areas, dropped off bundles for home-delivery carriers, stores, and businesses, and filled racks. These were adults who worked full time or regular part time. The home-delivery carriers, who were not included in the application, were youth. Using the control test to determine employment status, the board concluded that the motor-route carriers were independent contractors. In a more recent case, involving an unfair labour practice complaint arising from an organizing drive of bulk drivers employed by the *Times Herald Record*, the administrative law judge noted in passing that both carriers and motor-route drivers were independent contractors.[12] One glimmer of hope is a recent decision in which newspaper carriers for the *St. Joseph (Missouri) News-Press* were found to be employees covered by federal labour law (Stanger 2002, 207).

In sum, American publishers have successfully resisted efforts by most newspaper distribution workers to obtain statutory employment status for any purpose. This has been accomplished by obtaining statutory exclusions and by convincing administrative decision makers to treat these workers as independent contractors. To facilitate these measures, newspaper managers are trained to structure their relations with carriers in ways that will preserve their "little merchant" status under the law (Fink 1988, 203–5). Although early decisions by the NLRB opened up the possibility of extending access to collective bargaining more broadly by leaving it to the NLRB to determine who was an employee for the purposes of the NLRA and by supporting an "economic reality of dependence" test, the subsequent statutory exclusion of independent contractors and the board's application of that exclusion have made it relatively easy for publishers to structure their relations with drivers and carriers to deprive them of employment status.

The Canadian Experience: A New Hope? The employment status of newspaper distribution workers for the purposes of minimum-standards legislation was considered in Ontario in *Re Telegram Publishing Co. Ltd and William Amm and Others*,[13] a case involving district circulation managers whose work entailed contracting with and supervising carriers, taking financial responsibility for the wholesale value of the newspapers distributed through them, and obtaining new customers. Payment was determined by results, not by time. Noting the difficulty of fitting disparate fact situations into "neat legal compartments," the referee opted for the four-factor test first stated in *Montreal v. Montreal Locomotive Works Ltd*[14] to distinguish between employees and independent contractors. The four factors were: control, ownership of the tools, chance of profit, and risk of loss. In applying the test, however, the referee focused on the extent of these workers' organizational and economic dependency on the *Telegram* and on whether they were primarily contracting to supply their own labour rather than a broader array of services. The referee also had to grapple with the relationship between the district managers and the carriers, and its implications for their status. The award implicitly assumed that the carriers were the circulation managers' employees. Could an employer also be an employee? According to the referee, "the mere fact that a person hires casual labour to assist him in the performance of certain functions should not determine the issue,"[15] but rather it was just one factor to be placed in the balance. In this case, the referee determined that the circulation managers were not in business for themselves and thus were employees for the purposes of the *Employment Standards Act (ESA)*.

This approach is similar to the one endorsed by the United States Supreme Court in *Hearst*, and it lends itself to a broadening of the scope of employment status. The most recent reported decision, *Roltek Holdings Inc.*, involved a claim by a driver whose principal task was to deliver newspapers to "hand carriers." His contract, like that of the other drivers, identified him as an independent contractor, but over the years, the claimant had assumed additional responsibilities, including the supervision of other drivers. Using the *Telegram* approach, the referee found that this particular driver was an employee largely because he had assumed additional supervisory duties in relation to the other delivery drivers.[16] Despite the handful of favourable precedents, there have been few employment standards cases involving newspaper distribution workers, and officials with the Employment Standards Branch of the Ontario Ministry of Labour report that they cannot recall any complaints from newspaper carriers. They also have not undertaken proactive work on the industry.

In at least one province – British Columbia – the entitlement of newspaper carriers to minimum standards has been addressed by regulation. Prior to 1995, regulations exempted newspaper carriers from the ESA, even if they were employees. In 1995, the NDP government changed the regulations, following recommendations made in a report by Mark Thompson (1994). The exemption was narrowed to apply only to carriers who were students and worked less than fifteen hours a week. Fearful that this would turn their adult carriers into protected employees, some publishers contracted out their entire home-delivery operation. As well, newspaper publishers applied to the Employment Standards Tribunal, requesting that it make a recommendation to Cabinet to exclude newspaper carriers from coverage under the act. Following hearings, the tribunal recommended a partial exemption, and as a result, in addition to the general exclusion of student carriers from the BC ESA, non-student carriers working fifteen hours a week or less were also excluded from some hours of work and overtime provisions. Of course, news carriers must be employees and not independent contractors in order to claim any ESA benefits, and the director of the Employment Standards Branch, using a variety of tests, has consistently held that carriers are employees. These determinations have never been challenged, so there is no formal decision of the tribunal on point (Thompson 1994, 77).[17]

In contrast, news distribution workers have usually been found to be independent contractors for the purposes of tax and social wage legislation. This has been beneficial for newspaper publishers, who avoid liability for CPP/QPP and EI deductions. The interests of the news distribution workers are more ambiguous: as independent contractors, they can deduct more expenses incurred in earning income or more easily misreport their income; as employees, they would gain access to social wage programs. The divided interests of news distribution workers in gaining employment status has been an impediment to union-organizing efforts, although workers may retain their status as independent contractors for tax purposes while being employees for the purpose of collective bargaining.

Although tax authorities seemed content to accept the characterization of carriers as independent contractors notwithstanding the resulting revenue leakage, in recent years they have begun to challenge this claim. Following a determination by the Manitoba Labour Relations Board that the carriers of the *Winnipeg Free Press* (*WFP*) were employees for the purpose of collective bargaining, the Minister of National Revenue ruled that they were also employees for social wage purposes. The *Winnipeg Free Press* challenged this reclassification, and the question was considered in *Thomson Canada Ltd* (Winnipeg Free Press) *v. Canada (Minister of National Revenue)*.[18] In the course of reaching his decision, Mr Justice Porter of the Tax Court of Canada considered a wide range of issues and evidence, including the way that tax authorities addressed the employment status of news carriers in two prior rulings, one involving the *Kingston Whig-Standard* and the other the *Calgary Herald*. In the former, the minister ruled that the carriers were independent contractors, in the latter that they were employees. When the *Calgary Herald* appealed, however, the minister reversed his ruling. Justice Porter also cited an agreement reached between the Canadian Daily Newspaper Association and the minister over the calculation of the goods and services tax (GST) on newspapers. The result is that GST is calculated on the wholesale rate the newspapers charge to vendors or carriers, and it is an implicit acceptance of the theory of a sale to carriers and a resale by the carrier to the customer.[19] Justice Porter was also cognizant of the ruling by the Manitoba Labour Relations Board that the WFP carriers were employees for collective bargaining purposes.

In his summary of the case law, Justice Porter held that the correct test is one that integrates the four *Montreal Locomotive* factors (control, ownership of tools, chance of profit, and risk of loss) with integration into a business. Notably absent was any discussion of the purposes of social wage legislation or the reality of economic dependence, although some Federal Court of Appeal jurisprudence that spoke of a relationship of subordination as being the hallmark of employment was cited.[20]

The relations between the carriers and the WFP were typical of current practices within the newspaper industry. Carriers signed agreements that identified them as independent contractors; they used their own vehicles to pick up papers at drop-off depots and deliver them to customers; their time frame for performing the work was stipulated, but they were otherwise free to make whatever arrangements they chose, including engaging substitutes. They paid a wholesale rate for the papers and were credited with the retail price. In applying the test, Justice Porter found that the WFP exercised little direct control over the performance of the work. This was sharply distinguished from contractual stipulations regarding the outcomes to be achieved, a factor that is not indicative of an employment relation so long as there is no direct involvement in means adopted to reach the required result. He also found that the only tool used in the performance of the work was a vehicle that was supplied by the driver. With respect to the risk of loss and expectation of profit, Justice Porter found there was no entrepreneurial aspect to the purported sale/resale of the newspaper, and that in reality this was just an accounting measure. There was little risk of loss, except with respect to the vehicle, and Justice Porter strained to find some entrepreneurial opportunity to make a profit, pointing to the effect that good delivery could have on maintaining customers and the right under the contract for carriers to distribute other products while delivering papers. Finally, with respect to integration, Justice Porter emphasized the lack of supervision as evidence of the lack of integration of home delivery into the WFP's business.

Having completed his review of the factors, Justice Porter turned to the overall assessment. He acknowledged "other pressures" lurking in the background, recognizing that this was, in effect if not by intent, a test case that would determine the entitlement of carriers across the country to employment benefits. He accepted that they were not "typical entrepreneurial types" but rather individuals who performed "tough part-time work at inconvenient hours." Balanced against this was "the administrative nightmare and costs that would be faced" by newspaper publishers if they were required to calculate and remit EI and CPP premiums. However, these were cast aside as "political matters" that had no place in the court's decision, although they might provide a basis for exercising the power that exists in both schemes to deem groups of workers to be covered employees. Having surveyed the carriers' working situation from the magisterial heights of the bench, Justice Porter summarized his view: "I see far more of the picture of independent contractors working under individual contracts for services than employees working under a contract of service."[21]

We will return shortly to compare this decision to that of the Manitoba Labour Relations Board, but the most striking feature of Justice Porter's reasoning is the absence of any discussion of the economic realities of dependence. Not only is economic dependence not specified as an independent factor in the test, but also under the headings where it would most likely be considered – for example, in the chance of profit/risk of loss factor – the failure to touch upon economic dependence gives an unreal quality to the analysis. This was not an oversight. In concluding his discussion of the control factor, Justice Porter ruled that economic dependency was legally irrelevant: "The simple fact of economic imbalance does not amount to subordination."[22] Furthermore, there was no place in the judgment for any purposive analysis of social wage legislation and how that might affect the determination of entitlement. While these alternative approaches would not necessarily have led to a different result, they might have helped break down the artificially sharp distinction drawn by the judge between legal considerations on the one hand and political and economic ones on the other, as well as making more legally salient the vulnerability of the workers in question (Tucker 1985).

One other component of social wage legislation is workers' compensation. In Ontario, coverage is extended to most workers who are employed by employers in scheduled industries, and employers are required to pay the premiums. Independent contractors or sole proprietors in scheduled industries may apply for coverage, but the law specifies that they will be their own employers, personally liable for premiums.[23] To determine the scope of employment, the Workplace Safety and Insurance Board (WSIB) uses an organization or "business reality" test that examines three features: control, chance of profit/risk of loss, and "other applicable criteria." Its operational policy manual provides more detailed guidance on the application of the test, and the WSIB has also issued directions and orders specifying whether some occupational groups are covered workers or not (Dee, McCombie, and Newhouse 1999, 29–33; Gilbert et al. 1995, 3–6).[24] News distribution workers are not explicitly identified in any board order or direction; and in the only reported appeal decision, a newspaper delivery driver was held to be a covered worker. The WSIB position is that it will decide the status of newspaper carriers on the merits of each case, but it appears that carriers are generally not considered employees for the purposes of workers' compensation. For example, the *Star* was not paying premiums for its carriers.[25]

Collective bargaining legislation covers both employees and dependent contractors (see the introduction to this book). In Ontario, a dependent contractor is defined as a "person, whether or not employed under a contract of employment, and whether or not furnishing tools ... owned by the dependent contractor, who performs work or services for another person for compensation or reward on such terms and conditions that the dependent contractor is in a position of economic dependence upon, and under an obligation to perform duties for, that person more closely resembling the relation of an employee than that of an independent contractor."[26] As a result, almost all disputes over employment status revolve around whether the workers in question fit within the dependent contractor definition. However, because the law also stipulates that a unit of dependent contractors is an appropriate one for collective bargaining purposes, in some instances it may be necessary to distinguish between dependent contractors and other employees. In either event, the OLRB has developed a multifactor test that is applied with an eye to the purpose of the legislation (Sack, Mitchell, and Price 1997, paras 2.43–56).

In 1985, unions seeking to represent newspaper delivery drivers for the *Ottawa Citizen* and *Le Droit* applied to be certified. These were the first applications from newspaper distribution workers in Ontario. All the drivers owned their vehicles and were paid according to formulas worked out by the newspapers. In *Citizen*, the board identified three "clusters of factors" relevant to determining dependent contractor status: identification of the company with the contractor; ownership of the vehicles; and financial arrangements between the parties. It also referred to an earlier decision, in *Algonquin Tavern*, that identified eleven more specific factors, including the right to use substitutes, whether the services were sold to the market generally, and the degree of specialization. In applying these factors, the board concluded that the *Ottawa Citizen* drivers were independent contractors. However, in *Journal Le Droit*, the board applied the same test and came to the opposite conclusion, largely on the basis that these workers were more closely controlled, less able to take on other work because they spent more time delivering newspapers, and more integrated into the newspaper's operation.[27] The lesson was clear: small differences in contract language could have great legal significance.

Newspaper publishers and their legal advisers have applied this lesson, and since 1985, no other newspaper delivery drivers have successfully claimed dependent contractor status. In *Ajax Pickering News Advertiser*, the board reproduced the carefully drafted "contractor agreement," which stated explicitly that the contractor was not an employee and gave the contractor the right to engage employees or subcontract. The board found that the newspaper did not control the means by which the work was performed but was only concerned that the result met its requirements. It also pointed to the fact that the majority of drivers claimed self-employment status for tax purposes as evidence of entrepreneurial activity. Similarly, in *Kitchener-Waterloo Record*, the board applied the multitude of factors to three classes of drivers under contract with the newspaper and found that there was not a relationship of economic dependence. The drivers were not impeded from working for others and were not controlled in the performance of their tasks.[28]

Against this background of unfavourable decisions, it was somewhat surprising that CEP was even willing to take on the task of organizing the *Star* carriers when first approached in 1998. There were, however, a number of factors that presumably encouraged the union to accept the challenge. Aside from strategic calculations about their ability to organize and the potential bargaining power of the carriers, perhaps the most important was that carriers in two other jurisdictions, British Columbia and Manitoba, were being organized by other CEP locals and had successfully claimed employee status.

In British Columbia, outside news distribution workers had been far more successful than their Ontario counterparts in obtaining dependent contractor recognition, notwithstanding the similarity of the legal tests.[29] The reasons for the different outcome are difficult to discern. Perhaps the Manitoba Labour Relations Board's comparison of the cases says it best: "A review of those decisions shows that the British Columbia Labour Relations Board apparently is in favour of certification in such cases as this, and the Ontario Labour Relations Board apparently is not."[30] In any event, the British Columbia jurisprudence made the province a propitious location for the first modern-day Canadian newspaper carrier organizing campaign, which began in April 1997 among the carriers for Semiahmoo Management, a company to which Pacific Press, a division of the Southam newspaper chain and publisher of the *Vancouver Sun* and *Province*, had subcontracted delivery. Fifty-seven carriers worked for Semiahmoo pursuant to written purchase/distribution agreements. In typical fashion, they were required to provide their own vehicles and permitted to use substitutes and work for other companies (including competitors). Shortly after the organizing drive commenced, Semiahmoo circulated newsletters threatening to downsize in the event the union was certified and terminated a union supporter. As a result, the union brought an unfair labour practice complaint, and in response Semiahmoo raised the question of the carriers' employment status. The board listed ten factors that were relevant to that determination: the way the industry operates; the type of work involved and its source; the nature of the applicant's operations; the organization of the employer's operations and the degree to which the contractors are a continuing part of it; the contractual relations between the parties and others; the type and extent of control exercised by the employer; the nature and manner of compensation and how it is determined; the percentage of income the contractor derives from the employer; the opportunity for the contractor to make a profit through independent entrepreneurial judgment; and the contractor's opportunity for economic mobility, and whether the contractor solicits customers elsewhere.[31] When applying these factors, the board found they pointed in different directions, so that, at the end of the day, a marginal judgment had to be made. The board concluded that the carriers were more akin to employees than to independent contractors. It went on to uphold the unfair labour practice complaints, although it rejected the union's contention that the inclusion of an independent contractor provision in the contract of hiring in itself interfered with the right to organize.[32]

In the spring of 1997, there was also an organizing drive by CEP among the carriers of the *Winnipeg Free Press*, a member of the Thomson newspaper chain. The union won a certification vote by a large majority, but it had to await the outcome of a hearing into the workers' employment status. The board's July 1998 decision emphasized that in Manitoba, unlike in Ontario and British Columbia, there was no longer a dependent contractor provision. As part of the NDP's 1984 labour law amendments, it had adopted the Saskatchewan approach, which empowers the board to designate persons as employees. As a result, the question of who is an employee is no longer a question of law and fact, but rather a matter of policy. This means that the board can focus on the question of whether a group of persons ought to be able to bargain collectively, not whether they fit within a class of persons legally entitled to do so.[33]

Despite this legal difference, the Manitoba Labour Board approached the designation issue in much the same way that labour boards determine legal employment status. Indeed, in some ways the board chose a more conservative formulation of the criteria, emphasizing the importance of control over the work and ignoring the economic reality of dependence. Nevertheless, the board followed Semiahmoo, designated the carriers as employees, and certified the union.[34]

Thus, by the time CEP started organizing the *Star* carriers, in October 1998, there was a small body of Canadian precedent supporting the view that newspaper carriers were employees for the purposes of labour law. In its decision, the OLRB painstakingly applied the multifactor test to the circumstances of the *Star* carriers. Of particular significance was its emphasis on "the structure of the relationship between the individual and the employer" and whether "the relationship renders the individual economically dependent upon the employer."[35] The board found that there was little independence or scope for entrepreneurial activity: carriers were largely limited to one route; the gains from generating new business were minimal; "the use of substitutes [did] not create the possibility of profiting from the labour of others which is a hallmark of the entrepreneurial engagement of employees"; and the fact that some carriers had other businesses was irrelevant, since it did not alter the relationship between the carrier and the newspaper.[36] This finding, in conjunction with the board's view of the degree of integration and level of control over the work performance, led the board to conclude that the carriers were more akin to part-time employees than independent contractors.

In sum, the experience of newspaper distribution workers generally, and carriers in particular, illustrates the indeterminacy of the legal distinction between employees and independent contractors, even when a multifactor test is deployed. However, recent labour board decisions indicate that the test can be applied to extend employee status to some groups of precarious contract workers, enabling them to gain access to the collective bargaining system. While we cannot be too sanguine about the broader significance of these cases, they suggest that the doors to collective bargaining are being pried open.

B. Organizing Appropriate Bargaining Units

In order for a union to become certified as a bargaining agent, it must win majority support among a group of employees who comprise an appropriate bargaining unit. As observed in the introduction, organizing workers is never an easy task, but it is particularly challenging when contractors are the target population. As well, the definition of the appropriate bargaining unit can cause serious problems, which are often exacerbated in the context of precarious workers. The experience of newspaper distribution workers is illustrative.

Appropriate Bargaining Units As discussed in the introduction, labour board decisions on the appropriate bargaining unit have produced a highly fragmented bargaining structure. The newspaper industry provides a good example of this phenomenon. Historically, the earliest unions in the printing trades represented groups of workers organized by skill or craft – including compositors, printers, and graphic artists. Each craft had its own union and bargained separately from other groups of workers. Later, the newspaper guild generally represented more broadly defined groups of workers, including editorial, clerical, and sales staff. Often, these employees were certified on a departmental basis, but in recent years, labour boards have generally favoured more inclusive bargaining units to avoid excessive fragmentation, which was found to impede stable industrial relations (Sack, Mitchell, and Price 1997, para. 3.340).[37]

Workers involved in outside distribution were not usually included in these more inclusive units and were, with few exceptions, unorganized. Until recently, neither the printing trade unions nor the guild – or other unions, for that matter – evinced much interest in these workers. Since the mid-1980s, however, organizing drives among district circulation supervisors and delivery drivers have been conducted by a variety of unions, while the CEP has conducted all the recent Canadian organizing campaigns among newspaper carriers.[38]

Disputes over the appropriateness of a bargaining unit of newspaper delivery workers have arisen in two contexts. The first is at the organizing stage, where the question is whether the group that the union has applied to represent is appropriate for collective bargaining. The answer will affect whether the union enjoys majority support. But apart from the usual strategic behaviour on the part of unions trying to exclude non-supporters and employers seeking to include them, there is often an additional problem when contractors are the target group: the diversity of contractual arrangements. This can make it difficult to construct or identify a group of workers who share a community of interest. For example, a 1999 application by the teamsters' union to represent the wholesalers of the *Toronto Sun* failed because the OLRB held that "it is not possible for the Board, on the basis of the union's submissions, to configure a clear, coherent and objectively determinable bargaining unit."[39] This has been less of an issue in the carrier cases, although some minor disputes over the definition of the bargaining unit have arisen.[40]

The second context in which bargaining unit determinations play a vital role is related to bargaining structure. Each bargaining unit that is recognized for the purpose of certification will remain distinct for bargaining purposes, unless an alternative arrangement is agreed to by the parties or an amalgamation of units is ordered by the board – in jurisdictions where that is permitted. Where the proposed bargaining unit is composed of workers who are dependent contractors, the law deems them to be an appropriate bargaining unit with a distinct community of interest. However, it permits dependent contractors to be part of a more inclusive unit if the majority of dependent contractors favour this arrangement.[41] As well, in Ontario, the board historically certified part-time and full-time employees separately, although more recently it has rejected the axiomatic view that the two groups lack a community of interest.[42] For small groups of workers in the newspaper distribution chain, a separate unit can be problematic because it is unlikely to enjoy significant bargaining power, and therefore the gains from collective bargaining may be minimal. Moreover, the board will not impose a multi-employer bargaining structure that would enable unionized workers employed by different newspaper companies to bargain together.

One possible way of allowing smaller groups of workers to be certified while avoiding fragmentation is to allow labour boards to combine or alter bargaining units after certification has occurred. The power to combine bargaining units of a single employer existed under the Ontario NDP's labour law, in force from 1993 to 1995, after which the newly elected Conservative government retroactively repealed it, thus undoing all the combinations previously ordered by the OLRB. During this small window of opportunity, unions representing newspaper workers made a number of successful applications.[43] In British Columbia, the board retains the power to bring new groups of workers into existing bargaining units, but it has resisted the amalgamation of dependent contractor units into broader-based newspaper units on the ground that the applicant unions failed to demonstrate the existence of reasonable procedures for integration.[44] This heightened concern frustrated the democratic wishes of the majority of dependent contractors who favoured amalgamation and the general policy supporting inclusive bargaining units. These decisions also ignored the existing legal obligation on trade unions to fairly represent all their members.

In the case of the *Toronto Star*, it might be argued that because the carrier unit was larger than the rest of the local membership, fragmentation was less of an issue. Still, as we shall see, the fact that the news carriers were in a separate bargaining unit from the other workers represented by the CEP may have impaired the union's ability to oppose the employer's post-certification actions. For example, these other "core" workers were not permitted to withdraw their labour in an effort to pressure the *Star* to reverse its decision to contract out distribution.

Organizing The limited response of the law to the structurally unequal positions of employers and workers has affected some, but not all, of the recent organizing drives among newspaper distribution workers. For example, during the organizing drive of the carriers at Semiahmoo Management (a subcontractor of Dolphin Delivery, to whom Pacific Press contracted distribution of the *Vancouver Sun* and the *Province*), the employer was found to have committed several unfair labour practices, including firing a carrier who supported the union and telling workers that unionization could lead to a reduction in the number of carriers. Despite this legal victory, the organizing drive fizzled due to the dampening effect of employer threats and to the fact that another contractor for Pacific Press convinced the British Columbia

Labour Relations Board that its regular delivery of some newspapers outside the province brought it under federal jurisdiction. This meant that the organizing drive had to be initiated all over again, and by then enthusiasm had waned.[45]

While the legal ground rules often impede union organizers' access to workers, because of the structure of distribution, this did not loom large in the carrier organizing campaigns. The case of the *Toronto Star* was typical. Carriers queued up at approximately fifty delivery drops in the Greater Toronto Area in the early morning hours to pick up their papers. These sites provided a natural opportunity for organizing activities; organizers were not on private property controlled by the *Star*, so they could approach carriers. Moreover, because there were delivery delays approximately 20 per cent of the time, the carriers often had downtime for which they were not paid, making them particularly amenable to the union's message. Finally, the district representatives were CEP members and many supported the carrier campaign.[46]

Apart from legal impediments, the task of organizing requires a significant commitment of resources on the part of the union, especially when the target workers are from diverse linguistic and cultural communities that do not already have roots in the local labour movement. In the case of the *Star* carriers, for example, the union estimated that 20 per cent of the carriers were Tamil, and that there were also sizable groups from India, Poland, Ghana, Vietnam, and South America. The CEP responded to this situation by hiring a Tamil-speaking organizer and one who had emigrated from Ghana. A well-planned organizing campaign for a receptive audience of disgruntled workers resulted in a quick and successful drive, completed in about two months.[47]

C. *The Empire Strikes Back: Property Rights and Restructuring*

As noted in the introduction, the Canadian collective bargaining system remains firmly rooted in a voluntarist model that leaves employers' freedom of contract and property rights largely untouched. While they have a duty to bargain in good faith, employers are free to agree only to terms and conditions that they find acceptable. Because many newly certified unions are unable to overcome this hurdle, some jurisdictions make first-contract arbitration available in certain circumstances. Carriers of the *Winnipeg Free Press* benefited from such a provision but then had to conduct a five-day strike, in November 2000, to obtain a second agreement.

In contrast, the *Star* carriers could not resort to first-contract arbitration because of the Conservative government's 1995 labour law reforms limiting access to it.[48] Their situation, however, was further complicated by the *Star*'s exercise of its property rights to contract out the delivery operation, a power that is particularly potent in relations with contractors, such as newspaper carriers, whose work is already marginal to the core business of the employer. Employers' freedom to redeploy their property as they see fit is partially limited by the law: it protects bargaining rights when there has been a sale of a business as opposed to a contracting out; it stipulates that employers cannot contract out for the purpose of avoiding unionization; and it may require employers to disclose plans to contract out as part of the good-faith bargaining requirement or pursuant to a statutory structural adjustment or technological change provision. But because the law is so weak, some unions have negotiated for additional protection in the collective agreement.

Newspaper unions faced with contracting out have attempted to use whatever protection was available to them, with limited effect. Efforts to argue that contracting out amounts to a sale of business and that acquiring entities are bound by the existing collective agreements have been largely unsuccessful, although in at least one case a labour board held that the disposition by a newspaper of its wholesale distribution constituted the sale of a business.[49] Unions have also faced an uphill battle in characterizing contracting out as an unfair labour practice. For example, when Pacific Press outsourced its wholesale operations, the British Columbia Labour Relations Board rejected the union's argument that contracting out per se interfered with the formation, selection, or administration of a trade union without proof of specific anti-union animus. Moreover, there was no anti-union animus when the employer contracted out because the cost of the collective agreement was too high. Indeed, the board relied on a Coopers and Lybrand report commissioned by the employer that showed considerable saving could be achieved by contracting out as evidence of an innocent motivation.[50] The matter came up again when Pacific Press contracted out supervision of home delivery. The board again rejected the union's claim that contracting out in itself interfered with trade union rights guaranteed under the law. The fact that Pacific Press was expressly motivated by a desire to avoid being found to be the employer of newspaper carriers under the *Employment Standards Act* following the change to the regulations that eliminated their wholesale exclusion did not in any way taint its decision in the eyes of the board; indeed, it constituted a valid business justification for their action.[51]

Good-faith bargaining and other statutory notice requirements have also provided little protection against contracting out. For example, in the Pacific Press cases, the Labour Board was called upon to interpret the effect of the provision in the BC *Labour Code* requiring employers introducing significant changes to give sixty days' notice and to meet with those concerned to discuss adjustment plans in good faith. In the wholesale distribution case, the board held that the section does not prevent the employer from making an irrevocable agreement to contract out prior to notifying the union, provided that notice of the irrevocable change is given sixty days before it is to take effect.[52] Presumably, a similar interpretation would apply to a notice requirement in a collective agreement. Few unions, however, have either procedural or substantive protection in their collective agreements against contracting out. As a result, newspaper distribution workers have been forced to rely on work jurisdiction provisions that define the scope of bargaining unit work. Arbitrators, however, have rejected the argument that a work jurisdiction clause limits contracting out, but they have been willing to enforce specific limitations, such as ones designed to protect the job security of bargaining unit members.[53]

The difficulty of obtaining effective protection against contracting out is spotlighted by events at the *Star*. The issue first arose in 1992, when the *Star* decided to outsource primary distribution by delivery drivers. The guild went on strike and won contract language that placed some substantive and procedural limitations on the right of the *Star* to contract out bargaining unit work where it would result in the loss of jobs. Specifically, the *Star* was required to give the union ninety days' notice; meet with the union to discuss alternatives; offer voluntary termination options if no alternative was found; and lay off in accordance with the provisions of the collective agreement if staff-reduction targets were not met on a voluntary basis. The agreement specifically excluded juvenile or adult carriers from these protections, even though, at the time, the guild did not represent these workers.[54]

The *Star* began exploring the option of contracting out its home delivery some time after the union won the representation vote, in January 1999. It commissioned PricewaterhouseCoopers to prepare a report on its distribution costs. That study, delivered in January 2001, found that the *Star*'s distribution costs were the highest in Canada, and that it could save approximately $6 million by outsourcing its secondary distribution to homes and vending boxes. Because of the extraordinary delay at the OLRB, no decision had yet been reached on whether the carriers were dependent contractors.[55] On 29 January 2001, the *Star* formally announced its plans to outsource its newspaper distribution. Not only did this entail the layoff of approximately two hundred unionized *Star* employees who supervised secondary distribution, but it also meant that even if the OLRB found that the carriers were employees, they would not be the *Star*'s employees after the outsourcing took place. Four days later, and over two years after the certification application, the board finally issued its decision that the carriers were employees and that the certification application was successful.

The union now had to juggle two processes simultaneously: the contracting-out procedures in the collective agreement that covered the delivery supervisors; and the negotiation of a new collective agreement for the carriers who stood to lose their employment relationship with the *Star* and their collective bargaining rights if contracting out went ahead. In respect of the carriers, the union commenced bargaining immediately in order to put itself into a legal strike position as soon as possible. A strike vote was conducted on 20 February 2001, with 95 per cent of ballots cast in favour, and the union was in a legal strike position on 17 March. At the same time, it began meeting with the *Star* to discuss alternatives to contracting out under the collective agreement. The third prong of its strategy was to launch a complaint with the OLRB alleging that the contracting out was an unfair labour practice motivated by an anti-union animus – the desire to rid itself of unionized carriers. In order to prevent the *Star* from taking further steps to implement its contracting-out plan, the union also sought a judicial injunction preserving the status quo until the board could deal with the matter.[56] On 14 March, the court dismissed the injunction application because the union was not prepared to give an undertaking that it would compensate the *Star* for damages if its application to the board was ultimately unsuccessful. Moreover, the court would not relieve the union of this obligation.[57] Because of this decision and the limited protection offered by the outsourcing provision in the collective agreement covering the distribution supervisors, the union was left with two weapons to combat the outsourcing plan: the complaint before the OLRB and strike action by the carriers. Although the OLRB complaint stood a reasonable chance of success, the union was unable to get an expedited hearing and decided that it could not risk another lengthy delay.[58] The only alternative was a strike.

The union began job actions on 20 March and only called for a full-scale walkout at the beginning of April. The response from the carriers, however, was less than overwhelming. Although some union activists felt that not enough had been done to keep the membership mobilized, union leaders emphasized the difficulty of sustaining high levels of grassroots activity while waiting for more than two years for a determination on whether the union would be certified as bargaining agent. As well, during this period, there had been a 40 per cent turnover in the membership of the bargaining unit. Finally, the contracting-out issue was a divisive one, as many of the newer carriers viewed the compensation being offered by the *Star* as a windfall.[59]

In negotiations, the *Star* made it clear that its decision to contract out was irreversible, and the union soon accepted that it could not force the newspaper to back down. As a result, it focused instead on getting the best compensation package that it could, both for the carriers and the district representatives who would be laid off. A tentative deal was reached on 11 April, and it was ratified by a two-to-one margin after a stormy meeting on 14 April. The collective agreement provided laid-off carriers with between $3,000 and $4,000, depending on years of service. Carriers were further guaranteed a job offer from the successor contractors at the current rate until 28 February 2002. A deal was also reached giving circulation employees affected by the contracting out increased severance payments. In return, the union agreed to withdraw its OLRB complaint and to refrain from pursuing a successor rights claim against the new contractors.[60]

In sum, the union was unable to use the contracting-out provisions of the existing collective agreement or the carrier collective bargaining process to stop the *Toronto Star* from contracting out bargaining unit work. It did, however, get the *Star* to increase the payout to the affected workers. It is highly unlikely that better organization and more resources could have produced a different result. The *Star* took a $27-million writedown for the cost of contracting out before the strike and absorbed another $20-million loss to win the strike (Acharya 2001a, 2001b).[61] But the larger and more important point is that current law places all workers at risk of losing their relation with their employer, and possibly their employment status altogether, to outsourcing. Precariously employed workers are especially at risk. The legal freedom that employers enjoy to restructure their operations, in conjunction with their superior economic power, results in a situation where collective bargaining rights and other entitlements contingent upon maintaining an employment relationship are all too easily lost.

CONCLUSION

Collective bargaining offers workers the opportunity to improve the terms and conditions of their employment, but under our current law, workers experience increasing difficulty accessing and benefiting from it. This is especially true for precarious workers such as newspaper carriers. On the positive side, labour boards have given newspaper carriers access to the system by expanding the boundaries of the employee/dependent contractor category. As well, given their number and strategic location, newspaper carriers have some bargaining leverage, even where certified as a separate bargaining unit from other newspaper employees. Moreover, because many carriers are dissatisfied with their current conditions, they have become receptive to the appeals of unions trying to organize them.

There are, however, significant obstacles to overcome. Unions must learn to work more effectively with multi-ethnic workforces and to develop innovative organizing and mobilization strategies that respond to the specific situation of precarious workers (Erickson et al. 2002; Ghosh 2003). But even strongly committed and highly innovative unions will not be able to bring the benefits of collective bargaining to newspaper carriers and other precarious workers unless some fundamental structures of the law are changed. A fuller set of principles for reform will be offered in the conclusion to this book, but this case study clearly shows the vulnerability of any rights that are attached to the existence of a contract of employment with a particular employer rather than to the performance of work in an industry. A more expansive definition of *employee* will not address this problem, because employers can respond in the same way that many newspaper publishers have: faced with the possibility that their carriers would gain employee status for the purposes of collective bargaining, they contracted out their entire home-delivery operation. Of course, it is possible that the carriers will be held to be employees of the successor contractors, but even where this happens, the cost and difficulty of organizing smaller employers increases, and the likelihood of bargaining improved terms and conditions decreases, as does the ability of workers to enforce minimum standards. There are no panaceas in a social formation that values private property rights so highly, but a good beginning is to put (back) onto the political agenda some form of broader-based bargaining that establishes industry-wide standards for all persons performing the same work, regardless of their employment status.

2

Deemed to be Entrepreneurs: Rural Route Mail Couriers and Canada Post

The poor Country Cousins of the Canada Post,
Are the Rural Route Couriers who give their utmost.

They service the Country, those in need of the mail,
They seek a fair wage, but to no avail.

To meet those in charge we must all unite.
And we'll get a fair wage,
Or they're in for a fight.

The poor Country Cousins will no longer sit still,
And let this big Corporation push them at will.[1]

Each day, about 6,000 rural route mail couriers sort millions of bills, letters, cards, newspapers, parcels, and advertisements and then drive hundreds of thousands of kilometres across rural and suburban Canada to drop them into private postboxes, group boxes, and super-mailboxes. Prior to 1 January 2004, the couriers used their own vehicles, paid their own operating expenses, and found replacements when they were unable to personally deliver the mail. If they were injured, rural route mail couriers were not entitled to workers' compensation benefits (unless they were self-insured), and if they lost their mail delivery contracts they were not allowed to claim employment insurance benefits. Canada Post was under no legal obligation to abide by occupational health and safety legislation or to adhere to minimum employment standards when it came to rural route mail couriers. Nor did it have a legal duty to bargain collectively with the couriers or their elected representative. Because rural route mail couriers were deemed to be independent contractors and not employees under specific postal legislation, they were not entitled to labour protection or labour rights.

On an individual basis, rural route mail couriers have almost no bargaining power against Canada Post. The vast majority are individuals living in rural or suburban Canada for whom delivering the mail is the primary source of income. By contrast, Canada Post operates one of the largest communications networks in the country. It is Canada's seventh-largest employer (with 57,500 employees), and it ranks forty-sixth among Canadian businesses in consolidated revenues.[2] It is also a Crown corporation with a public policy mandate, and it is therefore subject to political control. Canada Post has the power to dictate the terms of its relationship with rural route mail couriers. For these reasons, the couriers have regarded themselves as "the poor Country Cousins of the Canada Post."

The idea of collective representation was conceived in 1985 by a small group of mail couriers who were disgruntled about the deterioration of their working conditions and their low remuneration. In the mid-1980s, Canada Post's attempt to restructure the rural network, which was a central element in the Conservative government's plan to commercialize the post office, prompted rural route mail couriers to organize. But it was the Canada Labour Relations Board's 1986 review of the bargaining units at Canada Post that gave the rural route mail couriers the opportunity to challenge their legal status, and that attracted the attention of the postal unions.

There have been three separate campaigns to unionize rural and suburban-route couriers. The first, fueled by the Canada Labour Relations Board's decision that the rural route mail couriers were employees under the *Canada Labour Code*[3] (the legislation providing for collective bargaining in private sector enterprises within federal jurisdiction), was derailed when the couriers' association was abandoned by the postal unions after the Federal Court of Appeal overturned the board's decision. The court held that subsection 13(5) of the *Canada Post Corporation Act*, which deems mail contractors – including those people who deliver to rural routes – to be independent contractors, trumps general labour law.

The second and third campaigns to unionize the couriers involved the Canadian Union of Postal Workers (CUPW). The first of CUPW's campaigns was based upon a union-building model designed to develop the capacity of rural and suburban couriers to organize and represent themselves. Established in 1997 with the assistance of CUPW, the Organization of Rural Route Mail Couriers (ORRMC) signed up rural and suburban mail couriers and embarked on a political campaign to persuade the Liberal government to change the law deeming rural route mail couriers to be entrepreneurs. In 2002, CUPW changed its tack, sending 160 organizers into the field to persuade couriers to sign CUPW membership cards. While the couriers and the large postal union continued to bring political pressure to bear on the federal government, the campaign for representation rights shifted to the bargaining table. CUPW made contracting in rural and suburban mail couriers a key demand in the 2003 round of negotiations with Canada Post, and it backed this demand by applying to the Canada Industrial Relations Board (the tribunal that replaced the Canada Labour Relations Board) to represent the rural and suburban couriers and have them placed in the broad postal operations bargaining unit. This strategy proved successful, and on 1 January 2004, Canada Post recognized rural and suburban mail couriers as employees and CUPW as their bargaining representative.

The poor economic status of rural route mail couriers was directly attributable to their legal designation as independent contractors and not employees. This case study recounts their struggle to secure legal status as employees and the right to bargain collectively. It demonstrates that the distinction between employees (who are entitled to legal protection under employment standards and collective bargaining legislation) and independent contractors (who are subject to commercial law) is not based on principle. Instead, the scope of collective bargaining legislation is subject to political fiat and depends upon the amount of economic and political power a particular group of workers wields. The study also shows how support from institutions such as unions, labour boards, courts, and political parties influences the power of precarious workers.

Part 1 describes the socio-economic status of rural carriers and links it to their legal status as independent contractors. Beginning with the transformation, in the early 1980s, of the post office from a government department to a Crown corporation, part 2 focuses on the extent to which the decision to continue to deny rural route mail couriers employee status was a political one based on an imperative to keep labour costs low. After describing the economic and political changes in the mid-1980s that prompted the couriers to challenge their legal status, part 3 shows how union support for the couriers' struggle was tenuous and reveals the limitations of the predominantly legal campaign. Starting with CUPW's 1995 decision to assist rural carriers, part 4 illustrates that despite the problems the prevailing legal regime poses for precarious self-employed workers, with the help of powerful unions they can secure collective bargaining rights. The chapter concludes by emphasizing the lessons to be learned from the campaigns to represent and secure collective bargaining for rural and suburban mail couriers.

1. POOR COUNTRY COUSINS: THE ECONOMIC STATUS OF RURAL ROUTE MAIL COURIERS

Rural route mail couriers have been categorized as independent contractors since the first rural route opened in Ancaster in southwestern Ontario in 1908. The rural delivery system expanded dramatically in the first half of the twentieth century, and the number of rural contractors also increased. Not much is known about the early contractors or their terms and conditions of work; they did not receive much attention until the 1940s and 1950s, when allegations of patronage in the awarding of rural contracts were frequently raised in the House of Commons (Campbell 1994, 78).

Patronage was also a problem when it came to selecting the postmasters who ran the rural post offices out of which rural couriers worked. However, the federal government's methods for dealing with complaints made by postmasters and those made by rural route couriers were very different. Historically, most postmasters were men who enjoyed considerable standing in their local communities and thus had some political power. They also exercised some control over rural couriers – postmasters have traditionally been responsible for ensuring the quality of rural couriers' work by fielding customer complaints, and they have had the power to influence the couriers' working conditions since they control their access to the post office. In 1948, the postmasters managed to persuade the government that they should be recognized as employees and treated as civil servants. Despite this legal recognition and the benefits that came with it, postmasters had ambivalent views about employee status and trade unions. According to the official history of the Canadian Postmasters and Assistants Association (CPAA), the union representing the postmasters, "the postmaster is not exactly an employee though he works for the Canada Post Corporation. He is a manager the same way someone may manage a bank staff. He is a member of a union, but likes to consider himself a step above unionism" (Canadian Postmasters 1983, ii).

Historically, most rural route mail couriers have been women with little political clout. In the early 1950s, rural route mail couriers banded together in a short-lived organization. Although they were not able to secure employment status, they managed to win some protection from unfettered competition. When the public tendering system for contracts with the post office was introduced in 1956, the rural couriers obtained an exemption for contracts valued at under $10,000, which enabled them to retain their contracts after the five-year term expired without submitting them to public tender.[4]

Although rural route couriers perform many of the same tasks as the letter carriers who sort and deliver mail throughout urban Canada,[5] their legal status and terms and conditions of work have been, and remain, very different. The vast majority of letter carriers have been men, they have been employed in urban centres, and they have worked in groups out of a central depot. They have always been recognized as postal employees, and they have been represented by a trade union since 1891. By contrast, rural contractors have been dispersed in rural offices where, traditionally, one or two women have worked under the direction of a male postmaster. Today, about two-thirds of the rural and suburban mail couriers work out of offices staffed by members of the CPAA, and about one-third work alongside CUPW members in letter carrier depots. There are about 5,000 couriers who deliver along traditional rural routes, and another 1,000 with routes in the suburbs, which is why the couriers have come to refer to themselves as "rural and suburban" mail couriers. Approximately 60 per cent of rural and suburban letter carriers are women. The majority of rural route mail contractors receive a rate of pay that hovers around the minimum wage, and they are not entitled to employment-related protection.[6]

But even within the rural market, other workers do better than the rural couriers who work for Canada Post. Postmasters and their assistants, who are recognized as employees, earn higher wages than do couriers, receive employment-related benefits, and bargain collectively with Canada Post (Canadian Postmasters 1983, 49). Moreover, in the United States, where rural route mail couriers are recognized as employees and have the right to bargain collectively, wages are much higher and benefits much better than those allotted to their Canadian counterparts. Rural letter carriers' wages in the United States are approximately three to four times the level of the US minimum wage, and the collective agreement between the United States Postal Service (USPS) and the National Rural Letter Carriers' Association provides for vehicle expenses and a range of contractual benefits and social entitlements.[7]

The dispersed nature of rural route mail couriers' work has made it difficult for them to organize to bring collective pressure to bear on the post office. Moreover, the fact that most rural route mail couriers have been women has contributed to their marginal status. The way the work is organized and located has combined with the marginal political status of women workers to create a legal classification that perpetuates the precarious status of rural route mail couriers.

2. ENTREPRENEURS: THE LEGAL STATUS OF RURAL ROUTE MAIL CONTRACTORS

The precarious economic status of rural route mail couriers is attributable to their explicit designation as mail contractors and not employees under subsection 13(5) of the *Canada Post Corporation Act*, the 1981 legislation that transformed the post office from a government department into a Crown corporation. It states: "Notwithstanding any provision of Part I of the *Canada Labour Code*, for the purposes of the application of that Part to the Corporation and to the officers and employees of the Corporation, a mail contractor is deemed not to be a dependent contractor or an employee within the meanings of those terms in subsection 3(1) of that Act."[8] This provision overrides the definitions of *employee* and *dependent contractor* in the *Canada Labour Code*.[9]

The exclusion of rural route mail couriers from the legal status of employee under the *Canada Labour Code* had its origins in the *Post Office Act*, which governed the post office when it was a federal government department. The *Post Office Act* legislatively enshrined the political compromise that the government fashioned by balancing the legal status of rural route mail contractors against contractual security.[10] The definition of *postal employee* excluded "a mail contractor or an employee of a mail contractor," while the provisions regarding "contracts for the conveyance of mail" exempted contracts that did not exceed $10,000 a year from the public tendering system if "the Postmaster General is satisfied that it is in the public interest that such contract be renewed."[11]

In 1980, the rural couriers' economic and legal status was raised during the discussions about the transformation of the post office from a government department to a Crown corporation. One rural member of Parliament pointed out that $10,000 was worth much less in 1980 than in 1956.[12] Rural couriers' solution to the problem of diminishing income was for the government to increase the value of contracts exempted from the public tendering process. However, the Canadian Labour Congress (CLC) and the New Democratic Party (NDP) proposed another answer: they argued that rural route mail contractors should be considered employees, since they did much the same work as other postal employees who were represented by unions.[13]

There were strong labour relations reasons for abolishing the exclusion. One of the main reasons the government gave for crowning the post office was to improve labour relations. Third-party advisors and the postal unions, especially CUPW, had long advocated changing the post office from a government department to a Crown corporation in order to liberate postal employees and their unions from the straitjacket of the *Public Service Staff Relations Act*, which governed collective bargaining in the federal public service (Campbell 1994, 183–5). Moreover, it was the federal government's express labour policy to extend the scope of collective bargaining legislation to include "dependent contractors," a term coined by Harry Arthurs in the mid-1960s to describe workers who were not employees in the traditional common-law sense (Arthurs 1965), but who were in a position of economic dependence similar to that of employees. Although the *Canada Labour Code* definition of this group of workers changed over time, by 1984, it encompassed working people like rural route mail couriers who, although they used their own vehicles, were economically dependent upon a single entity to purchase their service.[14]

But instead of allowing the legal status of mail contractors to be determined under the *Canada Labour Code*, the government continued to treat these people as independent contractors under the legislation that changed the post office from a government department into a Crown corporation. When asked to justify this exclusion, Postmaster General André Ouellet (later the president and chief executive officer of Canada Post) told the members of the Parliamentary Standing Committee:

There are a number of reasons. One of the big ones obviously is that the override of the *Canada Labour Code* must continue in this proposed *Canada Post Corporation Act*, because without this override we believe the tendering system that exists presently would be destroyed. The present land mail service contracts that we have are valued at about $90 million. If we were to carry this to the extreme – and I do not want to exaggerate the figure – the possibility of increased expenditures could be doubled or even tripled. Thirdly, the rural route mail contractors represent about 69 per cent of all land mail service contracts. Approximately 60 per cent of these work fewer than four hours per day, therefore, if we were to have these people pressing for unions the next step would be for the union to press for equalization of work and full-time employment with, obviously, the triple effect in terms of the escalation of costs. These are just a few of the reasons why I think it would be risky at this time to change this clause.[15]

However, in order to mollify the unions and the NDP, the minister promised to give the rural route contractors what they wanted by investing the new postal corporation with the power to review the $10,000 limit on contracts excluded from the tendering process.[16] But the government's failure to ensure that Canada Post did in fact increase the amount for contracts exempted from public tendering from inflation undermined the economic basis of the compromise.

3. "THEY FORCE YOU TO UNIONIZE": RURAL ROUTE COURIERS ORGANIZE, 1985–1994

On 22 April 1985, Sue Eybel, a rural route mail courier for over ten years, sent out about 100 letters to rural route couriers in the Hamilton, Ontario, area to arrange a meeting to discuss their common problems. Her letter tapped couriers' pent-up frustration with Canada Post. Many couriers were angry at the corporation's 1982 decision to stop Saturday delivery across Canada,[17] which had resulted in a 10 per cent reduction in their remuneration, despite the fact that they would have a greater workload on Mondays. They were also frustrated that the Crown corporation had not increased the value of contracts exempted from the public tendering process.

Receiving a positive response to her letter, Eybel organized a small meeting of couriers in Ancaster (where the first rural route was established, in 1908), at which the Association of Rural Route Mail Couriers (ARRMC) was founded. The couriers planned to contact Canada Post and the Conservative government to see if something could be done to compensate them for the increased work caused by the rising volume of unaddressed household mail and to resolve other work-related grievances. The ARRMC also contacted an organization that represented rural route contractors in Quebec. Initially, the ARRMC operated as a grassroots political pressure group.[18]

Canada Post's response to the association's demands was to modify some of its practices and policies, though not in the way couriers wanted. In December 1985, the corporation informed rural route mail couriers that it would no longer be issuing them T4 slips, which had been an indication that the couriers were treated as employees for the purposes of income tax.[19] At a series of fifty-six meetings held across Canada in the spring of 1986, Canada Post officials told couriers that rural routes would be amalgamated and that the tendering system would be simplified.[20] In September 1986, Canada Post announced that all contracts, no matter how small, would be put up for public tender. Increased competition led rural couriers to complain of lower wages, more onerous working conditions, and less economic security.[21] Moreover, Canada Post proposed major changes to the rural route network in its 1986–87 five-year plan.[22] In 1987, it abolished the residency requirement for holding a rural delivery contract, which opened up the possibility of subcontracting the couriers' work to other courier companies.[23] The corporation justified these changes as consistent with its tradition of treating rural route mail couriers as entrepreneurs: "In rural areas, delivery has traditionally been effected through rural route contractors; this has been an efficient and cost-effective way of operating for the Corporation and the department before it. It provides local entrepreneurs with an opportunity to become involved in the operation of the postal service, without becoming part of the Corporation and retaining maximum flexibility to keep their involvement in other businesses or occupations."[24]

When Canada Post's controversial five-year plan was introduced in Parliament in November 1986, the Conservative government was caught off guard by the extent of the opposition to the proposed restructuring of the rural network. Fearing a revolt within the Conservative caucus, Prime Minister Brian Mulroney directed that the plan be sent to a parliamentary committee chaired by Felix Holtman (Campbell 1994, 306). The committee hearings provided an opportunity for grassroots organizations to debate Canada Post's plan for rural service. The most visible of these organizations was Rural Dignity, a non-partisan, populist group founded on 14 December 1986 in eastern Quebec by Gilles Raymond to oppose Canada Post's plan to transform rural services.[25] Although Rural Dignity was primarily concerned with preserving rural post offices, Raymond asked Sue Eybel to serve on the organization's board of directors. Appearing before the Holtman Committee with Raymond, Eybel spoke of the rural route mail couriers' low wages and poor working conditions and explained why the couriers had formed an association. She also predicted that Canada Post's plans for rural delivery would lead to deterioration of service. Although the Holtman Committee recommended that Canada Post hold back on some of the most profound changes in its plan for rural service, it said nothing about the ARRMC's request that couriers be recognized as employees.[26]

The ARRMC's political tactics, which included traditional forms of lobbying such as letter-writing campaigns and petitions, as well as media draws like Valentine's Day rodeos, failed to make either the government or Canada Post take the association seriously. Eybel became convinced that the only option was to have association members recognized as employees and to persuade a union to represent them. According to her, "our first idea was to organize so we could go to Canada Post and ask to be recognized and to be appreciated and to be paid for [our work]. But they force you to unionize. They won't listen to you. They won't talk to you."[27]

Finding a union to represent rural route mail couriers was not an easy task. Eybel initially approached the International Brotherhood of the Teamsters for help with a national organizing drive of rural route mail couriers, but they suggested that an existing postal union would be the appropriate representative.[28] The Letter Carriers Union of Canada (LCUC), which represented urban letter carriers and urban mail delivery drivers, was the obvious choice. Charles Maguire, a retired business agent with the LCUC, was invited to the couriers' first meeting. He was an experienced trade unionist, and he was aware of Canada Post's plan to restructure its bargaining units and reduce the number of unions with which it had to bargain. He told the couriers about the bargaining unit review and explained how it created an opportunity for them to appear before the Canada Labour Relations Board to make their case for employee status. The LCUC also offered to provide some modest support for this endeavour.[29]

The couriers saw the board's global review of the bargaining structure at Canada Post as a golden opportunity to test their legal status as employees. Moreover, their involvement in the unit review provided a huge incentive for the postal unions to take the idea of organizing rural route mail couriers seriously.

A. *The Opening Legal Salvo*

On 2 May 1986, Maguire applied on behalf of the ARRMC for standing to participate in the bargaining unit review. The application claimed that the rural contractors were employees and that they fit into the external group's bargaining unit, which, at the time, was represented by LCUC. It also alleged that subsection 13(5) of the *Canada Post Corporation Act* violated the *Canadian Charter of Rights and Freedoms*.

Since the association could not afford a lawyer, Maguire appeared before the board, on 22 September 1986, to argue for standing. He testified that the association had 460 members in Ontario, was seeking members in other provinces, and had a membership potential of between 8,000 and 10,000. While all of the postal unions supported the association's right to participate in the hearings, Canada Post vigorously opposed it.

The board decided to deal with the issue of the association's standing in a step-by-step manner rather than with one comprehensive ruling.[30] Dismissing Canada Post's preliminary objections, it issued an oral ruling on 7 October 1986 granting the association standing. The board stated that the question of whether rural route couriers were mail contractors within the meaning of subsection 13(5) of the *Canada Post Corporation Act* should not only be determined by reference to the nature and function of their work and the terms and conditions of their governing contracts, but also by the principles of statutory interpretation.

Canada Post's application to review the postal bargaining units eventually precipitated a full-scale war between the two big rival postal unions. Both wanted to represent an amalgamated postal worker bargaining unit consisting of all of the operations employees. The fight over the right to represent rural route mail couriers was merely the first skirmish in a larger battle. The Canada Labour Relations Board had already decided that the separate units of inside plant and wicket workers, who were represented by CUPW, and outside workers involved in delivery, who were represented by LCUC, should be amalgamated. When the two big postal unions could not resolve the issue of representation, the board ordered a run-off vote. The possibility that the board would rule that the couriers were postal employees meant that this hitherto ignored group of workers could tip the balance in the struggle between LCUC and CUPW over which union would become the exclusive bargaining representative of an amalgamated operations postal unit. LCUC clearly had a head start on CUPW in the race to sign up couriers – both the ARRMC and the CPAA urged the couriers to sign LCUC cards. Once the Canada Labour Relations Board decided to give the ARRMC standing, CUPW began to help a group of couriers located in Elmwood, Ontario, challenge the ARRMC's claims to represent rural route couriers.[31]

The CLC stepped in to stop the two large postal unions from fighting over the rural couriers. It issued a direct charter for a local representing the rural couriers, which was called the Rural Route Mail Carriers of Canada, Local 1801 of the CLC. The question then became who would fill the executive positions in the new local. At a 1987 meeting convened in Ottawa by the CLC, representatives of the three courier groups (the ARRMC; the Country Mail Association of Canada, based in Quebec; and the Elmwood-based faction, aligned with CUPW) and the two postal unions (LCUC and CUPW) attempted to thrash out the issue of representation. They were unable to reach a consensus, so a vote to fill the executive positions of the new local was held between the rival courier groups. Eybel was elected president of Local 1801; the president of the Quebec association, with whom Eybel had been in contact since 1985, was elected vice-president.[32]

While the couriers, postal unions, and the CLC were working out who would represent the rural route mail couriers for the purpose of collective bargaining, the bargaining unit review was winding its way through the Canada Labour Relations Board proceedings. As chapter 1 of this book illustrates, the way in which labour boards exercise their discretion over the timing and structure of their decision-making processes is crucial to the success of union-organizing campaigns. This case confirms the significance of the board's discretion over timing. Although the board initially decided to postpone the final resolution of the courier question until after it had completed the hearings on the reconfiguration and issued its decision, the association was in luck. As the main hearings unfolded, it became clear to the board that the issue of the couriers would have to be dealt with sooner rather than later in order to enable the parties to determine what evidence would be needed for the rest of the review. Consequently, it reserved January dates for a "mini hearing" to deal with the couriers.

The board also indicated that it would proceed with the association's application for its members to be considered employees in two stages. The first involved two major issues: whether the rural route mail couriers were employees under the *Canada Labour Code*; and if so, whether subsection 13(5) of the *Canada Post Corporation Act* negated that status. The first issue was a mixed question of fact and law, with which the board had a great deal of experience. It required the board to identify the essential criteria enunciated in the statutory definition of *dependent contractor*, to develop and to articulate tests for implementing the definition, and to apply the tests to the facts under consideration. By contrast, the second issue required the board to interpret a statute with which it was unfamiliar, and this may explain why the board's discussion of the issue was so brief. The parties agreed that the board would only consider the second stage – the charter challenge to subsection 13(5) of the *Canada Post Corporation Act* – if it decided that the subsection deprived couriers of employee status under the *Canada Labour Code*.[33]

The board approached the first issue by discussing the policy behind, and the jurisprudence surrounding, the definition of *dependent contractor* in the *Canada Labour Code*. It began by quoting extensively from an earlier board decision that canvassed the relevant scholarly literature on the concept of dependent contractor, especially the seminal article by Harry Arthurs.[34] Next, it turned to the relevant part of the definition of *dependent contractor* in the *Canada Labour Code*: "any other person who, whether or not employed under a contract of employment, performs work or services for another person on such terms and conditions that he is, in relation to that other person, in a position of economic dependence on, and under an obligation to perform duties for, that other person."[35]

The board concluded that the definition set out two essential elements: economic dependence and an obligation to perform duties for another person. According to the board, the test used to determine economic dependence was a "stand alone" test, and the test used to evaluate the obligation to perform services required a consideration of administrative and other forms of control over the contractor and the degree to which the contractor was integrated into the employer's organization, as well as a comparison of the work being performed by the contractor and other persons within the organization.[36]

The evidence that the board considered was the testimony of individual rural route contractors and Canada Post officials responsible for rural transportation services, the corporation's handbook entitled *Rural Mail Delivery Service in Canada*, and a recent contract between the couriers and the corporation. It found that "Not only is no outside employment permitted contractually while functioning as a courier, but as a question of fact the nature and length of time it takes to perform the work that needs to be performed by the couriers for the Corporation effectively precludes any regular outside employment."[37] The board also decided that until 31 March 1987, when the new tendering system was introduced, the five-year term was merely a formality, since the contract would be extended automatically without retendering on terms essentially established by the corporation. Thus, the board concluded that the couriers were, in fact, economically dependent on Canada Post.

Next, the board considered whether rural route mail couriers were under an obligation to perform services by looking at two other tests: administrative control and integration. In response to the postal corporation's argument that the rural route couriers had freedom to determine how and when to deliver the mail, the board stated that the day-to-day supervision, in conjunction with the strict terms of the contract and handbook, "provide no leeway for the manner in which the courier is to perform his or her services."[38] According to the board, the degree and manner of control exercised by Canada Post over the couriers was the same as that exercised by it over any employee performing a similar function. As well, the board was satisfied that the couriers were fully integrated into the organizational structure of the corporation and that there was a marked similarity between their job functions and those of letter carriers – and, in some instances, of rural postmasters.

In order to counter these findings, Canada Post argued that since the couriers were permitted to, and often did, hire replacements, the services they rendered were not of a personal nature, and thus they fell outside the scope of the dependent contractor provision. This argument led the board to a wide-ranging consideration of the impact that the ability to hire substitutes had on employment status in a variety of jurisdictions. The key factor, according to the board, was whether the ability to hire substitutes enabled the contractor to develop a customer base and go into the business of providing the sorts of services that are the subject of the contract.[39] In the couriers' case, it found, "There is nothing in the facts which demonstrates that the replacement is done in an entrepreneurial sense; it is done as a convenience, without profit, to relieve the contractor of the burden of having to work while sick or having to completely forego any vacation time."[40]

The board concluded that the couriers were dependent contractors and, as such, employees under the *Canada Labour Code*. But it was careful to ensure that its decision was limited to those persons who actually performed the work as described in the documents it viewed and the witnesses it heard. While the board was content that couriers who both performed the work as described and held a second contract where the work was performed by someone else would be considered employees, it was careful to state that this finding "does not mean that all persons who have signed contracts with the employer as couriers are in fact employees. For example, there may be many companies or organizations that do not themselves perform the function of couriers but nonetheless tendered for and have been awarded contracts. This decision is not meant to encompass such cases."[41] Thus, the board emphasized personal service as the feature that distinguished dependent contractors, who would be treated as employees, from independent contractors, who would be considered entrepreneurs.

Moving to the second issue, the board invoked the canons of statutory interpretation to provide a narrow and technical reason why subsection 13(5) of the *Canada Post Corporation Act* did not trump the *Canada Labour Code*. According to the board, if the effect of subsection 13(5) was to limit rights, and its meaning was ambiguous, the narrowest interpretation of the provision should be adopted. But while it was clear that the effect of subsection 13(5) was to limit rights, it was not obvious that subsection 13(5) was ambiguous. In fact, Canada Post sought to persuade the board that the intent of the provision was clear by introducing Postmaster General Ouellet's statement to the Parliamentary Standing Committee that the purpose of subsection 13(5) was to exclude rural route mail contractors from employee status. But the board refused to allow the corporation to introduce this evidence of legislative intent.[42] Instead, after a tortuous reading of subsection 13(5) and a close comparison of the English and French definitions of *mail contractor*, the board found that the definition contained latent ambiguities.[43] It concluded that subsection 13(5) did not apply to the mail couriers and that they were employees within the meaning of the *Canada Labour Code*. Moreover, by employing this technical approach to the interpretive issue, it avoided having to deal with the charter issue, which raised directly the policy question of whether this group of workers ought to be excluded from collective bargaining legislation.

The Canada Labour Relations Board's decision, which was promptly handed down on 29 April 1987, evoked predictable responses. André Villeneuve, the vice-president of communications for Canada Post, claimed that it threatened "the fundamental basis of free enterprise in Canada."[44] Another corporate spokesman declared, "What's at stake here is a matter of principle. The decision undermines the whole nature of using competitive forces in the marketplace to get the best service at the best prices."[45] By contrast, ARRMC was delighted with the decision, but cautious. When it was released, Sue Eybel told reporters, "I have to wonder if [Canada Post] won't throw us a curve and somehow manage to turn it around."[46] She also indicated that the association had a two-step strategy. The first would be to seek reinstatement of those long-term couriers who had lost their contracts under Canada Post's policy of competitive tendering and to put an end to the new tendering policy. The second would be to secure the association's certification as the couriers' bargaining agent. The CLC had appointed a full-time union organizer to help organize the rural route couriers. In December 1987, Local 1801 had over 2,600 members, and it applied to the Canada Labour Relations Board for certification.

B. The Legal Setback and the Political Struggle

Eybel had good reason to be cautious. Canada Post successfully sought judicial review of the Canada Labour Relations Board's decision before the Federal Court of Appeal. Because the court decided that the board's interpretation of *mail contractor* under subsection 13(5) of the *Canada Post Corporation Act* was incorrect, it did not even consider the issue of whether the couriers were employees under the *Canada Labour Code*. Judge Hugessen characterized the issue of whether subsection 13(5) applied to the couriers as jurisdictional in nature,[47] which meant that he could easily substitute his interpretation of the controversial provision without having to defer to the board's greater expertise in, and sensitivity to, labour relations.[48] He also dismissed the alleged charter violation on the ground that there was no evidentiary record on which to resolve it.[49]

The Federal Court of Appeal's December 1987 decision was a huge setback for the rural route mail couriers. While Canada Post applauded it for upholding "a long-standing relationship between Canada Post and private entrepreneurs," the couriers appealed it to the Supreme Court of Canada. But in May 1988, the court refused leave to appeal (Canadian Press 1987, 1988). Canada Post was under no legal obligation to recognize Local 1801, despite that fact that the local had managed to recruit over 2,600 members. To make matters worse, once it was clear that there would not be a quick resolution to the couriers' status and that the couriers were no longer relevant to the outcome of the representation battle at Canada Post, the postal unions lost interest in them and stopped funding and supporting their attempts to achieve employee status.

Canada Post's plan to revise the rural route system threatened Local 1801. Under the public tendering system introduced on 1 April 1987, incumbent couriers were no longer entitled to have their contracts renewed upon expiry or have their routes transferred during the term of the contract. Moreover, the requirement that the courier reside in the area was abolished, paving the way for greater use of subcontracting. Courier turnover made it difficult for Local 1801 to retain members.[50]

Some couriers who were members of Local 1801 suspected that Canada Post's decision to restructure routes and introduce the new tendering system was prompted by the LCUC's organizing drive for rural route mail contractors. In 1987, seven rural route mail couriers in New Brunswick complained to the Canada Labour Relations Board that Canada Post had discriminated against them in the awarding of contracts because they were members of a trade union.[51] Eybel also lodged an unfair labour practice complaint after she lost her contract, on 22 June 1988.

But the complaints of unfair labour practice were unsuccessful. The board heard the New Brunswick complaints, since its decision that rural route mail couriers were employees had not yet been overruled. Canada Post argued that it had good business reasons for not awarding the routes to the former contractors and thus had not committed an unfair labour practice. It claimed that the decision not to construct a new post office triggered an examination of the rural routes, which in turn led to their restructuring and the change in contractors. The corporation also testified that while it did not object to union organizing per se, it did object to the rural route couriers' organizing on the ground that they were not employees within the *Canada Labour Code* definition and therefore were not entitled to the statute's protection against unfair labour practices.

In establishing an unfair labour practice under the *Canada Labour Code* it is the motive behind, not the impact of, the impugned action that counts. After reviewing the evidence of the timing of Canada Post's decision to restructure the routes and the awarding of contracts, the board held that there was no evidence of anti-union intention. According to it, the change started before the organizing drive, the routes were restructured to reduce costs, some of the complainants were not awarded contracts because they did not submit the lowest bids, and the complainant who submitted the lowest bid did not receive the contract because he had trouble performing his job. The fact that Canada Post could demonstrate a compelling economic rationale for its decision – even though that decision had a negative impact on union organizing because it increased contractor turnover – was sufficient to rebut the unfair labour practice complaint. The corporation's admission that it opposed the unionization of rural route mail couriers did not constitute an anti-union intention because there was no evidence that its opposition influenced the awarding of contracts on the restructured routes.

Eybel's unfair labour practice complaint was never heard. The board adjourned her case after Canada Post applied to the Federal Court to stop it from proceeding on the ground that it had no jurisdiction to hear the unfair labour practice complaint. According to the postal corporation, the Federal Court of Appeal's decision that the *Canada Labour Code* did not cover rural route mail contractors meant that Eybel could not bring an unfair labour practice complaint.[52] Without the protection of collective bargaining legislation, workers who believe they are being punished for trying to organize a union have no legal recourse to challenge their employer's actions.

Despite these setbacks, Local 1801 pushed ahead on the legal and political fronts to achieve employee status for the couriers. It initiated a charter challenge to the legislative exclusion of couriers from the *Canada Labour Code* while lobbying politicians to repeal the offending provision. The couriers did not, however, undertake any work-related action. This tactic was particularly difficult for them; rural route couriers work alone or with one or two others in isolated offices, and Canada Post had the right to unilaterally terminate their contracts if they failed to perform the services for which they had contracted.

On 23 March 1989, Local 1801 filed a statement of claim in the Federal Court alleging that subsection 13(5) of the *Canada Post Corporation Act* unfairly discriminated against persons employed as rural route mail contractors and denied them the equal protection and benefit of the law guaranteed by section 15(1) of the *Canadian Charter of Rights and Freedoms*.[53] Because the challenge was to a federal statute, Local 1801 was up against the Attorney General of Canada as well as the postal corporation. Although the Canada Labour Relations Board served notice of its intent to participate in the action, the association was responsible for carrying the costly legal action.

On 25 May 1989, the Deputy Attorney General of Canada filed a motion to dismiss Local 1801's action on the ground that its statement of claim failed to disclose a reasonable cause of action. The government's position was that the rural route mail contractors' equality rights were not violated because the Supreme Court of Canada had already decided that employment status was not a prohibited ground of discrimination under the charter.[54] On 3 August 1989, the Federal Court granted the government's motion and allowed the couriers forty-five days to amend their statement of claim. In response, the couriers claimed that the exclusion was discriminatory on the basis of sex, since the majority of rural route mail couriers were women, and residency, since the rural couriers were denied rights available to their urban counterparts. However, in the spring of 1990, the Federal Court struck down the amended statement of claim. Madame Justice Reed stated that the allegation that subsection 13(5) discriminated on the basis of sex was frivolous. Moreover, she characterized the claim that the section discriminated on the basis of residency as a disguised attempt to resurrect the earlier and unsuccessful claim of discrimination on the basis of occupation.[55] Although the rural couriers were given ten days to appeal the order, they abandoned the case because they did not have enough money to pursue it.[56]

Before the charter litigation stalled, Eybel and Maguire appeared before the Standing Committee on Consumer and Corporate Affairs and Government Operations, which was holding hearings into Canada's postal system. They told the committee about the ARRMC, how it had been transformed into Local 1801, and the effect that the new tendering system was having on long-term rural route mail couriers. They asked the committee to recommend that rural route mail couriers be recognized as employees of Canada Post and that the public tendering system be halted.[57] Although the chairman of the committee congratulated Eybel and her organization for the good quality of rural route service, he expressed his frustration with the ARRMC over its failure to produce statistics on the average number of calls and the average compensation per route, dismissing the estimate that couriers were paid four dollars an hour on average as unfounded.[58] Other Conservative members of the committee had little sympathy for the association; one member wondered how the ARRMC could criticize a tendering process that resulted in greater competition.[59]

On top of the legal and political reversals, Charlie Maguire's death following a heart attack at a Rural Dignity meeting in July 1990 had a dispiriting effect on the fragile association. For a few months, Eybel managed to keep the association and its campaign for employee status alive. She persuaded her local member of Parliament, Bob Speller, to introduce a private member's bill to repeal subsection 13(5) of the *Canada Post Corporation Act*. Although the bill received first reading in December 1990, it never went any further.[60] Discouraged by the lack of support from the labour movement and the lack of attention from the media and politicians, Eybel decided to disband Local 1801. In 1994, she sent out a newsletter to that effect.

Rural route mail couriers were unable to sustain their campaign for employee status without the help of the postal unions. But union assistance was conditional on a quick legal victory, and once it was clear that litigation was neither quick nor successful, the couriers lost the financial and institutional support of the postal unions and the CLC. When the CPAA withdrew its financial backing from Rural Dignity after the Liberal government announced a moratorium on the closure of rural post offices, the grassroots political organization was no longer able to mobilize events designed to bring the rural mail system to public attention. Thus, there was little grassroots opposition for the rural route mail couriers to tap into in order to sustain their political campaign for employee status.

4. THE UNION MAKES US STRONG: CUPW ORGANIZES THE RURAL COURIERS, 1995–2003

A. *The Union-Building Model: Separate Organizing*

The second campaign to have rural route mail couriers recognized as employees, which began in 1995, was markedly different from the first. The distinguishing feature was CUPW's financial and institutional support. The postal union, not the rural route couriers, initiated the second drive, and this time it was not fueled by the bargaining unit review and union rivalry. This campaign, unlike the one that followed and the one that preceded it, did not involve a certification application. Thus, it was not as vulnerable as the first to the vagaries of the legal process and unfavorable judicial and labour board decisions. The focus of this campaign was to develop the organizational capacities of rural route mail couriers and familiarize them with unions. CUPW helped the couriers to establish a separate organization that was accountable to the couriers, although financed by CUPW. The postal union's long-term strategy was that once the couriers had organized and become familiar with unions, the separate organization would merge with CUPW. Thus, it was a union-building, as opposed to a traditional organizing, campaign.

CUPW saw the achievement of employee status for rural couriers as the outcome of a decade-long campaign that would have to be waged on three fronts.[61] The first was organizational: CUPW had to develop the capacities of rural couriers to organize and represent themselves and its own institutional structures to represent and service them. The second was political: it had to put pressure on the federal government to change the provision in the *Canada Post Corporation Act* denying rural couriers employee status. And the third involved negotiating an agreement with Canada Post about the terms and conditions of rural couriers' work.

The political context of the second organizing drive was radically different from that of the first. Unlike the Conservative government, which was willing to endure a great deal of conflict in order to transform the post office into a private sector business, the Liberal government, elected in 1993, tried to blend public service with private enterprise to calm postal relations. The moratorium on the closure of rural post offices, which was announced in 1994, was the first and most obvious example of the new emphasis on the public responsibilities of Canada Post. In 1998, the Liberal government announced that Canada Post would not be privatized, although it still required the Crown corporation to behave like a profitable private sector corporation (Fudge 1999a; Janzen, White, and Lipseg-Mumme 2001).

This shift in the political direction of postal policy coincided with a dramatic change in the economic circumstances of Canada Post. When the Conservative government took power in 1984, the corporation was running a huge deficit. As well, it faced international competition in the services for which demand was increasing and a contraction in letter mail – the only market in which its position was protected by law.[62] In 1993, the Liberal government inherited a Crown corporation that had already been forced to operate according to the principles of the private sector. With the economic recovery of the 1990s, the corporation's balance sheet improved; not only was it showing a profit, but it also began to pay dividends and taxes to the federal government. And, in 1995, it managed to negotiate a collective agreement with CUPW without a strike. The only cloud on the horizon was the complaint of its competitors, especially the international courier companies and the newspapers, that Canada Post was not competing fairly with the private sector (Fudge 1999a; Janzen, White, and Lipseg-Mumme 2001).

Just as dramatic as the transformation in the political and economic context of Canada Post was the shift in focus of CUPW. Ever since CUPW narrowly won the 1989 Canada Labour Board–ordered vote to determine whether it or LCUC would be the exclusive representative of the amalgamated urban postal operations bargaining unit, it had been busy staving off LCUC raids and resolving internal dissent. The internecine union battle diverted a huge amount of CUPW's resources during a period in which the Crown corporation, with the Conservative government's blessing, embarked on a labour relations policy that repeatedly brought it into conflict with its unions. Preoccupied with the rearguard actions of disgruntled letter carriers and its battle with Canada Post, CUPW simply ignored the rural couriers after the 1987 Federal Court of Appeal decision denying them employee status. However, by 1995, CUPW had resolved its internal problems, which coincided with a reduction in the level of conflict in its relations with Canada Post. But fresh challenges loomed; new postal technology, combined with competition from other forms of communication and international courier companies, would gradually undermine the union's size and strength. CUPW considered a number of options: it could remain a "small, perfect" postal workers' union, it could merge with another union, or it could start organizing any worker who had contact with the mail.[63]

The 1996 national convention ratified the union executive's recommendation that CUPW begin a campaign to organize all workers who had contact with the mail. It focused on workers employed by contractors who were involved in mail delivery and rural route mail couriers. Its strategy was simply to sign up the employees of courier companies as members, which was possible because the employee status of these workers was not in question. As long as CUPW signed up a majority of the employees, it had the right to represent them and bargain on their behalf with the courier company. The situation of rural couriers was altogether a different matter. Not only would CUPW have to persuade the widely dispersed rural couriers that it could represent them, but it would also have to persuade the Liberal government to change the law. To sustain what it predicted would be a ten-year campaign that would cost about $250,000 annually, the union decided to organize the rural route mail couriers into a separate organization in order to develop their capacity to represent themselves. CUPW adopted a strategy to set up a separate union in part because of the legal status of the rural route couriers.[64] The plan was that once the couriers had developed the capacity for self-representation and negotiated a collective agreement, they would vote on whether to merge the Organization of Rural Route Mail Couriers (ORRMC) with CUPW.

CUPW's rural courier campaign was risky. Its success depended not only on persuading the couriers to join the ORRMC, but also, once they were organized into a separate organization, persuading them to merge with CUPW. Furthermore, it had to convince the government to change the law so that the couriers could insist that Canada Post bargain with their representative. And obtaining the right to represent the rural couriers might be just the beginning of CUPW's problems. Deborah Bourque, the national officer responsible for the rural route mail couriers' campaign (and later CUPW's national president) compared representing the couriers to "dog catches car."[65] The infusion into CUPW of 5,000 rural route and 1,000 suburban couriers, dispersed across the country in regions not traditionally supportive of unions, could dilute the union's traditional militant orientation. It could also increase conflict within the union, since any gains for rural couriers would likely entail some trade-offs at the expense of other groups of postal workers. Moreover, it could provoke conflict with the CPAA over the right to represent couriers.

In 1995, CUPW embarked on the first stage of its campaign, which involved contacting couriers to see if they wanted CUPW's help to win employee status and engage in collective bargaining. This stage lasted until 1997, when the ORRMC was officially established. One of the union's initial goals was to convince rural route couriers that it would not abandon them. CUPW contacted Sue Eybel and sent a letter to all the couriers on Local 1801's old membership list.[66] It also began trying to persuade its existing members that it was in their interest to devote considerable union resources to organizing rural couriers.[67]

In a letter to rural route mail couriers and CUPW local presidents and secretary treasurers, CUPW's then–national president Darryl Tingley explained why the union wanted to organize rural couriers and the different options available to it.[68] Faced with the possibility that Canada Post would gradually contract out more and more of its delivery network and postal worker jobs, the union adopted the position that all aspects of letter delivery should be performed by unionized employees of Canada Post – this solution included rural couriers. Nor was the idea of organizing rural route couriers far-fetched; in the US they were unionized. According to Tingley, unionizing rural couriers was a win-win situation: in the short term, it was good for rural couriers; in the long term, it was good for all postal workers. He also outlined the different ways to achieve the goal of having rural delivery contracted in: CUPW could organize the rural route mail couriers and ask Canada Post for voluntary recognition; it could bring a legal challenge to subsection 13(5) of the *Canada Post Corporation Act*; it could convince the postal corporation to contract in the rural work under appendix T of the collective agreement; and it could petition Parliament to permit unionization.

CUPW initially decided not to pursue a charter challenge to the legislation excluding rural route mail couriers from the definitions of *em-*

ployee and *dependent contractor*, since this tactic had failed once, and CUPW's lawyer advised that the chance of winning such litigation was virtually nonexistent.[69] At the time, the Supreme Court of Canada's interpretation of the freedom of association protected under the *Charter of Rights* was limited to the right to join a trade union, and the government had no obligation to protect this right. Couriers already had the freedom to organize; what they wanted was protection from employer retaliation and the right to make Canada Post bargain with their union. And while it was obvious that the *Canada Post Corporation Act* denied rural route couriers treatment equal to that of other employees of the postal corporation, the Supreme Court of Canada had decided that the equality rights in the charter do not protect individuals from discrimination based upon employment or occupational status.[70]

CUPW's decision to attempt to contract in all aspects of mail delivery work was given a big boost in 1995, when Canada Post agreed that the approximately 10,000 temporary and part-time workers who delivered unaddressed ad mail would be recognized as part of CUPW's bargaining unit. But while voluntary recognition was an important concession to the union, CUPW still had the difficult job of organizing a group of workers whom the letter carriers' union had historically ignored and who, because of their employment relations and work patterns, were difficult to organize (Janzen, White, and Lipseg-Mumme 2001).

Rural route mail couriers were in the opposite situation: CUPW started to organize them before it had the right to represent them. It received 200 favourable responses to the 2,500 letters it sent out to couriers in 1995. In a follow-up letter, Bourque explained that since litigation was the method least likely to change the legal status of rural route mail couriers, CUPW would focus on persuading the postal corporation to agree to recognize the union as the couriers' bargaining representative and on convincing the government to change the law.[71]

Obtaining Eybel's support for the organizing campaign was an important factor in CUPW's success. Despite the failure of the ARRMC to improve the conditions of rural couriers and to form a lasting institution – which led some couriers to doubt whether unionization was possible – it enjoyed a degree of legitimacy and support because it was created and controlled by couriers.[72] CUPW's connection with the ARRMC and Eybel's involvement lent credence to the union's claim that it would respect the couriers' wishes, and it supported CUPW's contention that the couriers wanted to change their legal status in order to able to bargain collectively.

The government's decision to appoint George Radwanski, a former aid to Prime Minister Jean Chrétien and a past editor of the *Toronto Star*, to conduct a review of Canada Post's mandate provided CUPW with an opportunity to launch the public face of its campaign to organize rural route mail contractors. Along with CUPW and Rural Dignity, Sue Eybel, on behalf of the ARRMC, complained to Radwanski about the unfairness of excluding rural route mail contractors from collective bargaining. She also gave many examples of the poor terms and conditions of work that couriers endured as a result of their legal status. With the union and Rural Dignity, she urged the government to change the law and allow rural mail couriers to bargain collectively.[73]

But Radwanski's report and the government's response suggested that there would be no quick and easy victory for CUPW in its campaign to contract in all mail delivery.[74] Although the government did not follow Radwanski's general recommendation to limit Canada Post to services not profitable for the private sector, it heeded his specific advice that the postal corporation be ordered to get out of the business of delivering advertising mail. In October 1996, the corporation gave 10,000 ad mail workers notice, as required by law, that their employment would be terminated in six months' time (Janzen, White, and Lipseg-Mumme 2001).

CUPW was unable to keep the ad mail work in its bargaining unit and preserve the ad mail workers' jobs, even though it adopted militant tactics to persuade the government to reverse its decision. The union organized a series of demonstrations at Liberal constituency offices, made it an issue in its 1997 strike, and even threatened to take unlawful job action. However, CUPW was in a weak position because it had only signed a few hundred ad mail workers since it was voluntarily recognized by Canada Post (White and Janzen 2000).

But CUPW did devote a great deal of effort to organizing rural route mail couriers. In 1997, its national executive board decided to help the couriers establish a separate organization. CUPW had Eybel's assistance in this endeavour; she asked former members of the association's executive to participate in a meeting in Ottawa, paid for by CUPW, to establish the new organization. In March 1997, the ORRMC was established. Although it was a separate organization under the democratic control of rural route couriers, the ORRMC depended upon CUPW's financial and institutional support. As it worked with the rural couriers, CUPW explained to its members why it was helping the couriers establish a separate organization and urged them to get involved in the campaign. CUPW also trained its members to sign up rural couriers for the ORRMC.

The ORRMC held its first general members' meeting in March 1998. At this meeting, an executive was elected, the constitution was amended, the organization's relationship with CUPW was fleshed out, and a campaign strategy was developed. ORRMC membership, which was dues-based, was open to all rural route and suburban service mail couriers as well as persons working for rural route or suburban service contractors. The ORRMC adopted a national structure, with an executive committee composed of couriers, upon which CUPW had one ex-officio position. The nature of the working relationship between the ORRMC and CUPW was never formalized. The ORRMC embarked on its second membership drive in autumn 1998, and by the end of the year it boasted 3,500 members.[75]

With the ORRMC up and running, CUPW concentrated on applying political pressure to the Liberal government to change the law. This pressure took two forms. The first was a complaint to the National Administrative Office (NAO) in the United States that the federal government was violating the North American Agreement on Labour Cooperation (NAALC) – commonly referred to as the "labour-side agreement" under NAFTA – by excluding rural couriers from employee status. The second form of pressure was traditional lobbying directed at members of Parliament. The ORRMC organized parliamentary petitions and a private member's bill to change the law, tactics that Rural Dignity had used to preserve the rural postal service and postmasters' jobs.

Although CUPW was not optimistic that the NAALC complaint would be successful from a legal point of view, it hoped that it could be used to generate support from unions across North America for the couriers' campaign while at the same time attracting some media attention and embarrassing the Liberal government. As a legal process for enforcing basic labour rights, the NAALC is toothless: the complaint process is cumbersome; the rights it protects are limited and their scope is open to a wide range of interpretations; and the enforcement mechanism is weak (Compa 1999). However, since it provides an opportunity for a public hearing to investigate a union complaint, CUPW decided to invoke the NAALC process.

The complaint, which was signed by a coalition of twenty-one unions and social justice groups in Canada, the United States, and Mexico, was one of only two lodged by unions against Canadian governments under the NAALC, and it was the first targeting the federal government for violating basic labour rights. Thus, CUPW roused some media attention when it filed the complaint on 2 December 1998 in the US National

Administration Office in Washington (McKenna 1998). The submission claimed that by denying rural route mail couriers employee status, the government of Canada interfered with their freedom of association; denied their right to bargain collectively; discriminated against them; and denied them protection from, and compensation for, occupational injuries and illnesses. According to CUPW, the Canadian government was violating NAALC principles and obligations, and the US NAO should hold public hearings on the matter, request co-operative consultations with the Canadian NAO, convene ministerial consultations, urge the Canadian federal government to repeal subsection 13(5) of the *Canada Post Corporation Act*, and request the Secretariat of the Commission for Labour Cooperation to undertake a wide-ranging and far-reaching report on the freedom of association of rural route mail couriers and the nature and conditions of their work.

In its response to the complaint, Canada Post emphasized that rural route mail couriers had always been treated as independent contractors and that Canadian courts had repeatedly dismissed the legal challenges to this status. In particular, it made much of the fact that the Supreme Court of Canada had interpreted the freedom of association protected in the Canadian *Charter of Rights* as an individual right that does not protect the activities of associations. According to Canada Post, both Parliament and the courts made a "clear determination that rural route mail couriers are not considered employees or dependent contractors for the purposes of Part 1 of the *Code*."[76]

The US NAO refused to accept CUPW's submission on the ground that it did not raise "questions regarding the application or enforcement of the law."[77] Under the NAALC, the failure of a country to apply or enforce its own labour law is the only basis on which the NAO is required to accept a submission for review. In a letter to CUPW dated 1 February 1999, Irasema Garza, secretary of the US NAO, wrote that she had discretion to decline a submission if it would not constitute a failure of another party to comply with obligations under the agreement. Since the "federal courts ruled that the *Canada Post Corporation Act* does not contradict the *Canada Labour Code* or the *Canadian Charter of Rights and Freedoms*," she wrote, the submission does not raise "issues concerning the application or enforcement of the law."

Although CUPW was disappointed with the decision, it was even more upset by the NAO process. The letter notifying the union of the decision refusing to review the submission stated that the decision was based on information provided by the Canadian NAO and Canada Post.

CUPW did not receive Canada Post's response to its submission until it received the NAO's decision, and thus it did not have an opportunity to challenge any of the postal corporation's claims. On 8 March 1999, then–CLC president Bob White complained on CUPW's behalf to the US NAO and asked it to reconsider it decision.[78] While acknowledging that the US NAO was not required to follow a judicial process, White emphasized the need for transparency, since the NAO was the only point of contact with the public in the NAALC complaint process. Not only had Canada Post made controversial claims (such as the assertion that subsection 13(5) of the *Canada Post Corporation Act* did not contradict the *Canada Labour Code*), upon which the US NAO's decision seemed to rest, but it also failed to address a range of issues (including that of discrimination and the role of international obligations). He concluded, however, by suggesting that if the US NAO decided not to reconsider its decision, it might assist the secretary of labour in developing cooperative activities. In particular, he asked that the situation of the Canadian rural route mail couriers be used as a case study to examine the scope of the principle of freedom of association and the issue of discrimination on occupational status.

The upshot of the NAALC complaint was a public workshop organized by the US and the Canadian NAOs on the right to organize and bargain collectively. The workshop, held in Toronto, would address the general scope of the protection of these rights as well as legal limits and enhancements in the two countries. Over two days in February 2001, panels comprised of academics, trade unionists, and industry spokespeople discussed generally the scope of the freedom to associate and bargain collectively, and the rights of particular groups of workers. Sharing the lineup with rural route mail couriers were other non-standard workers, such as temporary workers, and other groups of excluded employees, including front-line managers, supervisors, Crown employees, and agricultural workers. While the workshop gave CUPW and the ORRMC an opportunity to publicize the plight of rural route mail couriers, it had little impact on the federal government.[79]

The campaign that targeted members of Parliament, while slower to heat up than the NAALC complaint, put greater pressure on the government to change the law. It was coordinated by Cynthia Patterson, who had honed her grassroots political mobilization skills with Rural Dignity, and it involved the rural route mail couriers. First, in early 1999, after obtaining some favourable news coverage for the rural route mail couriers' campaign, ORRMC members and their allies collected signatures for petitions complaining about the exclusion of rural couriers from employee status. Over the next two years, dozens of petitions were presented in the House of Commons. In the spring, members of the ORRMC executive lobbied parliamentarians in Ottawa, and on 14 April, more than 800 members of CUPW marched to Parliament Hill to support the bargaining rights of rural route mail couriers.[80]

The campaign culminated in November 1999, when Pat Martin, a member of Parliament and the NDP's labour and postal critic, tabled a private member's bill (Bill C-238) that would repeal subsection 13(5) of the *Canada Post Corporation Act*. Martin won the lottery that allowed his private member's bill to proceed to debate and a vote. On one side, the NDP and the Bloc Québécois supported treating rural route mail couriers like any other dependent contractors in the private sector and defended their rights to associate and bargain collectively. On the other, the Liberal government, together with the Conservative and Reform Parties, cautioned against changing the status quo on the ground that it would jeopardize entrepreneurship, reduce Canada Post's flexibility, and increase its costs. When the bill was attacked as a ploy by CUPW to make a grab for members, Martin claimed that nothing in it tied rural couriers to the controversial postal union. Although many members from every party acknowledged the generally poor treatment of rural route couriers, the solution they favoured was not to recognize them as employees, but to improve the contracting system. On 4 April 2000, Bill C-238 was narrowly defeated by a vote of 114 to 110.[81]

While the NAALC complaint and the parliamentary campaign were unfolding, Alice Boudreau, president of the ORRMC, together with Cynthia Patterson and Deborah Bourque, met with Canada Post officials to present the rural couriers' demands. André Ouellet, then president of Canada Post and former postmaster general, promised to look into the tendering process, but he stated that the rural couriers' problem was a political one – the existence of subsection 13(5) of the *Canada Post Corporation Act* – and he could not resolve it. According to Bourque, when members of the ORRMC executive met, in 2000, with both the minister responsible for Canada Post and the corporation's president, they promised that there would be improvements for couriers, but neither made a commitment to recognize the couriers as employees or CUPW as their bargaining agent.[82]

In 2000, Canada Post began to improve the tendering process and standardize work practices – changes that were designed to respond to couriers' complaints and dull their desire for unionization. The public tendering system no longer threatened couriers' contracts, the corporation no longer insisted on the lowest bid as a basis for awarding contracts, and it developed and distributed a comprehensive rural delivery service manual.[83] While these initiatives tended to undermine Canada Post's claim that rural couriers were independent contractors, the postal corporation also adopted other measures that promoted couriers' independent status. The couriers' contract no longer required them to provide personal service, although it prohibited them from delivering for any other courier company.[84]

Despite the stalemate over the status of the rural route mail contractors, CUPW and Canada Post signed a collective agreement in 2000 without resort to economic sanctions. They also faced a common threat: United Parcel Service (UPS) brought legal action against the government of Canada, claiming that the government had violated NAFTA by allowing Canada Post to engage in unfair competition and practice cross-subsidization of its competitive services with its protected activities. Labour peace in the postal service and Canada Post's business strategy depended upon expanding postal services in competitive markets as well as maintaining and strengthening universal service at a uniform cost across the country. The UPS legal action threatened to undermine the basis for postal peace and a public parcel service.[85]

B. United We Stand: One Big Postal Union

Deborah Bourque's acclamation as national president of CUPW at the union's national convention in April 2002 signalled a change in tactics for securing collective bargaining rights and employment benefits for rural route mail couriers. It also marked the beginning of the third campaign to organize the couriers. For five years, the ORRMC had sought to persuade the federal government to change the *Canada Post Corporation Act* in order to permit rural and suburban mail couriers to organize and bargain collectively. Although it was not giving up on political tactics – during the convention, CUPW organized a rally at the Prime Minister's Office to demand the right of rural route mail couriers to bargain collectively[86] – it was going to concentrate on Canada Post and the upcoming negotiations. CUPW decided that it should sign up rural route mail couriers as its members in order to increase pressure on Canada Post to contract in the couriers' work and voluntarily recognize CUPW as their representative. If a majority of rural and suburban route mail couriers were willing to join CUPW, this would enhance the legitimacy of the union's claim to represent them and enable it to apply to be certified as the couriers' bargaining representative. While the purpose of the certification application was to put pressure on Canada Post to voluntarily recognize the couriers as employees and CUPW as their representative, the application was neither a hollow nor a purely symbolic gesture. In December 2001, the Supreme Court of Canada changed its position on the relationship between the freedom of association protected by section 2(d) of the *Charter of Rights* and trade union activities.[87] Now CUPW could make a strong legal argument that, at the very least, the government had an obligation to protect rural route mail couriers from unfair labour practices.

The decision to focus on Canada Post and to put its energy into securing recognition through negotiation explains why CUPW changed its strategy from securing bargaining rights for ORRMC as a separate organization before asking the couriers to merge with CUPW, to asking couriers to join CUPW immediately. The timing of this change was critical; the campaign to sign up rural and suburban mail couriers as CUPW members would have to be ratified by the union's national convention in April 2002 to coincide with the expiry of CUPW's collective agreement in January 2003. The plan was to submit an application for certification for the rural route couriers when the collective agreement expired and to ask Canada Post to dovetail the couriers into CUPW's collective agreement.[88]

The single biggest question was whether the rural and suburban route mail couriers were ready to join CUPW. When Deborah Bourque asked the ORRMC executive this question at a meeting in Ottawa in October 2001, the answer was a resounding "No." But when Bourque repeated the question at the next meeting of the executive of the ORRMC, in January 2002, those in attendance unanimously agreed that rural couriers were ready to join the postal union. Alice Boudreau attributed this change in the executive's assessment of the couriers' willingness to join CUPW to a series of meetings in October and November at which couriers did not express fear at the prospect of joining CUPW. The strategy of having the couriers sign membership cards with an independent organization – the ORRMC – and CUPW's willingness to give the ORRMC a great deal of latitude during the campaign allayed couriers' fears that CUPW would simply swallow them up without recognizing their distinct interests. For five years, CUPW had demonstrated that it was willing to respect the wishes and interests of couriers, and it had also devoted a great deal of effort to educating rural couriers about the benefits of unionism in general and CUPW in particular. By January 2002, the ORRMC executive believed that the rural couriers were as ready as they would ever be to join CUPW.[89] CUPW's union-building strategy was a success.

Before the campaign began in earnest and the decision to organize rural route mail couriers directly into CUPW was made public, Boudreau and Bourque wanted to inform the CPAA of the change in strategy. Although relations between the ORRMC and the CPAA had been friendly, and the ORRMC kept the CPAA apprised of its campaign, there was a long history of suspicion between CUPW and the CPAA.[90] At a meeting in Ottawa on 5 March 2002, Boudreau, Patterson, and Bourque explained to the national executive of the CPAA that CUPW would soon be embarking on a member sign-up campaign for rural route and suburban mail couriers. The news that the couriers would no longer be attempting to establish a separate bargaining unit and a separate organization and would be joining CUPW instead was not welcomed by the CPAA. On 11 March, Leslie Schous, the organization's national president, wrote to Boudreau, "your decision to organize as members of another Canada Post Corporation bargaining unit has raised some concerns with respect to the relationship between our members and the rural route couriers that operate out of our offices." She continued: "while it is not our intention to do anything to impede your efforts to become unionized we do believe that there is a potential conflict with our desire to protect the work in our bargaining unit."[91] Although Boudreau and Bourque were disappointed with the CPAA's response, they were preoccupied with the membership drive and did not pay it much heed.

In March 2002, at the ORRMC annual general meeting in Ottawa, a resolution that the ORRMC be disbanded and that rural and suburban route mail couriers be urged to sign CUPW membership cards received unanimous approval. CUPW's national executive board approved the sign-up campaign in March, and in April the union's national convention endorsed it as a priority for the union. George Floresco, a former president of the Winnipeg local that was very active in organizing workers who were employed by courier companies holding contracts with Canada Post, was elected third national vice-president, and he became responsible for the rural and suburban mail couriers' campaign.

CUPW devoted considerable resources to the membership drive; Floresco estimated that it cost one million dollars.[92] In May, the union began training sessions for organizers, and they ran until the end of July.

An intensive and confidential organizing drive that would capitalize on momentum and limit costs was planned, and 1 August was selected as its official start date. Under the *Canada Labour Code*, union membership cards are simply considered an expression of the choice to be represented by a union for six months from the date the card is signed; membership cards older than six months are not counted in a certification vote. Since CUPW's plan was to apply for certification at the same time its collective agreement expired, which was the end of January 2003, it had to begin the membership drive no earlier than 1 August 2002. The drive deadline was set for 20 September, although membership cards could trickle in until the application was filed.

The campaign involved 160 organizers (whose wages were paid by CUPW) divided into two-person teams composed of one CUPW member and one rural route mail courier. These teams would meet with couriers in groups or one-on-one across the country. The official campaign kick-off was held at the New Brunswick side of the bridge linking Prince Edward Island to the mainland, a site chosen to symbolize the link between different types of postal workers. CUPW also conducted several mass mailings across the country. Organizers were careful to allay couriers' fears of employer retaliation by emphasizing the couriers' right to organize. According to CUPW, the Supreme Court of Canada's decision in *Dunmore v. Ontario (AG)* meant that rural route mail couriers had the right to join a trade union and that Canada Post could not lawfully retaliate against couriers who joined CUPW. Boudreau believed that many couriers felt emboldened to join CUPW once they were told that they had a charter-protected right to do so.[93] Moreover, Canada Post was content to see the campaign run its course as long as CUPW did not organize on the corporation's property. The CPAA advised its members who were confronted with couriers' questions to respond by explaining that the membership drive was an ORRMC and CUPW initiative. It told postmasters and assistants, "because of concerns with respect to work in the CPAA bargaining unit it would not be appropriate for us to take an active part in the campaign."[94] In mid-September, CUPW announced that the campaign had been successful and that more than half the rural and suburban couriers had signed membership cards. The executive of the ORRMC met in Ottawa to dissolve the ORRMC, and the members of its executive were offered positions as temporary technical assistants (TTAs) with CUPW.

Armed with the rural couriers' membership cards, CUPW began to develop the demands that it would present to Canada Post. Improving wages was not the only concern for the couriers; the most important issue for the majority of them was basic employment rights, such as the right to a paid holiday, and the right to take that holiday without first having to arrange for a replacement.[95] The ultimate goal was to persuade the postal corporation that CUPW should be recognized as the exclusive bargaining representative of the rural and suburban couriers, who would be part of CUPW's bargaining unit and covered by its collective agreement, though treated as a separate classification.[96] CUPW made justice and equality for rural and suburban couriers a key platform in its negotiations.

On 10 January 2003, CUPW applied to the Canadian Industrial Relations Board (CIRB) to be certified as the bargaining representative for rural route mail couriers.[97] It claimed that the majority of rural and suburban couriers had signed CUPW membership cards and asked to be placed in its large operations unit. The CUPW application also challenged the exclusion of the couriers from the *Canada Labour Code* as a violation of the charter's guarantee of freedom of association. Relying on the Supreme Court of Canada's decision that agricultural workers are a vulnerable group of employees to whom the government of Ontario owes a duty to provide legal protections of their right to join and participate in trade unions, CUPW claimed that rural and suburban couriers were a vulnerable group of (mostly female) workers and that their exclusion from the *Canada Labour Code* violated their charter-protected freedom of association.[98]

Canada Post's response had two parts. First, it filed an unfair labour practice complaint with the CIRB alleging that CUPW was in breach of the *Canada Labour Code* by compelling the corporation to bargain with the union over employees whom it did not represent.[99] The postal corporation also claimed that CUPW's demand to be recognized as the bargaining agent of rural contractors potentially impacted on the rights of the CPAA, and it asked the board to consider its complaint on an expedited basis. Second, it argued that the CIRB had no jurisdiction to hear CUPW's application regarding the couriers since they were not employees under the *Canada Labour Code*.[100] To CUPW's surprise and dismay, the CPAA filed an application to intervene in the certification application, arguing that rural *and* suburban couriers should be placed inside its bargaining unit.[101] In February, the CPAA asked its members to present a letter to the rural couriers in their offices asking for their support.[102] The letter claimed that rural and suburban couriers fell into the CPAA's, and not CUPW's, bargaining unit and attributed the CPAA's failure to conduct a sign-up campaign to the existence of subsection 13(5). The only explanation for such dramatic action is that the CPAA saw the possibility of CUPW members in CPAA offices as a threat to its survival. Not only could improvements in the terms and conditions offered to rural couriers undermine the job security and working conditions of CPAA members as Canada Post sought to reduce costs in other aspects of the rural system, but also the superior collective agreement and strength of CUPW might attract postmasters away from their union to their more militant rival.[103]

In the short term, the CPAA's intervention in CUPW's certification application created confusion for rural route couriers and complicated matters for CUPW. CUPW wanted to avoid the kind of destructive inter-union battle it had fought with LCUC from erupting with the CPAA, and it invoked the CLC's jurisdictional dispute resolution process to resolve the question of which union had the right to represent the rural and suburban couriers. The president of the CLC, Kenneth Georgetti, appointed a mediator to resolve the dispute. The mediator met with the presidents of the two unions, and when he was not able to resolve the dispute, he wrote to Georgetti supporting CUPW's right to represent the rural couriers.[104] In May 2003, Georgetti wrote to the presidents of CUPW and the CPAA to inform them of his decision: the CPAA would have to withdraw its intervention in CUPW's certification application.[105] Should the CPAA refuse to do so, the CLC would issue sanctions, such as expulsion from the CLC. Expulsion would open the CPAA up to a raid by CUPW once the CPAA's collective agreement expired.[106]

The CPAA's intervention complicated the negotiations between CUPW and Canada Post over the status of the rural and suburban couriers. Initially, Canada Post refused to discuss the demand to contract in rural route mail couriers as part of the negotiations. The corporation's official position was that it was necessary to get rid of subsection 13(5) before it could recognize CUPW as the rural and suburban couriers' bargaining representative. However, at an informal level, extensive negotiations about status, employment rights, and wages began early in the process. In March, the union applied for conciliation; in June, it began cross-country strike-vote meetings with its members.[107]

A number of factors indicated that the 2003 round of negotiations was a good time for Canada Post to recognize the right of rural and suburban mail couriers to bargain collectively and to accept CUPW as their bargaining representative. Business competitors were using supranational trade agreements to challenge Canada Post. UPS lodged a

NAFTA complaint against the corporation, and an international arbitration tribunal would consider UPS's complaint that Canada was violating NAFTA by letting Canada Post subsidize its competitive services with revenues from the monopoly it enjoyed.[108] UPS had a long history of attacking Canada Post for cross-subsidization, but its NAFTA complaint had a novel twist. It claimed, among other things, that the exclusion of rural and suburban route couriers from labour law was a form of subsidy, and thus it violated NAFTA.[109] The federal government defended the exclusion on the ground that it had existed before the post office was turned into a Crown corporation and that it related to Canada Post's universal service obligation.[110] While CUPW did not think that the rights of workers should be determined by investor-state litigation in which workers are denied any meaningful opportunity to participate and questioned why UPS did not invoke NAALC to deal with that aspect of its complaint, it agreed with UPS that the exclusion functioned as a subsidy to Canada Post.[111] One way that the postal corporation could avoid this issue in the UPS complaint was to agree to CUPW's demand that the couriers be recognized as employees and the union be recognized as their bargaining representative.

Moreover, Canada Post had strong reasons for avoiding a strike with CUPW. It was proud of having achieved an agreement in 2000 without a strike, and its business strategy, which depended upon expanding its competitive services, required the postal service to be seen as reliable, efficient, and modern. A postal strike would seriously undermine Canada Post's credibility. Ouellet, who had very good relations with the Liberal government and a very long history with the postal service, was appointed to another term as president in 2002. He denounced postal privatization and defended the public postal system.[112] Given the international climate of postal privatization and multilateral trade and service agreements, Ouellet's position was unusual. Canada Post's survival as a public postal service depends upon it maintaining its hold over the growing residential parcel business. The rural delivery network is an important component of this business, which is why the status of rural and suburban mail couriers was such a bone of contention between the corporation and CUPW.

CUPW made the status of the couriers a key issue in the negotiations – an issue that it was willing to strike over. Not only did the union believe that its long-term health depended upon its ability to represent every worker who came in contact with the mail, it believed that it had justice on its side. Moreover, its experience in negotiating on behalf of couriers working for small competitive companies had taught CUPW how to meet the challenge of bargaining on behalf of workers in radically different labour markets.[113]

CUPW did not abandon the political process during negotiations, although politics were placed on a back burner. Petitions calling for the repeal of subsection 13(5) continued to be filed in Parliament by federal members. A prominent NDP member, Bill Blaikie, sponsored a private member's bill calling for the provision's repeal.[114] But political lobbying was designed to reinforce, not supplant, the negotiations.

Backed by an overwhelming strike mandate, CUPW increased pressure on Canada Post to come to an agreement by establishing an 18 July strike deadline. The negotiations had been going on for seven months, and major issues remained unresolved. Tying the negotiations of the large operations unit's collective agreement to the issue of employment status and union recognition for the rural and suburban couriers complicated the process. Moreover, CUPW ran the risk that its members would reject the operations unit's collective agreement if it contained what they perceived to be concessions regarding their rights and entitlements in exchange for obtaining an agreement for the rural and suburban couriers. As the deadline loomed, officials with Canada Post and CUPW assured the public that they wanted to avoid a strike. The union agreed to extend the strike deadline, and after a framework agreement was achieved, it agreed to another extension. On 28 July, Canada Post and CUPW announced that they had secured a collective agreement for the operations unit. Among other things, the postal corporation agreed to contract in urban-expedited parcels, while the union made changes to the work rules of mail service couriers who delivered parcels and gave up severance pay for members of the operations' unit, although it preserved the severance entitlements that had accrued for individual workers.[115]

In addition, CUPW announced that it had achieved a historic agreement for the rural and suburban mail couriers. Canada Post's long-standing objection to treating rural and suburban mail couriers as employees because the postal legislation specifically excluded them from this status was easily finessed. Instead of waiting for the political process of amending the legislation to get rid of the subsection 13(5) exclusion, Canada Post agreed to offer rural and suburban mail contractors who had routes employee status that would take effect on 1 January 2004. The new legal status of these workers was signified by their new name: rural and suburban mail carriers (RSMCs). The collective agreement, which was for an eight-year term with a provision to reopen it for negotiation every second year, recognized CUPW as the exclusive bargaining representative of a separate bargaining unit comprising RSMCs, who would have their own unique classification.

The rural and suburban couriers indicated their overwhelming support for the collective agreement with an 86.79 per cent vote in favour of ratifying it. However, the response to the operations unit's collective agreement was much more mixed – the percentage of the vote in favour of ratification was only 65.41.[116] Some members of the operations unit felt that CUPW had sacrificed too much – future entitlement to severance pay – for the rural and suburban mail couriers' collective agreement, and that the union should either have gone on strike to save severance pay and obtain a collective agreement for the couriers or continued with the political strategy of obtaining employee status for the couriers.[117] Although the merit of this position is controversial,[118] the relatively low ratification vote indicates that union leaders put themselves in jeopardy when they link demands for precarious workers whom they have not traditionally represented to negotiations on behalf of their traditional membership. Any changes to the existing rights and entitlements of the traditional membership can easily be characterized as unwarranted concessions.

However, the change in their legal status resulted in a number of immediate benefits for the rural and suburban couriers: they were now covered under employment insurance, workers' compensation, and the Canada and Quebec Pension Plans without having to self-insure or make additional contributions; they were also entitled to basic bereavement, maternity, and parental leaves, paid statutory holidays, two weeks of paid vacation, and health and safety protections under the *Canada Labour Code*. As well, the agreement provided protection from unjust dismissal, a vehicle allowance, and a wage increase in the first year of the agreement. Under the agreement, "Canada Post will contribute $29 million in the first year and an additional $15 million each year thereafter, to finance the improvements in wages, benefits and working conditions."[119] A joint six-member transition committee, composed of three representatives each from CUPW and Canada Post, was appointed to oversee the introduction of the contract, which included setting up a work evaluation system and an hourly payroll. The committee also had to resolve issues such as establishing dates of hire, a seniority system, and workload. Moreover, CUPW took on the difficult task of integrating the workers who assist RSMCs (known as "helpers" before the integration and "replacement workers" afterwards) into the labour process, bargaining unit, and collective agreement. The union still faces the difficult task of developing political structures in its constitution for representing the RSMCs, devising institutional arrangements, and developing and adapting policies and practices in order to service them.

CONCLUSION

The success of CUPW's campaign to organize rural route mail couriers in order to achieve employee status, union recognition, and a collective agreement demonstrates that unions have the potential to attract and represent precarious self-employed workers. But it also shows that developing a strong and enduring base for self-organization and self-representation among precarious workers requires a great deal of financial and institutional support. Only a few unions are willing or able to invest such substantial resources in organizing campaigns in which the risks of being defeated at the certification stage or raided by another union are so high and success is easily reversed by contracting out. This case study also demonstrates that union leaders who link the negotiation of the collective agreements of their traditional membership to the recognition of precarious workers also face a potential backlash from the traditional membership if they make bargaining concessions, even if the concessions are not directly attributable to the rights won for precarious workers. Moreover, some precarious workers fit more readily into the collective bargaining regime than do others. Rural route mail couriers are a relatively fortunate group of precarious workers: they work for a single corporation that has a highly organized workforce, the lion's share of which is represented by a militant union committed to organizing all of the workers in the sector.

Two justifications were offered for excluding rural and suburban mail couriers from the labour protection and labour rights available to other workers. The first was ideological. The tradition and values of entrepreneurship were invoked by the Liberal government and Canada Post to defend maintaining the historical status of rural contractors. The emphasis on the legal form of the contracting arrangement with rural couriers to justify their treatment obscured the range of different social categories subsumed under the legal form. By treating mail contracting as a homogeneous category of independent contracting, the legislation equated rural and suburban mail couriers with large contractors such as trucking companies and Air Canada. However, the vast majority of rural and suburban couriers were own-account, self-employed individuals who did not employ others, received little remuneration, worked in a climate of great economic insecurity, and fell outside the scope of employment protection legislation and many employment-linked social benefits.[120] Rural route mail couriers and CUPW used a number of tactics, from legal challenges to political petitions to public interest news stories, to show the reality of the couriers' working lives and their precarious economic situations. Judicial recognition of the rights of vulnerable workers to associate freely combined with the depiction of rural and suburban mail couriers as precarious workers to challenge the validity of the rhetoric of entrepreneurship.

The second justification for the rural couriers' status as independent contractors was economic. The government emphasized the increased cost that their unionization could incur were the law changed. The corporation claimed that it would cost at least $90 million a year, the same amount that André Ouellet estimated in 1980 when he was the minister responsible for the post office.[121] However, the economic rationale for denying rural route mail couriers employment protection was no longer as compelling as it had been twenty years earlier. Since 1995, the postal corporation has earned a profit and paid income tax. In this context, it was difficult to justify maintaining the legislatively enforced precarious status of rural route mail contractors. The resolve of a majority of the rural and suburban mail couriers to join CUPW, combined with CUPW's willingness to strike over the status of these members, persuaded Canada Post that it had more to gain than lose by recognizing the employee status of these so-called independent contractors and bargaining with the union that represented them. Legal challenges and political lobbying proved insufficient to change the legal status of rural mail couriers; a union-building strategy backed by the economic power of a large union was required for the couriers to be recognized as employees.

3

From Precarious Workers to Unionized Employees and Back Again?: The Challenges of Organizing Personal-Care Workers in Ontario

People who do the work of bathing, toileting, feeding, and caring for those with disabilities provide a very important service. Most of these workers are women, and their positions are precarious. Some work at unrecognized, unregulated, low-paying (or often unpaid) jobs on a casual basis in private homes; others find better-paying, but generally part-time, employment through non-profit agencies or public sector institutions. The precariousness of this work stems from the fact that collective bargaining law is based on the norm of a direct and continuous employment relationship with one employer in which the work is performed at one formal work site (Fudge and Vosko 2001a). While personal-care workers who are considered employees have recently organized, others are considered either independent contractors or domestic workers and have little ability to organize for better wages and working conditions.[1]

This chapter examines a new model for delivering personal-care services to Ontarians with physical disabilities – called Self-Managed Care: Direct Funding – and compares it to the dominant model of service delivery by non-profit organizations. The primary methodology is a legal and policy analysis. Labor legislation, especially the Ontario *Labour Relations Act (OLRA)*,[2] relevant cases brought before the Ontario Labour Relations Board (OLRB), and new legislation to bring in direct funding are evaluated for their impact upon personal-care workers. This analysis is supplemented with an examination of relevant data from the Labour Force Survey and the census and interviews with five key informants. These informants make up a purposive sample, and they were chosen because they have worked and/or organized in the sector for many years.[3] Their deep knowledge of the issues facing personal-care workers adds credibility to the information they shared, but no attempt is made to generalize to Ontario personal-care workers.

The chapter is organized into five parts. Part 1 describes the emergence of community-based delivery models in Ontario within the context of privatization. Part 2 describes the economic and social status of personal-care workers, illustrating that gender, race/ethnicity, and immigrant status intersect to determine who does this type of work. Part 3 examines the mismatch between the nature of personal-care work and the conventional legal definition of *employee*, explains how this mismatch affects the ability of employers to argue that personal-care workers are either independent contractors or domestic workers, and describes the difficulties of organizing personal-care workers under Canada's industrial labour relations regime. Part 4 is an analysis of the first model of service delivery, in which workers are employed by non-profit agencies funded by the provincial government; it focuses on how part-time, shift, and on-call workers have won fair wages, extended benefits, and the ability to enforce fair labour standards by joining Local 40 of the Canadian Auto Workers (CAW). However, some people with disabilities have sought more "flexibility, choice and control" over service provision through Self-Managed Care: Direct Funding (Parker et al. 2000). Part 5 examines three possible regulatory scenarios that could emerge under this new model and the implications of each scenario for personal-care workers. The conclusion highlights how current labour law systematically disadvantages personal-care workers, who are predominately immigrant women of colour, as well as people with disabilities, and it suggests the need for a new labour relations regime that can bring security to workers and clients/consumers.[4]

1. PERSONAL CARE IN A CONTEXT OF PRIVATIZATION

Prior to the 1970s, most people with disabilities either lived in institutions, where they received care from paid medical professionals, or at home, where they received unpaid, unprofessional care from family and friends. In the mid-1970s, disability activists began to organize for more community-based options.[5] These new, community-based services were provided by non-profit agencies and funded by cost sharing between the federal and provincial governments. In Ontario, two programs were designed to provide more independent living options for people with disabilities: Social Support Living Units (SSLUs) and Outreach Attendant Services (Outreach). SSLUs, piloted in 1975, are accessible and affordable housing units linked to attendant services available twenty-four hours a day, seven days a week. The Ontario government established Outreach services in 1984 to provide more limited-care and housekeeping services to people with disabilities living in dispersed homes. Outreach services are only available for scheduled visits and are limited to ninety hours per month. In both of these programs, a single non-profit agency is the employer.[6]

The demand for attendant services far surpasses the supply through SSLUs and Outreach (Lord, Hutchison, and Farlow 1988; Roeher Institute 1993).[7] As of 1996, 93 SSLUs were providing services to approximately 1,423 people, while 43 providers were offering services to 2,071 people through Outreach.[8] In contrast, the number of people with disabilities in Ontario is estimated at over 1.5 million.[9] People with disabilities also use the general home-care program, but these services are not sufficient to meet the demand. Compared to institutionalization or living with one's family, SSLUs and Outreach services were regarded by disability activists as significant steps towards independent living (Dunn 1999; Parker et al. 2000, 24). Attendant services offered through SSLUs and Outreach are based on people with disabilities self-directing their own care, meaning that the individual with the disability directs the worker on how to provide services. Many agencies have people with disabilities on their boards of directors, including some who are clients/consumers of the agency's services (Lord, Hutchison, and Farlow 1988). Therefore, in some cases, people with disabilities are able to manage the services that they use, although their management role is performed within a corporate entity.

In the 1980s, disability activists began to call for personal-care options modelled on individualized[10] and direct funding. They argued that people with disabilities needed more control over where, when, and how personal-care services were offered as well as who provided the services. They also called for housekeeping and a range of services outside the home – such as shopping, banking, and assistance at one's place of employment – to be included in public-funded care (Lord, Hutchison, and Farlow 1988). As early as 1982, the Ontario Advisory Council for Disabled Persons called for an attendant-care allowance. In the mid-

1980s, the Attendant Care Action Coalition formed and began to look into brokering models for linking personal-care workers to people with disabilities (Parker et al. 2000). In 1988, two important reports – the *Lord Report*, commissioned by the Ministry of Community and Social Services and entitled *Independence and Control: Today's Dream, Tomorrow's Reality*; and a report by the Ontario Advisory Council for Disabled Persons entitled *Independent Living: The Time Is Now* – recommended direct funding to allow people with disabilities more flexibility and control and suggested a brokerage mechanism to facilitate it.

Provincial politicians also began to examine community-based service options in the late 1980s and the 1990s. Direct funding was promised by the Liberals, piloted by the NDP, and institutionalized by the Conservatives. In 1989, the Liberal government announced long-term-care reform and committed to testing a pilot project on individualized direct funding.[11] In 1991, the NDP government initiated a public consultation process to "redirect" long-term care towards the community.[12] The NDP plan included a commitment to look at individualized funding, but it also proposed that the government be considered the ultimate employer of personal-care workers and initially included increased funding of community-based services.[13] Bill 101 was passed by the NDP government in 1993, amending the *Ministry of Community and Social Services Act* to allow individuals with disabilities to receive funding directly from the government or to allow agencies to transfer such a grant on behalf of a person with a disability.[14] In 1994, the NDP government allocated $4.4 million to the Centre for Independent Living in Toronto (CILT) to administer the Direct Funding Pilot Program (Parker et al. 2000, 27). A year later, the NDP was voted out of office, and the new Conservative government began its own restructuring process. It institutionalized individualized direct funding in 1998 – creating the Self-Managed Care: Direct Funding Program – and it increased the budget to $18.7 million, allowing up to 700 Ontarians with disabilities to become "self-managers" (Parker et al. 2000, 27).[15]

In the restructuring of long term care, the politics between organized labour and disability activists have been intense. During the NDP consultation process, the CAW, the Canadian Union of Public Employees (CUPE), the Ontario Public Service Employees Union (OPSEU), and the Service Employees International Union (SEIU), all of which were engaged in organizing attendants, voiced their concerns about the impact of individualized direct funding on workers. One observer argued that the four unions had "banded together to oppose the implementation of

Direct Funding in the absence of what they consider adequate safeguards for attendant service workers."[16] The unions pointed out how direct funding represented a trend towards privatization, the divestment of government responsibility, and the erosion of unionized jobs.[17] They expressed doubt that the level of funding would be sufficient to allow clients/consumers to pay workers' wages equal to those paid by agencies and to fulfill all the labour-related statutory responsibilities of an employer. They were also concerned that workers under this program would not know their rights because they would lose their ability to organize collectively. In the words of one CAW activist, "I'm not saying that's all that this was, a cheap labour strategy, but that was definitely part of it."[18] In turn, while the target of labour's critique has always been the government, some disability activists believed that the labour movement assumed that people with disabilities were not capable of being employers.[19]

Neo-liberal policies of the Conservative government, heavily focused on privatization, set the terms of the debate, and this has had consequences for workers and for people with disabilities. Privatization not only involves the government selling the companies it owns, but it also involves the government contracting out the provision of services to the community services sector and downloading services to households and individuals – and all of this is combined with funding cutbacks (Armstrong, Armstrong, and Connelly 1997; Fudge and Cossman 2002). Since 1995, when the Conservative government took office, there have been considerable cuts to spending on accessible public housing, transportation, and support services for people with disabilities (Dunn 1999). Across Canada, including in Ontario, cuts to acute-care budgets have not resulted in equivalent spending on home care (Flood 1999). As the federal government has cut back funding for health and social services, the Ontario government has downloaded these services to municipal governments, resulting in a narrowing of attendant service options for people with disabilities and more precarious conditions for care workers. For example, with the shift to "managed competition," people with disabilities and the elderly must compete with sick people for home-care services, as the latter are pushed out of hospitals sooner (Armstrong and Armstrong 2003; Aronson and Neysmith 2001). These privatizations have had a particularly negative impact on female paid workers and unpaid caregivers (Armstrong and Armstrong 2002; Flood 1999; Morris et al 1999; Neysmith 2000; Roeher Institute 2001).

Within this context, Self-Managed Care came to be framed as an opportunity for the government to cut costs. The move from a pilot project to a regular program was heavily supported by an analysis of the cost-effectiveness of Self-Managed Care compared to the two other independent living options, SSLUs and Outreach. This analysis estimated that the cost for one hour of attendant services under the self-managed-care pilot was $16.28, compared to $24.29 for Outreach and $33.79 for SSLUs (Roeher Institute 1997). Some advocates of direct funding focused on the benefit to the Ontario government afforded by reductions in administration and labour costs. For example, the CILT argued that unlike the on-call, twenty-four-hour services provided by SSLUs, Self-Managed Care had no "hidden costs," such as wages for attendants who were "on shift but not being utilized" (Parker et al. 2000, 2, 43–4). Direct funding was also framed within a neo-liberal ideology about the free market and choice, as is the case in other jurisdictions (Imrie 1996, 61–6; Parker et al. 2000). Despite these arguments, disability advocates also recognized that neo-liberal policies could lead to insecurity for many people with disabilities due to inadequate levels of funding.[20] This case study suggests that privatization will lead to a more precarious status for personal-care workers.

2. THE SOCIAL AND ECONOMIC STATUS OF PERSONAL-CARE WORKERS

Personal-care work is intimate and intermittent. It involves two vulnerable populations: women and immigrants of colour. Most personal-care workers are either precariously employed or take on multiple clients or multiple jobs in order to earn a living. In addition, the precariousness of personal-care work is intensified by its social location (Neysmith and Aronson 1997; Roeher Institute 2001). The work takes place in other people's homes and involves assisting clients/consumers with such intimate daily activities as personal grooming, bathing, shampooing, and shaving; dressing and undressing; using the toilet, and bowel and bladder routines when a toilet cannot be used; turning in bed and moving from one position to another; stretching; eating; and sometimes communicating.[21] The intimate nature of personal care means that a good relationship between the attendant care worker and the client/consumer is essential. As scholars have long argued, care work also includes the invisible task of building and sustaining relationships (Armstrong and

Armstrong 2002; Daniels 1987; Meyer 2000; Neysmith 2000; Ungerson 1999). For attendant workers, this includes the "fumbling, middle-ground sort of work – clearing the air and communicating."[22] Many personal-care workers also play an advocacy role, which is unpaid and generally unrecognized (Williams et al. 2000).[23]

The fact that this is personal service tailored to the needs of the client/consumer means that the work is highly intermittent. It lends itself to part-time hours, split shifts, and other irregular work arrangements. However, the number of hours a personal-care worker has on the job and the stability of her work schedule depend on the model of service delivery and the existence of a union. This is how an employee of a non-union agency providing Outreach attendant services describes her work schedule: "For the Outreach, it varies, because you can be up this minute and the next minute your hours are down because of the clients – let's say they are hospitalized or anything like that, you know, then your hours will go down. So it's an up-and-down kind of thing. You've got to have the client to get the hours."[24]

The intermittent and intimate nature of the work often means that a personal attendant must undertake multiple domestic tasks. Disability activists and people with disabilities define care needs as physical assistance with the routine activities of living that clients/consumers would perform for themselves were it not for their physical limitations (Parker et al. 2000). This broad concept of attendant care includes housekeeping and sometimes child care. It also includes tasks previously done by medical professionals, such as giving medication. In the agency model, workers often accept additional tasks to increase their hours.[25] Arranging for additional hours is more difficult under the Outreach program, which funds fewer hours of care and little housekeeping; it is also difficult under Self-Managed Care, due to funding limitations.

Because of the insecurity of this work, many personal-care workers either take on multiple clients or have several jobs. The closest category to personal-care work in the publicly available data collected by Statistics Canada is "child-care and home-support workers." In 2001, child-care and home-support workers in Ontario earned a median wage of $11.50 an hour, yet their hours were intermittent due to their employment status and form. They were overrepresented among the own-account self-employed, as well as part-time and temporary employees, compared to the proportion of all Ontario workers. In Ontario in 2001, 16 per cent of child-care and home-support workers were part-time permanent employees, 7 per cent were part-time temporary, 22 per cent were full-time own-account self-employed, and 10 per cent were part-time own-account self-employed; compare this to 11 per cent, 4 per cent, 7 per cent, and 3 per cent, respectively, for all Ontario workers. These are the forms of employment most likely to be precarious in terms of regulatory protection, control, and wages (Cranford, Vosko, and Zukewich 2003). In addition, their median job tenure is thirty-six months (compared to fifty months for all Ontarians), and 7 per cent have multiple jobs (compared to 5 per cent of all Ontario workers).[26] Wages range widely, depending on the care model and the existence of a union. In the agency model, low wages push workers to take multiple jobs, particularly if they are non-union. The more individualized the care model, the more insecure the work, and the more likely the worker is to take multiple clients.

Most personal-care workers are in precarious social locations as immigrant women of colour (Neysmith and Aronson 1997; Roeher Institute 2001). This is particularly true in Greater Toronto, the site of the two case studies examined in this chapter. In the Toronto metropolitan area, 95 per cent of child-care and home-support workers were women in 2001.[27] The concentration of women in care work is due to both supply- and demand-side factors (Armstrong and Armstrong 2002; Fudge and Vosko 2001a). On the demand side, employers often justify hiring women part time or for split shifts by arguing that women put family first and are working only to supplement the household income. On the supply side, many women accept split shifts and part-time hours due to basic gender inequities – they must shoulder responsibility for the unpaid care work required in their own homes, and they lack power in the paid labour market. There are more men engaged in agency-provided attendant care than in other forms of care work, in part because some men with disabilities prefer to have services provided by other men, and the agencies accommodate this. Most men who do this work are from racialized groups, many are recent immigrants, and they also lack power in the Canadian labour market.[28] In the 1996 census of the Toronto metropolitan area (the CMA), 40 per cent of child-care and home-support workers were visible minorities, compared to 28 per cent of all employed. Immigrant workers made up a slightly greater share of child-care and home-support workers than did Canadian-born workers. Fifty-four per cent of child-care and home-support workers were not born in Canada, compared to only 46 per cent of all the employed.

People from the Philippines and the Caribbean were overrepresented in this occupational group.[29]

The percentage of women in personal-care work increases with the individualization of the care model (Keigher 1997; Ungerson 1999). The majority of workers represented by CAW Local 40 are women, yet the percentage of men is not insignificant, ranging from 35 to 45 per cent across the bargaining units. Racialized immigrant men have stayed in this job well past their first few years in Canada because they were able to mitigate the precariousness that generally accompanies the work through unionization.[30] In contrast, according to a 1997 survey, 86 per cent of the personal attendants in the Self-Managed Care pilot were women. In terms of ethnicity, 13 per cent of personal attendants working through Self-Managed Care had parents whose first language was French; 10 per cent had parents whose first language was neither English nor French; 16 per cent identified as a visible minority; and 4 per cent identified as Aboriginal (Roeher Institute 1997).

Due to the interpersonal nature of the work, the fates of the workers and the clients/consumers may be linked (Eustis and Rischer 1991; Neysmith and Aronson 1997; Roeher Institute 2001). As a group, people with disabilities are also vulnerable, but in different dimensions. They are stigmatized and excluded from many aspects of daily life, including employment, by physical and social barriers. When they do participate in the paid labour force, they are disproportionately concentrated in marginal, low-paying jobs, and as a result they are disproportionately poor (Bach and Rioux 1996; Barnes, Mercer, and Shakespeare 1999, 110–16). In addition, it is not uncommon for people with disabilities to be subjected to physical and sexual abuse by unpaid and paid caregivers (Morris 1993; Williams et al. 2000). These dimensions of social inequality have shaped the call from people with disabilities for more control over personal-care supports. The participants in the Self-Managed Care: Direct Funding pilot had higher incomes, more extensive employment backgrounds, and higher levels of education than people with disabilities as a whole; 55 per cent were men and 5 per cent identified as visible minorities (Roeher Institute 1997). However, within the context of privatization, workers and people with disabilities are likely to end up in more precarious situations. Workers' precariousness also stems from the fact that individualized employment relationships are more difficult to regulate under Ontario's collective bargaining regime.

3. PERSONAL-CARE WORKERS AND THE COLLECTIVE BARGAINING REGIME IN ONTARIO

Personal-care workers confront three barriers when attempting to organize collectively. First, employee status is the gateway to coverage under collective bargaining legislation, yet, like a growing number of workers, some personal-care workers fall into a grey area between the legal concepts of employee and independent contractor. Like dependent employees, they perform personal services, generally under conditions over which they have little control. However, with the trend towards privatization of care-related services, personal-care workers increasingly contract with multiple clients/consumers, leading some employers to argue that they are independent contractors. Even if they are classified as employees, personal-care workers may face a second problem due to inequalities within the definition of *employee* – inequalities relating to whether the employees in question work for large, formal employers or for individual householders. Pointing to the interpersonal nature of the work and its location in the home of the client/consumer, employers have argued that attendants are domestic workers. Domestic workers are excluded from the OLRA, which provides the basic legal protections for unions and collective bargaining. Even if domestic workers were included in the OLRA, as they were briefly under the NDP government, they would face a third barrier to attaining the benefits of collective bargaining due to the lack of fit between personal-care work located in homes and a labour relations regime premised on large, industrial workplaces.

A. Establishing Employment Status

In Ontario, a worker must be an *employee*, a term that is broadly defined to include *dependent contractor*, in order to unionize and bargain collectively. Like most pieces of labour legislation, the OLRA does not provide a clear definition of *employee*; instead, adjudicators rely on various tests to determine employee status. Historically, control was the single most important factor in determining employee status, but labour boards now examine the degree of economic dependence as well.[31] The concept "dependent contractor" is meant to capture the situation of persons who are legally contractors but who are economically dependent (Arthurs 1965; Sack, Mitchell, and Price 1997, 2.74–95). The OLRA defines a *dependent contractor* as "a person, whether or not employed under a contract of employment, and whether or not furnishing tools, vehicles, equipment, machinery, material, or any other thing owned by the dependent contractor, who performs work or services for another person for compensation or reward on such terms and conditions that the dependent contractor *is in a position of economic dependence upon*, and *under an obligation to perform duties for*, that person more closely resembling the relationship of an employee than that of an independent contractor."[32]

The OLRB draws on a host of factors to determine whether elements of control and the degree of economic dependence on a particular employer are sufficient to conclude that a worker is more akin to an employee than an independent contractor. The board has ruled that home-care workers, who have employment relationships similar to those we now see under some individualized funding arrangements, are dependent contractors.[33] For example, in 1998, when homemakers contracted to a Community Care Access Centre (CCAC) sought to unionize with OPSEU, the CCAC argued that the workers were independent contractors.[34] The homemakers worked on average one-third the hours of a full-time worker, and several were working for multiple agencies as well as independent clients/consumers. They could refuse assignments, make arrangements with clients/consumers to change times, and use other home-care workers contracted to the same CCAC as substitutes. They signed an annual contract that stipulated that they were providing services to the CCAC on a nonexclusive basis as independent contractors so that they could work for any other individual or agency. They were treated as independent contractors on the payroll.

Referencing the eleven factors set out in *Algonquin Tavern*, the board considered whether the relationship between the homemakers and the CCAC more closely resembled the relationship with an employee than with an independent contractor.[35] It concluded that the homemakers had some control over *when* they did their work, but little control over *how*, because this was set out in a CCAC manual and because they were assessed regularly "in a format which looks remarkably like an employee evaluation."[36] The board also pointed to the fact that wages and mileage rates as well as strict guidelines and timelines for invoicing were set by the CCAC as an indicator of the homemakers' lack of control over how they were remunerated. There was no scope for homemakers to profit or to incur loss; they were paid on an hourly basis (with mileage); the CCAC paid any substitutes; and the CCAC would collect any monies outstanding in the event that clients/consumers did not pay for the services. The board found that there was "simply no evidence of entrepreneurial activity on the part of the homemakers," and that the homemakers were integrated into the CCAC organization and were a "very stable group of service providers."[37]

The board acknowledged that the homemakers enjoyed some level of independence: they had non-exclusive contracts, they could accept or turn down work, they could express their weekend shift preferences to the homemaking coordinator, and they were treated as independent contractors on the payroll. It discounted the last factor on the ground that the form of remuneration was not significant in determining employee status for the purposes of collective bargaining, even though the Tax Court had classified the homemakers as independent contractors. The board argued that the first three factors were "not unlike the situation that usually prevails for part-time workers or dependent contractors who ... by virtue of not having sufficient hours of work available from one employer, may work for other employers as well."[38] The fact that homemakers perform, on average, only one-third of a full-time job and work for multiple agencies or clients was not a relevant indicator of the lack of integration into an employer's operations, according to the board. After reviewing all of the factors, the adjudicator concluded that, "on balance, I am of the view that the homemakers are in a contractual relationship of dependency with [CCAC]. They are therefore dependent contractors and are employees for the purposes of the Act."[39]

Dependent contractor provisions have been criticized for not expanding the coverage of collective bargaining law beyond those who would be considered employees under the standard factor tests (Bendel 1982). Indeed, in this case, the board's decision rested heavily on the traditional factor of control. A very similar case illustrates just how much attention the board has paid to the dimension of control in the application of the *dependent contractor* definition to care workers.

Three months after the board found that the homemakers were dependent contractors in *Hunstville District Memorial Hospital*, the same Community Care Access Centre (CCAC) argued that nursing service providers were independent contractors. OPSEU again challenged this interpretation of workers' status.[40] Interested in a quick determination of status, the parties proposed, and the board accepted, that the CCAC would set the basis on which it asserted that the nurses differed from the homemakers.[41] The differences between the two groups were considerable. Nurses, unlike homemakers, are part of a recognized profession; nurses have discretion in developing care plans and determining the number of visits; nurses provide more of the tools used in their work; nurses were subject to less direction from the CCAC due to their professional licensing; and nurses were paid by the visit, not by the hour. The Workplace Safety and Insurance Board (WSIB) had also ruled that one of the nurses was an independent contractor. Despite all of these factors, the OLRB ruled that the nurses were dependent contractors of the CCAC for the purpose of collective bargaining.

Several themes in the board's decision are important for personal-care workers generally. The board referred to the interpersonal nature of the work and its location in the home of the client/consumer in its interpretation of the extent to which various factors were indicators of independence. It argued that "while recognizing the nurses' ability to exercise independent judgment in the course of providing their services, including suggesting changes to the services being provided to a client, when considered in the context of the nature and location of the work being performed, we do not view such as a strong indicator of independent contractor status."[42] It concluded that the nurses' need to exercise independent judgment in providing services was more a reflection of the nature of the work itself than an indication that the nurses were independent contractors; they had to "make educated decisions on their own ... and to act on those decisions accordingly." The OLRB's consideration of scheduling is also significant for other care workers. While the board conceded that the CCAC coordinator had less control over the schedules of the nurses than the schedules of the homemakers, it argued this "may be a distinction without a difference," because nurses provide personal services to people. Focusing on the nature of the work, the board argued: "nurses must arrange their schedule around their clients' medical needs and availability. Given that many medical services have to be provided at particular times of the day and with a certain degree of regularity, it cannot be said that nurses have complete control over their own schedule."[43] This, the board asserted, limited the ability of the nurses to structure their schedules so as to maximize income and earn a profit. Significantly, the board maintained that these facts, combined with the belief that the nurses were well integrated into the home-care program, outweighed evidence pointing to entrepreneurial activity, such as nurses being paid by the visit rather than the hour. The board concluded that the nurses were involved in an employment relationship rather than a relationship between two businesses. In this case, the board essentially prompted a consideration of the role the client/

consumer plays in deciding workers' employee status, a consideration that is significant for workers under individualized funding.

Despite gains for these home-care workers, the dependent contractor concept is not broad enough to include many other personal-care workers. These homemakers and nurses are contracted to a CCAC, but the goal of individualized funding is to mitigate the role played by an agency. This approach may mean that workers who are dependent on multiple clients/consumers are considered to be independent contractors. At the same time, if the shift to individualized funding results in the person with the disability gaining more control over how the work is organized, then the workers may be classified as domestic workers. Those who are classified as domestic workers in Ontario are not entitled to the statutory protection of the right to organize trade unions and bargain collectively available to other workers. Indeed, some groups of personal-care workers have had to establish an organization as their employer in order not to be considered employees and thus to have access to collective bargaining legislation.

B. Establishing an Organization as the Employer

A second hurdle that personal-care workers have had to leap in attempting to organize collectively is establishing that their employer is not the householder to whom they provide services.[44] A care worker who is an employee of an individual householder and who works in that householder's home is excluded from coverage under the OLRA, which states: "This Act does not apply to a domestic employed in a private home."[45] Domestic workers are excluded from the OLRA as well as other pieces of labour legislation because the home is viewed as a site for private family relations (Fudge 1997; Hondagneu-Sotelo 2000). The privileging of family relations at this site results in the assumption that householders, not the government, should largely determine the social relations that occur there, even if they involve paid work. A domestic worker is not seen as a real employee but rather as "one of the family" (Bakan and Stasiulis 1997). These ideologies of privacy and domesticity combine to justify the lesser protection accorded to domestic workers (Fudge 1997, 123–4, 126).

The inability of domestic workers to organize in Ontario has prompted at least one employer in this sector to try to classify personal-care workers as domestic workers, even when services were provided through an agency.[46] In 1983, workers who provided services to people with disabilities through a small, community-based non-profit corporation called Nucleus Housing Incorporated began to organize with the SEIU. In response to an application for certification by SEIU Local 204, Nucleus argued that the attendants were employees of the people with disabilities and excluded from the OLRA by virtue of section 2(a). Nucleus was a non-profit corporation that used funds from the Ontario government to provide personal care to fourteen men with quadriplegia in a SSLU setting. The clients/consumers lived in separate apartments in a building also inhabited by non-disabled people. They told Nucleus how many hours of service they required each day, and workers were given their assignments on that basis. The client/consumer gave care instructions to the attendant, but he did not necessarily have the same attendant each day, and he would sometimes have more than one attendant in the course of a day. Nucleus was run by a board of directors, and six of the fourteen board members were tenants of the apartment building. Nucleus argued that it was merely an enabling agency set up to channel funding to the individual men because the government would not pay them directly to employ personal attendants. According to Nucleus, the employment relationship between the clients/consumers and their attendants was closer to that between an individual householder/employer and a domestic worker because its clients/consumers were individual tenants who self-directed their care, and because the attendants performed a range of domestic labour and care tasks.

The OLRB ruled that the attendants were employees of the non-profit corporation, not domestics employed in private homes within the meaning of section 2(a) of the OLRA. The decision of the OLRB rested on two facts. First, funding was only available to the people with disabilities through the non-profit corporation, despite the fact that they themselves had created this corporation and a number of them sat on its board of directors. Second, the OLRB argued that the fact that he directed the services he received did not make the individual with a disability an employer. The argument of the board on this second point was that "while counsel for Nucleus submits that each tenant is the master of the person or persons assigned to him as his daily personal attendant in terms of directing what services the attendant is to perform for him, all the other elements characteristic of an employee-employer relationship are clearly within the control of Nucleus ... Consequently, they are not domestics employed in a private home within the meaning of Section 2(a) of the Act."[47] Accordingly, the OLRB certified SEIU as the representative of the workers.

The board has focused more specifically on the extent to which the employment relationship is institutionalized, rather than occurring between two individuals, in determining whether personal-care workers are "domestic[s] employed in a private home" within the meaning of section 2(a) of the OLRA.[48] In a case concerning the maintenance, dietary, infirmary, and housekeeping staff who provided services to the nuns of the Sisters of St. Joseph, the OLRB rejected St. Joseph's argument that because the workers provided services relating to household affairs at a site that received no public funding and was perceived by the nuns as their home, they were "domestic[s] employed in a private home." Approximately twenty-five full-time workers and sixteen part-time workers provided services to sixty-seven resident members of the religious order. The workers – including registered nursing assistants and health-care aides – were supervised by a registered nurse. Those in the infirmary worked shifts – 7:00 a.m. to 3:00 p.m., 3:00 p.m. to 11:00 p.m., and 11:00 p.m. to 7:00 a.m. These workers bathed, fed, and distributed medicine to the sisters and helped with their general care. The dietary staff prepared meals and cleaned up after them. There was one full-time cook. Part-time workers generally had the same duties as full-time staff, and they replaced full-time staff on weekends or days off.[49]

The board accepted that the phrase "domestic employed in a private home" could have more than one meaning, but it rejected the definitions used by St. Joseph because they did not fit within the full context of the purpose of the statute. Citing the decision in *Nucleus Housing Inc.* as a precedent for interpreting section 2(a) of the act,[50] the board argued that it was more appropriate within the purposes of the act to exclude from section 2(a) "those households which bear 'institutional' elements and therefore resemble other workplaces where employees engage in collective bargaining under the Act."[51] By "'institutional' elements," the board meant that the relationship between each resident and the workers was "mediated through coordinating bodies consisting of lay supervisors and designated sisters." The board found relevant the facts that the employees worked set shifts, they had established duties, and the organization set certain routines, like meal times. It also pointed to the number of residents and the number of workers involved in the care of the sisters as evidence of the institutional nature of the employment relationship. These facts, the board argued, meant that "the degree of control that each of the residents has over the employees working there [is attenuated]."[52]

While these decisions were important for the groups of workers involved and for workers in similar situations, they also illustrate the limits of collective bargaining legislation for many other personal-care workers. The focus on the degree of institutionalization of an employment relationship leaves the door open for employers and governments to move care into private homes that do not have what the board would consider "institutional" elements: that is, they are places where unmediated, individual relationships occur; and they do not resemble workplaces where collective bargaining occurs. Indeed, this is what has occurred with more individualized funding. More broadly, the focus on institutionalized employment relationships reproduces the notion that there is a genuine private sphere within which government regulation should not interfere.

C. Structural Problems with the Industrial Labour Relations Regime

Personal-care workers face a third problem in gaining access to the full benefits of collective bargaining, one rooted in the lack of fit between personal services performed in homes and the contemporary labour relations regime premised on the large, industrial workplace.

The labour relations regime under which unions must today organize was not designed to provide collective bargaining for workers in the competitive service, retail, and manufacturing industries made up of small workplaces, or for those employed in private households – areas where women have historically been, and continue to be, concentrated (Forrest 1995; Fudge 1993; Ursel 1992). The regime emerged from the struggles undertaken by predominately male workers during the 1930s and early 1940s in oligopolistic manufacturing and resource-extraction industries characterized by large, bureaucratically organized workplaces. In exchange for recognition from employers, the industrial unions consented to a collective bargaining regime, which was largely taken out of their control and placed in the hands of labour boards (Ursel 1992, 199–201). The single-employer, single-location bargaining unit is the "cornerstone of labour board policy" (Fudge 1993, 235).

Personal-care workers labour in small workplaces, where it is difficult and expensive to secure strong collective agreements. In the late 1960s and the 1970s, there was a new wave of organizing in the public sector. However, unionization remained a challenge at the "periphery of the public sector," where the small non-profit agencies that contracted with the government existed (O'Grady 1992, 157; Haiven 1995, 244). Negotiating a collective agreement and enforcing it through grievance procedures is expensive, and thus it is difficult to fund with the dues generated by small workplaces (O'Grady 1992). Furthermore, since workers gain power in numbers, small workplaces produce less pressure at the bargaining table (Fudge 1993). These problems are multiplied as personal care moves into private homes. Even if domestic workers were not excluded from the OLRA, they would be nearly impossible to organize under Ontario's current collective bargaining regime for several reasons. First, the OLRA requires a bargaining unit to have more than one worker. Second, even if single-employee bargaining units were permitted, it would be very expensive to organize workers individually. Third, a bargaining unit of one would not have the power to negotiate better wages and working conditions (Fudge 1997). These problems undermine the incentive for unions to organize personal-care workers.

There is a "symbiotic relationship" between labour relations law and trade union structures and strategies (Fudge 1993, 242–3), and many industrial union strategies do not fit well with personal-care work. Workplace-based collective bargaining law has shaped a "job control unionism" focused on gaining job security with a single employer (O'Grady 1995). Job control unionism emerged partly in response to the organization of industrial workplaces along Taylorist principles. But Taylorism, per se, was not the foundation of job control unionism. That foundation consisted of Taylorism in combination with two other aspects unique to the labour relations regime that emerged in the post-war period in Canada: a common-law rather than statutory tradition of mandated consultation, and low commitments to employment security (O'Grady 1995, 44). A key aspect of job control unionism is the use of seniority with a single employer to regulate the assignment of jobs and schedules. In contrast, personal-care workers share several characteristics with waitresses and other service workers who, in the past, have practiced a variant of craft unionism – Dorothy Sue Cobble calls it "occupational unionism" (1991). Occupational unionism was characterized by representational rights and benefits tied to occupational membership rather than work-site or job-based affiliation. For example, waitress locals allowed employers wide discretion in discharging employees and instead assigned workers other jobs through the hiring hall (Cobble 1991, 424–6). As we shall see, security tied to seniority with a given employer can also be problematic for personal-care workers due to the efforts of clients/consumers to choose their own care providers.

Another characteristic that many personal-care workers share with those who have practiced occupational unionism is an occupational identity that includes concern with providing good services to clients/consumers and is not based solely on opposition to a single employer (Cobble 1991; Armstrong and Armstrong 2002; Donovan 1989; Meyer 2000). In contrast, the industrial labour relations regime regulates collective bargaining between a single employer and a bargaining unit of employees, and many secondary pressure tactics previously available to unions have been outlawed. When the employer is other than the entity that funds the services, it is useful to distinguish between the employer of record and the paymaster – that is, the government (Haiven and Haiven 2002). At the periphery of the public sector, while the union must bargain with the employer of record – for example, the agency – the government is a "ghost at the bargaining table," controlling the agency's budget through transfer payments and thus controlling both wages and the quality of service (Swimmer and Thompson 1995, 6). Personal-care workers face additional barriers in that the economic sanction available to them in the event of an impasse – a strike – could result in harm to the client/consumer. Finally, the fragmented bargaining structure also encourages unions to compete with one another for members, and they do so by focusing on tangible bread-and-butter issues rather than on issues of political, economic, and social change (Fudge 1993, 240–3). However, it is these broader changes that are necessary to bring about better employment and better care.

In sum, the intermittency of personal-care services pushes many workers to take either multiple clients or multiple jobs. The interpersonal nature of the work results in workers performing a range of intimate tasks in other people's homes. However, because collective bargaining law and labour legislation are based on the norm of a high degree of stability and longevity with one employer at a large, formal work site (Fudge and Vosko 2001a), those working within more individualized employment relationships in multiple and informal work sites confront significant barriers when attempting to organize collectively. This is the context within which the impact of individualized funding on workers must be understood. And it is the context that shapes unions' strategies in organizing personal-care workers employed by agencies.

4. ATTENDANT EMPLOYEES OF NON-PROFIT AGENCIES

Several unions are organizing personal-care workers, including the CAW, CUPE, OPSEU, and SEIU. While figures on the union density of this subset of home-care workers are not available, 31 per cent of all child-care and home-support workers in Ontario, and 25 per cent in the Toronto CMA, were covered by a union contract in 2001. These figures are significantly lower than those for other health occupations.[53] This study focuses on the experiences of Local 40 of the CAW, which has organized several bargaining units of personal-care workers.

A case study of personal-care workers organizing with CAW Local 40 shows how employees of non-profit agencies have been able to limit the insecurity that generally accompanies intermittent and interpersonal care work through collective bargaining. However, ambiguity in the employment relationship remains, due to the location and nature of the work. Local 40 has had to work within the structure of industrial unionism, a model premised on the relationship between an employer and employees at a single work site. The local has modified its tactics to accommodate the fact that the legal employer is a non-profit contractor funded by the government, the role that the client/consumer plays in the labour process, and the fact that the work takes place in other people's living spaces. Nevertheless, some of the more traditional means for gaining security are used — such as job security based on seniority with a single employer — which conflict with the desires of some clients/consumers for more control over how services are provided and by whom. This conflict suggests the need for a more significant break with industrial unionism. In this section, I draw on informant interviews, collective agreements between CAW Local 40 and non-profit service providers, relevant labour legislation and policy, as well as secondary reports and academic studies on the broader home-care sector to examine how collective bargaining functions for workers who provide personal care.

Local 40 represents workers employed under both the Social Support Living Units and Outreach Attendant Care delivery models. The SSLUs are apartment buildings that are sites for round-the-clock on-call care. These buildings generally house twelve to sixteen people with disabilities as well as people without disabilities. Workers provide assistance with daily activities and housekeeping to several people with disabilities who, in turn, receive services from several attendant workers. A small full-time core staff works eight-to-twelve-hour shifts and is supplemented by a larger number of part-time workers.[54] Outreach more closely resembles a worker-client relationship, yet an agency is still the legal employer. With Outreach, attendants call the agency to receive their schedules and then visit clients/consumers living within defined geographical regions. They work alone, and they are generally assigned to the same people. Since funding is limited in attendant care, workers provide services to multiple clients/consumers. However, the hours are less stable with Outreach than with SSLUs.

A. Difficulties and Successes with Organizing

Local 40 began to organize attendant-care workers in the early 1980s as part of the independent Canadian Textile and Chemical Union (CTCU), and it has represented workers employed by two agencies since the early 1980s. The CTCU merged with the Canadian Auto Workers (CAW) in 1992, and it continued to organize in this sector. Organizing has been facilitated through workers' networks, which extend beyond a given work site. Many part-time workers have more than one employer in this sector. These networks in between and outside the workplace have been essential for organizers in the face of employers' anti-union campaigns. One worker explains how they allowed him to organize in sites away from the workplace, "quietly, through people you can trust."[55] Since 2000, CAW Local 40 has organized four additional employers. The local now represents employees of six bargaining units in the Greater Toronto area, including those employed by the largest attendant-care provider in the province. The local plans to continue organizing in this industry, and occupational networks will be important assets.

The fragmented collective bargaining structure makes it difficult for unions to organize and represent personal-care workers. Instead of coordinating an organizing strategy, unions are competing for members in this sector. Each of the five bargaining units of Local 40 consists of part-time and full-time employees of an individual employer, but they do contain multiple work sites, albeit very small ones. However, one of the agencies employs workers at four buildings that are represented by the CAW and at two buildings that are represented by the SEIU, because another agency that employed workers who were already represented by the SEIU previously provided services in these two buildings. In addition, the workers at Nucleus Housing who were organized by the SEIU in the early 1980s are now represented by CAW Local 40.⁵⁶ In the mid-1990s, CUPE organized a workplace, but shortly after the employer amalgamated all of its separate locations the certification was discarded. This experience, combined with the employer's anti-union campaign, prompted the workers to seek out Local 40 when they decided that they needed a union for their second job.⁵⁷

The organizing drives of Local 40 have focused on "hot shops" – that is, workplaces where workers have sought out the union. The workers' reasons for doing so include low pay, lack of respect, and excessive workloads. One male attendant cited inadequate compensation as the motivation for organizing: "Look at the things we have to do when we come in the morning through a routine booking – all the stuff that is involved – it's like a nurse, and we're not getting any pay."⁵⁸ According to Jenny Ahn, president of Local 40, one group of workers was primarily concerned with the demands made by clients/consumers and their families that they perform tasks that did not fit their job description, and the agency's unwillingness or inability to intervene.⁵⁹ Workers at a more recently unionized workplace organized in part because they did not have a say; they believed that there were unwarranted firings and instances of preferential treatment – certain workers received better shifts and more hours. One worker explained that with the union, they were going to "regulate" these issues through seniority.⁶⁰ Although most of the workers' reasons for seeking unionization were related to the actions of supervisors, the role played by the client/consumer in daily work relations was also a factor. Some workers maintained that clients/consumers had too much influence on the supervisors, and they sought to rectify this by organizing a union.⁶¹ This points to a mismatch between the legal employment relationship and the social relations of work. Ambiguity in employment relations also makes it difficult to ensure good working conditions.

B. Difficulties and Successes with Ensuring Good Working Conditions

Local 40 has tried to make indirect links between the legal employer and the client/consumer and to enable workers to enforce labour standards through individual negotiations with clients/consumers. As well, the local has used the strike as a pressure tactic, but it has supplemented this with appeals to clients/consumers and to broader public opinion; it has also tried to reduce the impact of the strike on the clients/consumers, as do most health-care unions (Haiven and Haiven 2002).

In April of 2001, Local 40 launched its first strike against an employer in this sector. Since long-term care is not considered an essential service, it was not an illegal strike (Haiven 1995, 247), but mobilization strategies were complicated by the fact that the legal employer was a non-profit contractor funded by the government. Ahn explains that the workers "understood the reality of being funded under a Mike Harris government," and they would ask the union, "There is no money – how do we go to strike on that?" Local 40 focused on the solution of funding workers' wage increases through a reduction in management salaries. It argued that the executive director of one of the unionized non-profit agencies earned over $100,000 a year, and the program director about $70,000; the workers were paid $13 an hour. The union also questioned that the employer was planning to hire three additional assistant managers when there was already a manager at each work site, which consisted of fifteen to twenty workers. In addition, it revealed that workers had been receiving raises in lump sums while management received regular wage increases linked to inflation. Also, the workers hadn't been given a pension increase for roughly five years. When they received this information on the bigger picture, the members became politicized and began to believe that because they were employed at the periphery of the public sector, it didn't mean that they should be marginalized and underpaid. As Ahn recalls, "they started to learn, and they started to get a bit upset." The workers voted to strike.[62]

This focus on redistributing funding in favour of workers was also part of an effort to defuse conflict between workers and clients/consumers. This is a second example of how Local 40 slightly modified industrial union strategies during the strike to accommodate the workers' identity as care workers providing important services. During the strike, some clients/consumers felt that the union was striking against them.[63] Through one-on-one conversations with these clients/consumers, workers and organizers tried to illuminate the connection between better wages and working conditions on the one hand and better service provision on the other. A few clients/consumers were persuaded to join workers on the picket line, and others made statements to the press linking workers' wages and benefits to quality of care.[64] Another strategy to reduce the impact of the strike on the clients/consumers was to allow management and medical service providers to cross the picket line. As a result of the strike, the workers won wage increases and extended benefits.

Part-time, shift, and on-call workers have made significant material gains through the union. Depending on date of hire, wages now range from $12.40 to $15.20 an hour. Full-time and most part-time workers receive vacation pay and more paid holidays, and at a better rate than required by the *Employment Standards Act*. The employer pays 100 per cent of a benefits package for full-time employees that includes life insurance, long-term disability, dental, drugs, vision, and supplemental health care. The union has secured benefits for part-time employees from one of the employers; other part-time employees (who work sixteen hours or more in a two-week period) receive pay in lieu of some benefits. In addition to bringing personal-care workers better wages and benefits, collective representation is necessary to ensure fair labour standards. Before the union, several employers did not have pay equity plans, and the plans of those who did were not implemented. Through unionization, Local 40 members have received the pay due to them. However, other labour legislation has been more difficult to enforce.

Labour and collective bargaining legislation does not fit neatly with the nature and location of personal-care work due to the state's ambivalence towards regulating private homes (Fudge 1997).[65] The role the client/consumer plays in daily work relations impedes the establishment of good working conditions for personal-care workers in private homes because labour and collective bargaining legislation is based on the relationship between the worker and a single direct employer (the agency) in a formal workplace. The union has taken these ambiguities into consideration in formulating strategies to enforce the union contract. Like most people who use domestic help, people with disabilities prefer to view their apartments as a home rather than a workplace (Hondagneu-Sotelo 2000; Parker et al. 2000). According to the workers and the union, employers generally side with clients/consumers on this issue.[66] For example, there have been instances when a male client/consumer watches pornographic movies while a female worker is cleaning his apartment, but employers argue that by telling the client/consumer what to watch in his or her own home, one turns the home into an institution. In general, the employers take the position that the apartment is a home first and a workplace second. The union argues that when the worker is in the apartment, the apartment is a workplace,[67] but these lines are difficult to draw, making the union contract difficult to enforce.

One of the most difficult standards to enforce for personal-care workers is health and safety at work. The rate of back injury among workers in this occupation is very high (Denton et al. 1999).[68] The *Occupational Health and Safety Act* (*OHSA*) covers these workers; *workplace* is defined in the act as, "any land, premises, location or thing at, upon, in or near which a worker works," and thus includes the home of the client/consumer.[69] The problem is that health and safety is an employer responsibility under the *OHSA*, but clients/consumers also play a role in determining the safety of the work site, and thus the health and safety of workers, in the home-care sector (Neysmith and Aronson 1997; Denton et al. 1999). Workers have sought more control over the labour process by gaining the right of self-protection under the *OHSA* (Tucker 1995). However, clients/consumers fall outside of the purpose of the legislation. The *OHSA* regulates the relationship between workers and a single direct and formal employer. As a result, neither the *OHSA* nor the regulations covering this industry mention the clients/consumers of services as actors with an impact on health and safety issues.[70] When clients/consumers are mentioned, the legislation considers them passive recipients of care. These gaps between the purpose of the *OHSA* and the social relations of work make ensuring a safe and healthy work environment difficult in practice.

A good example of the complexity of ensuring a safe and healthy workplace is the issue of lifting people in a way that is safe for both parties. Consider how one worker explains the occupational safety concerns involved: "While you're lifting that person, that person could go into a spasm, like a shake, and it's gonna be bad for both me and the consumer. Because when the body is shaking they might slip right through your legs, and you fall on top of them, or they fall on top of you."[71] On account of these concerns, Local 40 has tried to allocate responsibility to the employer to ensure a healthy and safe work environment. In the case of SSLU workers, the collective agreement stipulates that no worker will lift a heavy person alone.[72] However, this does not work for Outreach, because its attendants work alone in private homes throughout the city. One collective agreement includes a passage on mechanical lifts, but it is rather weak: "the Employer will use its best efforts to encourage consumers to obtain and maintain necessary mechanical and other equipment. Support Care Workers will undertake to advise the Employer when new equipment or maintenance of equipment is required by a consumer." As a result of these difficulties, there have been work refusals involving lifts, as well as other issues.[73] Workers have the right to refuse to undertake unsafe practices under the *OHSA*, but the interpersonal nature of the work makes this tactic problematic for both workers and clients/

consumers. The OSHA accords this right unless "the worker's refusal to work would directly endanger the life, health or safety of another person."[74] Similar language appears in the collective agreements between CAW, Local 40, and the agencies. Ahn explains that it can be difficult to refuse unsafe work due to the relationship between the worker and the client/consumer: "There's a little bit more work involved in how do you ensure that the consumer is comfortable and safe first, which gets kind of tough, because in order to make them safe first, sometimes you are putting yourself at risk, a little bit." In short, the safety of the worker and the client/consumer are intertwined.

On account of these difficulties, the union has sought to prevent unsafe situations through education and training and building strong health and safety committees. However, employers and workers are required to participate in health and safety training but clients/consumers are not. Clients/consumers, and workers, who do not receive such training may not be aware of the health and safety issues involved in this work (Walters and Denton 1990). One worker points out that workers must have adequate experience to negotiate safe interactions with some clients/consumers: "There are the odd ones that want to do things a different way from the right way that it's supposed to be done. But then if you are an experienced person you know, and you have to get your point across and let them know that 'I'm concerned.' Most of the time, you can always talk with them and it works out." While these situations likely only occur on "odd" occasions, knowledge gained from speaking with colleagues may help workers negotiate those situations when they do occur. Such knowledge sharing would reduce the negative impact of individualized and interpersonal relationships on workers.

Studies on personal care and home care more generally have found that broader inequalities, including racism, often emerge in the interpersonal relationship between workers and clients/consumers (Roeher Institute 2001; Neysmith and Aronson 1997). This study reveals how some conflicts emerge in that interpersonal relationship due to inadequate funding. Workers have sought security in this context by using the strategies available to them within the industrial labour relations regime – that is, by seeking job security with their direct employers. However, these strategies cannot solve the funding problem.

Services provided through SSLUs and Outreach do not currently have the level of flexibility desired by some people with disabilities, in large part because there is inadequate funding to employ enough staff. In SSLUs, services are organized through scheduled bookings combined with on-call backup care. Clients/consumers can call for help with small tasks, such as bathroom assistance or help putting on a jacket to go outside. Workers are paid to be on-call to allow for round-the-clock service. However, help with personal-care routines – such as bathing, eating, and preparing for bed – is booked in advance. For example, if a client/consumer books an appointment to be helped out of bed at 10:00 a.m., and the attendant arrives to discover that the client/consumer prefers to get up later, then they can arrange a later booking. However, a long-time worker told me when I asked if bookings could be easily changed, "Yes, as long as there are openings, because sometimes there are no openings."[75] Since the ability of the client/consumer to change a booking depends on staff availability, clients/consumers often have to book well in advance and stick to that schedule.

This lack of flexibility in scheduling is a criticism that many people with disabilities make of agency-provided services (Lord, Hutchison, and Farlow 1988; Parker et al. 2000; Morris 1993). Slotting one's life into an inflexible schedule becomes even more difficult when one has to navigate multiple public services. This is how a self-manager who previously used agency-provided attendant services describes the drawbacks of agency-funded care: "Attendants worked hard, but by the time they got to me, to get me out of bed, sometimes I had missed the Wheels Trans. You see, in that kind of setting everything has to be about attendants' schedules, not yours" (Parker et al. 2000, 12). Such difficulties sometimes occur because the employer, rather than the consumer, schedules back-to-back bookings, allowing just enough time for the worker to get from one apartment to the next. Thus, if a particular client/consumer needs more than the allotted time, the worker cannot maintain the schedule.[76] Conflicts like these could be resolved if funding levels were increased to pay more workers to be on call; however, a union wage would be necessary to reduce the high turnover rate among attendants.

Some people with disabilities also believe that there is not enough flexibility in determining which tasks the workers in SSLUs and Outreach programs will perform, while many workers equate task flexibility with workload increase, particularly within a context of funding cuts. For example, many people with disabilities argue that a wide range of housekeeping tasks is an important part of their care. Outreach only provides personal-care services, but clients/consumers often ask workers to do some housekeeping. According to one worker, however, "you can't be a housekeeper and be the attendant at the same time. There is a conflict there."[77] The conflict mentioned by the worker might arise from allotting insufficient hours to each client/consumer, a broader trend that is "taking the care out of care work" (Armstrong and Armstrong 2002). The situation in the SSLUs, where housekeeping is part of the service provided, is slightly different. Although part-time workers often agree to do housekeeping to gain more hours, workers in the industry have sought to delimit the type and number of housekeeping tasks they do and identify the people for whom they will do this work. For example, before they were unionized, some workers were asked to do laundry and cook dinner for the able-bodied family members of the clients/consumers. These workers decided that they needed a union to negotiate the tasks that were included in their jobs, particularly since clients/consumers sat on the board of directors.[78]

Lack of task flexibility has become intertwined with the choice of who provides the services, but having the ability to choose the person who provides intimate services can also be an issue of basic dignity for the person with a disability. According to the union, it is not uncommon for a client/consumer to cancel a booking with one worker and allow tasks to accumulate until a preferred worker is available. Local 40 has tried to limit the number of workers who agree to do excessive tasks. Thus, the choice of service provider is sometimes used as a means to gain control over which services are provided and when they are performed, but this is arguably not always the case. Many people with disabilities insist that they have a fundamental right to choose their service providers and to base their choices on compatibility and trust (Roeher Institute 1997, 37). The union, however, maintains that attendants are not permitted to choose their clients/consumers, so clients/consumers should not be permitted to choose their attendants.[79] This position reflects the means available to unions to ensure job security – for example, by assigning shifts based on seniority and not on personal preference.

There have also been instances of clients/consumers wanting to choose particular workers due to racism, in this case study as well as others (Bakan and Stasiulis 1995; Neysmith and Aronson 1997). In Local 40 workplaces, some white clients/consumers have said they do not want to have a person of colour providing their personal care.[80] Although agency employees are protected against discrimination by the Ontario *Human Rights Code*, this legislation does not fully address the problem. A worker of Jamaican origin has suggested that when racism emerges in the interpersonal relations between attendant and client, that relationship should be severed. "I'm here to make my money. I can't stop you from being racist ... But if you don't want me, you don't have to step on my toe. You could just say: 'I don't want you.'"[81] This issue, perhaps more than any other, demonstrates the need for models of collectivization that allow workers to gain security through a broader labour market rather than through seniority with an individual employer or client.[82] In the interim, Local 40 has addressed this problem by working with the employers and by undertaking broader, anti-racist educational and organizing efforts.

This case study illustrates how attendant workers employed by non-profit agencies have gained security within the industrial union model, with slight modifications to consider intermittent and interpersonal care work in the non-profit sector. The union has also regulated the labour supply, because the higher wages and benefits that come with unionization have reduced worker turnover.[83] This should benefit people with disabilities as well as workers by ensuring both secure employment and reliable service. However, still bound by the industrial model, some of the means for gaining security – including job security based on seniority with a single employer – do not fit comfortably with this interpersonal work. The work-site-based labour relations regime that shapes union strategy is even more at odds with the employment relationships emerging under direct funding.

5. SELF-MANAGED CARE: DIRECT FUNDING

The Direct Funding program is intended for people with physical disabilities who are able to serve as employers of their own personal attendants. However, the legal status of workers for the purpose of collective bargaining is not yet clear. The available evidence suggests that three regulatory scenarios are possible. The first is that the workers remain employees of an agency, but the agency changes to become the Centre for Independent Living in Toronto (CILT); second, workers become employees of the individual self-manager; third, workers become self-employed contractors. The latter two scenarios would cause considerable insecurity for workers, since, as either self-employed contractors or domestic workers, they would lose their access to collective bargaining. In describing these scenarios, I draw on an evaluation of Self-Managed Care: Direct Funding at the pilot stage, which included a 1997 survey of self-managers and some personal attendants, as well as a description of a current Self-Managed Care program by its administrators and primary documents from the program.

A. Regulatory Scenario 1: Employees of the CILT

The first scenario is that the workers remain employees of an agency for the purpose of collective bargaining, but the employer changes to the CILT. As the funder, the Ontario government would ultimately determine the wages and working conditions of the workers as well as the quality of service (Swimmer and Thompson 1995). However, Self-Managed Care is structured by a set of regulations and contracts that allow the government to position the CILT between itself and the workers and thus distance itself from employer responsibilities. Amendments to the *Ministry of Community and Social Services Act* allow for individuals to receive funding directly from the government, but they also allow for organizations to enter into an agreement with the government to "transfer the grant to or on behalf of person who has a disability." [84] The CILT plays this transferring role (Parker et al. 2000, 2, 32). Nevertheless, it is difficult to disentangle the roles and responsibilities of the CILT and the government. The most significant contribution of the Ontario government is setting the funding levels. During the tenure of the NDP government, 180 funded hours per month was proposed as a satisfactory maximum for all Ontario long-term-care programs. Although this never became a regulation, the program has adopted it as policy (Parker et al. 2000, 36).

Both the CILT and the government play a role in determining the level of funding allotted to each manager, since both play a role in governing the program through the steering committee. The steering committee includes representatives of the Ontario ministries of Health and of Citizenship, Culture and Recreation as well as representatives from the CILT and other Independent Living Resource Centres (ILRCS) (Roeher Institute 1997, 4; Parker et al. 2000, 29). Applicants to the program submit proposals stating the frequency of their attendant service need (Parker et al. 2000, 36–7).[85] Selection panels – made up of a CILT staff member, an elected representative of the applicant's regional ILRC, and a community representative – review the application package and make recommendations to the steering committee (Parker et al. 2000, 36). In many cases, the funding request is negotiated down, but panels have occasionally recommended more funding than was requested (Parker et al. 2000, 36–7).

Another key function of the steering committee is to set the wage at the provincial average. A wage of $13.33 an hour was estimated, and this is the maximum allowable under Self-Managed Care; a minimum wage of $11.39 an hour was also set. Self-managers are allocated 15 per cent of the workers' wages to cover statutory benefits, such as Canada Pension Plan, Employment Insurance, Workplace Safety and Insurance Board contributions, vacation pay and holiday pay under the *Employment Standards Act*, as well as other benefits, including extended healthcare coverage (Roeher Institute 1997). Self-managers are theoretically able to budget other benefits under the heading "optional arrangement costs," including one-way travel to work for attendants. However, the application guide for the program encourages self-managers to hire people who live close by and reminds applicants that most workers are not paid for travel to work. The CILT has also played a key role in developing enabling legislation, regulations, and guidelines for the program with Ontario government officials (Parker et al. 2000, 29).

While the government helps to determine funding levels and maximum wages, it seeks to place full responsibility and accountability for the financial and other administration of the program on the CILT. A contract between the CILT and the Ontario government sets out four specific areas of administration: resource development, project development, ongoing support, and general administration (Parker et al. 2000, appendix C). Resource development is centred on the CILT's role in providing information to the person with a disability concerning employer responsibility. This encompasses information on labour and employment standards, federal and provincial tax obligations, payroll, and recruitment of employees – including the use of employment and referral agencies, hiring and firing, and developing support networks. Similarly, general administration involves undertaking "all necessary administrative and financial arrangements with participants." This includes administering legal agreements and transferring funds.[86]

The devolution of responsibility from government to the CILT, combined with the fact that the CILT transfers funds to the person with a disability, may make it more likely that the CILT rather than the government is identified as the employer for the purposes of collective bargaining. As discussed earlier, the OLRB decision that Nucleus Housing was the employer for such purposes was influenced in part by the funding relationship.[87] Like Nucleus, the CILT also plays a role in developing care plans and determining the number of hours funded, a role that was important in other cases in which home-care workers were found to be dependent on the intermediate agency.[88] The OLRB has also found the degree of involvement of a government-funded agency in setting the wage rate of workers to be an important factor in determining dependent contractor status.[89] If workers were to become employees of the CILT for the purposes of collective bargaining, then they would be able to organize collectively. The employment relationship would be akin to that found in Outreach or many Community Care Access Centres (CCACs). The previous section shows that CAW Local 40 has the will to organize employees in dispersed workplaces/households when there is a single employer, and the SEIU is organizing home-care workers contracted to CCACs. However, it is difficult to predict who will be identified as the employer for the purposes of collective bargaining, since while the government is devolving responsibility to the CILT, the CILT is shifting responsibility to the self-manager.

B. Regulatory Scenario 2: Domestic Workers

One of the many positives of this arrangement is the relationship between myself and my attendants. They are directly accountable and committed to me as their employer; and I respect them as competent employees.[90]

Wouldn't that be going back to where we started?[91]

The second scenario is that the workers become employees of the individual person with a disability and are considered domestic workers for the purposes of collective bargaining. Participants not only self-direct their care, as in the agency-provided service model, but they also self-manage, taking on many responsibilities of an employer. Unlike the government and the CILT, self-managers embrace the idea of being the employer and argue that it has brought them "flexibility, choice and control" over when, where, and how the work is done and by whom (Parker et al. 2000; Roeher Institute 1997, 38).[92]

Participants in the program are called self-managers because they are responsible for a number of personnel management tasks, and this responsibility involves several factors often used by labour boards to determine who has control. Detailed regulations stipulate that the self-manager must recruit, hire and fire, train, supervise, and instruct workers, as well as schedule their services (Parker et al. 2000, 39–40).[93] Despite the fact that the government sets funding limits and the CILT largely determines the level of funding, the regulations require that self-managers manage and account for the funds that they are granted.

Participants must register with Revenue Canada for a business number, sign paycheques, and keep records of employee hours and level of pay for tax purposes.

Participants enter into a contract with the CILT that sets out their obligations, including, "sole responsibility for their attendant service arrangements and full legal liability as the employer of their attendant(s)" (Parker et al. 2000, 38; Roeher Institute 1997, 4). However, the intent of a particular statute, the individual facts of each case, and the broader political ethos all weigh on a ruling of employee status for a given purpose. The degree to which the CILT plays a matching role and takes on some of the coordination of workers' schedules could mean that the CILT is seen as the employer for the purposes of collective bargaining.[94] Indeed, during the pilot project, self-managers asked that brokering for self-managers in hiring attendants be designated as an area for further development and support by the CILT and the ILRCs (Roeher Institute 1997, 61). The CILT informs self-managers about statutory employment-related contributions in its financial guide. The CILT also requires that self-managers extend their home insurance to $2 million to cover liability for an employed domestic (Roeher Institute 1997, 7, 10). Even if these workers are found to be employees of self-managers for the purposes of income tax or the *Workplace Safety and Insurance Act*, determining whether they will be the employees of the individual self-manager for the purposes of collective bargaining – and thus considered domestic workers, excluded from the *OLRA* – is another issue, since the intent of the law is to facilitate organization.

The individual self-manager's control could be limited in that he or she has little influence over the funding level and therefore little ability to raise wages to keep an attendant. The program's application guide implies that self-managers have some discretion, suggesting they could pay a flat rate of $25 to $60 for a sleepover, "depending on how much 'hands-on' work the attendant is expected to do." The guide also suggests that self-managers either roll short visits into larger blocks of time by including additional tasks or pay a better rate for short visits.[95] Yet this discretion is slight, as it would have to fit within the minimum wage (of $11.39) and maximum wage (of $13.33) set by program policy. Nevertheless, given the distancing strategies of the government and the CILT's devolution of responsibility to the individual self-manager, evidence of control by either of these entities to supplement evidence of economic dependence will be hard to come by.

As employees of the individual self-manager, these workers would have no ability to organize a trade union or to bargain collectively, because domestic workers are excluded from the OLRA, which protects these rights for Ontario workers. The ability to organize collectively is particularly important for such workers, because there is confusion over whether they are fully covered by key pieces of employment-standards and social-wage legislation. For example, the program administrators argue that the self-manager is liable in instances of wrongful dismissal of an attendant and state that self-managers must abide by the Ontario *Human Rights Code*.[96] However, if the self-manager is considered to be the direct employer of the attendants, then the attendants do not have the right to equal treatment without discrimination under the code, since the code excludes people who directly employ a person to care for themselves or for a family member.[97] Similarly, the CILT states on its Web site that self-managers must abide by the *Occupational Health and Safety Act*.[98] However, if the attendants are considered employees of the self-manager, then this work is not covered by the act.[99] Despite the fact that the CILT instructs self-managers to make deductions from attendants' paycheques for the Workplace Safety and Insurance Board, the *Workers' Compensation Act* covers only full-time domestic workers, which means that few attendants are covered since most work part time.[100]

There is also confusion over the level of coverage of these workers under the *Employment Standards Act (ESA)*. CILT pilot materials inform the self-manager of the decreased coverage of domestic workers who work fewer than twenty-four hours. However, it appears that these distinctions do not exist under the ESA 2000.[101] All key areas of the act cover domestic workers, although special rules apply to the minimum wage.[102] There is more confusion surrounding the need of many people with disabilities for twenty-four-hour backup services. At least one householder/employer with a disability has argued that the personal-care worker she hired to "sleep over" was a "residential-care worker" and thus not entitled to overtime pay under regulation 285/01 of the *ESA*.[103] In one such case, the employment standards officer agreed, but at the worker's request the OLRB reviewed the decision. After making a painstaking attempt to fit the worker and the client/consumer into the vaguely defined categories to which the legislation applies,[104] the board ruled that the worker was not a residential-care worker because she could be called to work at any time, even if she was sleeping. Nevertheless, further decisions would be based on the individual facts of each case, and some of these facts could lead to a ruling that the workers are self-employed contractors.

C. Regulatory Scenario 3: Workers as Self-Employed Contractors

One of my attendants told me that working for me and two other consumers is a lot like being self-employed. She says she has flexibility to go shopping or look after her kids between appointments.[105]

I was considered self-employed ... And you don't want to ask them for a wage increase because you know for the last five years they've also got the same amount of funding ... And they never brought up wage increases. In fact, they asked if I would take a decrease in my wages because the needs were increasing and there was less funding.[106]

The third scenario is that the workers become self-employed contractors. Although being a personal attendant may in some ways be "a lot like being self-employed," there is little evidence that these workers have the necessary capital to profit from their labour the way entrepreneurs do. As the quoted self-employed contractor explains, funding levels impacted the ability to negotiate wage increases. Nevertheless, these workers may well fall out of the narrow concept of employee as someone dependent on a single employer.

Although hourly wages have been set at the provincial average, since most self-managers only hire attendants for few hours, many workers contract with multiple clients or take multiple jobs in order to earn a living. According to the 1997 survey done during the pilot program, the mean number of hours worked per week for the individual self-manager surveyed was seventeen; 27 per cent of the self-managers had main attendants who worked fewer than ten hours, 36 per cent had main attendants who worked ten to fifteen hours, and 36 per cent had main attendants who worked sixteen hours or more (Roeher Institute 1997, 52).[107] Since the maximum hourly wage allowable is $13.33, the average worker is only earning $226 a week, and some are earning as little as $130 a week. Thus, it is not surprising that 12 per cent of the attendants worked for more than one individual self-manager, and 31 per cent had a second job with an agency that delivered services to people with disabilities. Some workers have an infrequent and casual relationship with their self-managers. A common situation is for a self-manager to hire one or two persons as main attendant(s) and another as a casual backup. Self-managers employed on average three attendants. A full 44 per cent of the self-managers hired at least one attendant in a backup-only capacity in a very casual manner. In contrast, 15 per cent of the sixty-one self-managers hired just one attendant (Roeher Institute 1997, 52).

There is evidence that some attendants have achieved a degree of flexibility, allowing them to turn down work, yet there is little to suggest that the workers are able to earn a profit from their work as entrepreneurs do. Of the attendants surveyed who worked for an agency in the year before the pilot project, a few cited more flexibility as a benefit of working as a personal attendant compared to working for an agency. Yet others noted too few hours, short shifts, lack of advance notice, and inadequate scheduling as drawbacks of working under Self-Managed Care (Roeher Institute 1997), indicating that many do not have the ability to structure their schedules to make a profit. The application guide suggests that prospective self-managers plan for backup emergency assistance by "asking their attendants to take responsibility for arranging temporary replacements for themselves if they are sick or otherwise unable to work as scheduled."[108] However, given that the maximum wage is set by program policy, there is little margin for profit, even if there is slight variation in fees charged. Other factors often cited by labour boards are less relevant to this type of work. For example, the number of tools required for this work might increase slightly to include syringes and perhaps cleaning products and latex gloves, yet ownership of these tools hardly amounts to capital. Similarly, while interpersonal care is skilled work, it involves a highly gendered set of skills that are generally not recognized by employers or the Labour Board.

A client/self-employed contractor relationship might allow the parties to negotiate flexibility in arrangements and tasks, but negotiating security for workers would require either a very strong position in the labour market due to financial capital or valued human capital, neither of which are evident here, or some kind of collective pressure on the entity that controls funding, and thus wage levels and hours of work. Collective pressure is certainly needed, since many of these workers will be precariously employed. Self-managers are hiring workers who have discontinuous attachments to the labour market, such as mothers of small children, students, and unemployed people, as well as backup workers on a casual basis (Parker et al. 2000, 4, 11, 13).[109] These workers have difficulty qualifying for employment insurance unless they can piece together sufficient hours by taking multiple clients.[110] However, the more clients they take, the more likely they are to considered independent contractors rather than dependent contractors who have the ability to organize collectively. The OLRB jurisprudence is clear: the term *dependence* is not meant to convey dependence on a large number of purchasers or an entire industry. Instead, the number of purchasers must be very small, and they must have control over the labour market – "an oligopoly in economic terms, if you will."[111]

Many of these workers have multiple jobs rather than multiple employers, and so they may fall into the category of dependent contractor. Yet the question would still be this: Dependent on whom? If the board were to give more weight to economic dependence, it might conclude that the CILT or the government should be considered an employer of the attendants, given their roles in determining funding levels and setting wages. Section 1(4)) of the OLRA gives the OLRB the power to treat two or more individuals or firms who engage in related activities as one employer for the purposes of the act. In order for the OLRB to rule that two or more entities are a single employer, three preconditions must be met. First, there must be more than one entity. These entities are defined by the facts of each case, not by whether they are legal or corporate entities. Second, the activities or businesses must be under "common control or direction." The OLRB has used five criteria to determine this: common ownership or financial control; common management; interrelationship of operations; representation to the public as a single, integrated enterprise; and centralized control of labour relations. However, not all of these criteria are always met, and the OLRB has considered a laundry list of factors to be relevant in different situations. Importantly, however, common control must be managerial. The financial dependency of one entity on another is generally not sufficient for a declaration of related employer (Sack, Mitchell, and Price 1997, 6.88, 6.90). Third, the activities or businesses must be associated or related, but they need not be conducted simultaneously. Certain criteria are used to determine whether two businesses are related. They are related if they are of the same character, serve the same general market, employ the same mode and means of production, utilize similar employee skills, and are conducted for the benefit of related principals. As it does in rulings on whether a worker is to be classified as an employee or an independent contractor, the OLRB makes decisions on a case-by-case basis, weighing a multitude of factors. With the individualization of care, each case is different, making the drawing of lines by labour boards particularly problematic for personal-care workers.

The analysis of Self-Managed Care: Direct Funding illustrates three possible regulatory scenarios for the purposes of collective bargaining: the workers could be regarded as employees of the CILT or another agency, as independent contractors, or as domestic workers. Given the distancing strategies of the Ontario government in contracting with the CILT, it is unlikely that the workers will become employees of the government, despite the fact that it ultimately controls working conditions. However, securing enough funding to ensure flexibility in scheduling and tasks without causing insecurity for workers would likely mean that the Ontario government would also be viewed as an employer. The role of the CILT in developing care plans for clients could mean that the attendants are found to be employees of the CILT. However, given that the individual self-manager is responsible for such things as hiring and firing, scheduling, training, and payroll, the workers could also be considered employees of the individual self-manager. Finally, since many of these workers provide services to more than one client/consumer, it is highly likely that they will be classified as independent contractors.

CONCLUSION

Security for the most precarious workers depends on collective organization, yet the model of representation that emerged in the post-war period does not fit well with many forms of personal-care work. Within the confines of the industrial union model, workers have decoupled precariousness and interpersonal, intermittent work – securing compensation for travel time and for on-call and night-shift work, winning decent wages and benefits, and gaining the ability to enforce fair labour standards and pay equity legislation through unionization. For some people with disabilities, only a slightly larger modification of the dominant service delivery model – to allow for more flexibility in scheduling and tasks – would be sufficient to ensure security for both themselves and their attendants. Yet for others, a more significant break with the current industrial relations model is necessary. Furthermore, unions must move beyond one of their key strategies – namely, security tied to seniority with a single employer. In every province but Ontario, there has been a regionalization of health care, and in many, the regional health authorities have become the employers of record. This may facilitate union organizing and also allow workers to move between jobs, taking their security with them (Haiven and Haiven 2002). However, individualized funding presents additional challenges.

Personal-care workers must undertake collective action in order to limit the precariousness that characterizes the way they earn their living. However, if they are classified as domestic workers or independent contractors, they cannot organize a trade union and bargain collectively. Of the three possible scenarios cited earlier – classification as agency employees, domestic workers, or independent contractors – the second is arguably the most precarious, because domestic workers, aside from being unable to organize collectively under the *OLRA*, also fall outside the protection of important pieces of employment standards legislation under which even independent contractors fall. The narrowness of the employee/dependent contractor concept combined with the unequal treatment of domestic workers under labour legislation has given the government the incentive to cut costs through direct funding mechanisms long advocated by people with disabilities.

In the debates over individualized funding leading up to Self-Managed Care, workers and people with disabilities were pitted against one another. However, workers' inability to organize for security could result in insecurity for people with disabilities in two ways. First, concerns about turnover and the difficulty of finding attendants were raised during the pilot program due to lack of two-way travel allowances, discrepancies between urban wages and the provincial average, and the lack of extended health plans (Roeher Institute 1997). Indeed, in the general home-care sector in Ontario as well as other jurisdictions, lack of parity with the institutional sector in the area of wages and benefits has led to high turnover and inadequate services (Flood 1999; Morris et al. 1999; Morris 1993; Williams et al. 2000). This analysis points to the necessity of parity, not just in hourly wages but also in hours of work, benefits, and the right to organize. Second, if direct funding coincides with continued underfunding of other support services and social housing – a likely scenario in Ontario – people with disabilities who are unwilling or unable to become employers may have little choice but to do so. There is an extensive literature on the way that vulnerable intermediaries, as a survival strategy, transfer their vulnerability onto their workers in the form of poor working conditions (Cranford 2001; Hondagneu-Sotelo 1994; Light and Bonacich 1988). If most funding is transferred to individualized funding, the service-provision options for people with disabilities will also be reduced.

These problems are political and historical, not inevitable. This case study highlights the need to include workers and clients/consumers alike in a broader community unionism, one that recognizes the important role played by the government as funder. In the short term, autonomous yet allied associations of personal-care workers and clients/consumers could pressure the government to raise funding levels to pay for flexibility of services without bringing insecurity to the workers. In the long term, reregulation is required to allow domestic workers, employees with multiple employers, and independent contractors to organize collectively. Unions could help facilitate this and mediate conflicts between two vulnerable groups: people with disabilities and their attendants, predominately immigrant women of colour. Reregulation would remove the incentive for governments to download employer-related costs onto intermediaries and households. It would allow personal-care workers and their clients/consumers to organize for security with flexibility.

4

The Precarious Status of the Artist: Freelance Editors' Struggle for Collective Bargaining Rights

On 1 November 2002, after a protracted struggle for legitimacy, the Canadian Artists and Producers Professional Relations Tribunal (CAPPRT) certified the Editors' Association of Canada (EAC/ACR) as the representative artists' association for a sector of editors[1] under the federal *Status of the Artist Act, 1992*.[2] Over two decades after its formation, in the face of considerable opposition from other artists' organizations, the EAC/ACR won the legal right to negotiate scale agreements on behalf of a segment of its membership – agreements that it hopes will benefit its entire membership, but especially freelance editors in precarious situations.

Although the CAPPRT rescinded two of its previous decisions and a certification order granted to the EAC/ACR in 2001 in response to a request for reconsideration filed by the Writers' Union of Canada (TWUC),[3] the certification of the EAC/ACR is unprecedented for freelance editors. Taking advantage of the unique dimensions of the *Status of the Artist Act*, specifically its introduction of a collective bargaining regime centred on the creation of artistic works, the EAC/ACR certification pushes the boundaries of the prevailing federal collective bargaining regime in the arts to their limits. Still, the outcomes of the freelance editors' struggle are complex and contradictory. While the certification enables a group of professional freelance editors to negotiate scale agreements with federal producers – a credit to the CAPPRT's skilful navigation of its narrow jurisdiction – its terms, which grew narrower and narrower as the certification and reconsideration process proceeded, fail to displace the troublesome distinction between *employees* and *independent contractors* at the heart of Canadian labour law. They also amplify labour law's ambiguous treatment of professionals and aggravate jurisdictional tensions between artists' associations. The EAC/ACR certification thus highlights the pitfalls of fashioning an alternative regime extending legal collective bargaining rights to artists (narrowly defined) on the basis of the creation of products, rather than on the performance of personal service, to avoid challenging problem aspects of the dominant regime. Echoing a central premise of this book, the nature of the certification reveals that addressing the precarious status of many workers in work relationships deviating from the standard employment relationship calls for a plurality of representational forms.

This chapter probes the *Status of the Artist Act (SAA)* as a potential model for extending collective bargaining rights to marginalized workers – specifically, independent contractors – through a case study of the EAC/ACR's struggle on behalf of freelance editors. It unfolds in five parts. Part 1 begins with a description of the precarious and gendered character of freelance editing and a short history of the EAC/ACR; it links the socio-economic situation of freelance editors to their legal status as independent contractors and their ongoing struggle for professional status, complicated by the ethic of invisibility central to the editing process. Situating the case of freelance editors in the context of Canada's federal collective bargaining regime, part 2 describes how two threshold definitions of *employee* and *dependent contractor* in the *Canada Labour Code* limit freelance editors' ability to organize and bargain collectively.[4] It also describes the definition of *professional* in the code and corresponding provincial legislation, since the notion of *professional* in the SAA is based partly on such definitions. After identifying the barriers to collective bargaining confronting freelance editors at the federal level, part 3 examines the SAA, crafted principally to extend collective bargaining rights to independent professional artists who produce artistic works rather than performing work under conditions of economic dependency. It devotes particular attention to the reason artists were singled out as requiring special collective bargaining legislation, how their employment situation influenced the shape of the resulting act, and why the federal government adopted such a limited model, riddled with potential for jurisdictional conflict. Part 4 then turns to examine the EAC/ACR's struggle to gain certification under the SAA. The EAC/ACR certification is a unique case, since freelance editors are not typical of artists' groups seeking certification under the act. They are the only group to seek coverage to date that has been forced to demonstrate that they are "artists" who create artistic products, and this has involved the painstaking process of proving authorship while defending the distinct roles of editors and writers. To attain certification, the EAC/ACR was compelled to establish freelance editors' status as artists. Initially, it was certified to represent freelance editors who are authors of original literary works in the form of compilations or collective works and authors of literary works of joint authorship, despite opposition from artists' groups centring on the definition of *authorship*. Upon reconsideration, freelance editors' status as artists was at issue once again, especially in light of the CAPPRT's initial determination that editors can be joint authors. Part 5 concludes the chapter by evaluating the SAA as a model for reregulating work relationships, finding its approach to competition policy and its introduction of scale agreements promising, but its conception of *professional artist* and its focus on the production of artistic works limiting.

1. FREELANCE EDITING: A GENDERED FORM OF PRECARIOUS EMPLOYMENT

Seldom paid for each hour they work ... [workers in the female-dominated freelance editing sector] confront the same problems of low wages and low status as women in other areas of the labour force, but the freelance nature of their work has meant that they have rarely been a target of unionization attempts. (Kates and Springer 1984, 238)

Editors who work freelance in Canada – performing functions ranging from developmental editing, structural/substantive editing, and copyediting, to proofreading, indexing, markup, and fact checking – confront a set of profound problems tied to their employment situation. Predominantly women, they work in isolation, frequently in their own homes, where they juggle child care and other family responsibilities with waged work. As independent contractors, they lack the benefits and entitlements typically attached to a standard employment relationship and, in most instances, the ability to organize and bargain collectively. At the same time, freelance editors are not often treated like professionals. Despite constituting a well-trained segment of the workforce, their incomes are relatively low given their educational levels and given that they are responsible for covering their own overhead and investing in equipment in order to serve authors and/or publishers.[5] Yet freelance editors' autonomy is manifest mainly in the removal of direct supervision, limited control over working hours, and the spatial arrangements of work. As one commentator notes: "Freelancers in publishing ... are 'disguised wage labour' with very limited autonomy and freedom ... [they] are unlikely to grow their businesses. They typically employ no one, own little or no capital, and have no capacity to extract surplus value and accumulate capital" (Stanworth and Stanworth 1995, 227).

According to a survey of 1,650 editors conducted by the EAC/ACR, freelance editors earn on average $23,869 annually, even though they report that their hourly rates technically range from $28 to $40 (Lahey 1999, 16).[6] The disjuncture between yearly and hourly wages is explained by two interrelated factors: first, many editors are effectively paid by the piece – by the number of words, the page, the chapter, or the book – and many underestimate the hours of editing required under this system; second, editing work is highly intermittent. Moreover, freelance editors are not paid to attend meetings or take breaks; unlike in-house editors, they bill clients strictly for work undertaken at the desk or the computer.[7] There is also a problem of controlling the flow of the work. Editors are generally crunched between the demands of the publisher and the writer, so they are naturally under a lot of stress to complete work.[8] Editors report further that these stresses are exaggerated by a reliance on a narrow client base, which is explained partly by a convention in the industry whereby small clients opt to deal with a handful of freelance editors and partly by the limited number of clients in the publishing industry – editors estimate that 20 to 30 per cent of freelance editing work is in book publishing (text and trade) and magazine publishing, and the rest is with large institutions like governments, banks, corporations, and hospitals. Freelance editors' work stresses are also aggravated, paradoxically, by the need to create the illusion that a given project is their top priority, even though most editors work on several simultaneously. It is either feast or famine in the freelance editing business: the fear of no work prompts most editors to take on multiple projects; many also rely on subcontracted work, much of it at lower wages, a trend that is likely to continue given publishers' growing resort to subcontracting.[9]

Freelance editors report that editing work is sporadic, often generating economic uncertainty. Mirroring the conditions of employment endured by other groups of workers described in this book, freelance editing is precarious. It involves atypical employment contracts, limited social benefits, and statutory entitlements, as well as job insecurity, low job tenure, and a high risk of ill health. Yet freelance editing is unique among other forms of precarious work, since editors may be better paid than other workers in precarious work relationships, and since editing is highly skilled work, demanding a range of professional qualifications. In the editing process, the editor wears many hats. The tasks involved are far-reaching, ranging from acting as a first reader who suggests changes to the manuscript to rewriting or even writing substantial sections of the text.[10] Editors, moreover, routinely report that authors often underplay their contributions. As one editor notes, "Probably the most common thing that a writer says to an editor is, 'This won't take much work.' No writer comes and says, 'This is really a mess – help me.'"[11]

Editing work is undervalued by many writers and the publishing industry as a whole, since editors' professional qualifications often go unrecognized. Yet this undervaluation also reflects the fact that freelance editing is a peculiar form of artistic work. Freelance editors are not writers in a conventional sense – nor do they aspire to be – yet their work lies in the sphere of the arts. They contribute to producing artistic works, but their profession rests upon an ethic of invisibility – the notion that the editor should be invisible in the text and should not play a public role in the creation and promotion of the work.[12] While essential to the preservation of their profession, the ethic of invisibility contributes to removing editing work from view. Hence, where collective bargaining is concerned, it aggravates tensions between writers and editors over the appropriate jurisdiction of various artists' associations and raises contradictions for the many writers who are also editors, and vice versa. In combination with freelance editors' independent contractor status, which excludes them from a range of labour and social protections, these tensions heighten their precarious socio-economic status.

Freelance editors in Canada have not passively accepted their precarious status, however. Keenly aware of the importance of the ethic of invisibility to preserving their role in the publishing business, yet concerned with securing professional status, they have a unique history of pursuing collective representation, most notably through the creation of the EAC/ACR. Initiated by a group of five Toronto-based freelance editors in 1978, the Freelance Editors' Association of Canada held its founding meeting in 1979. David Homel, an early editor-organizer, reflects on the nature of the group at the time: "We were marginal and we knew it. We worked with lead pencils, some of which were a little dull. Our hourly rate was unimpressive. But we were part of the book world, and that's where we wanted to be. It's important to understand that. We wanted that intersection between culture and commerce. We believed in it; we thought we ought to be able to make a living working in an intellectual pursuit, but not a pure one; we didn't want to be college professors ... All of us, I remember, came out of the left wing of Toronto politics; the NDP was our border on the right. We conceived of the Freelance Editors' Association of Canada as something along the lines of a trade union, or a grass-roots community organization" (1999, 4–5). Early organizers drew about twenty-five editors to their first meeting, thirty-five to their second, and fifty-five to their formal inaugural meeting in May 1979. As Jane Springer, who helped organize the initial meeting with support from Joanne Kates, reports, "after all these years, what stands out for me is the euphoria of the first meeting ... we managed to get more than 25 people to attend. The effect on the publishers was immediate and incredible – we all raised our rates. The publishers were terribly nervous" (1999, 4).

In the twenty-five years after its inception, the Freelance Editors' Association of Canada struggled with its identity, moving through a number of stages. Several of the initial organizers came together to build a union, yet they quickly realized that "the fact that everyone was freelance made a union model a little bit dicey," and that organizing outside the law for standardized minimum rates was still critically important (Homel 1999, 4). Sandra Gulland, another organizer involved in all the initial meetings, remembers heated debates over whether to form a professional association or a union, and "whether we were an association of editors or of freelance editors," yet she also recalls that the decision to go the way of the professional association was the only alternative, given the split within the group as well as the fundamental obstacles to organizing freelancers at the time (1999, 1).

Following its formal establishment, the Freelance Editors' Association of Canada focused its efforts on attaining professional status for editors and expanded its membership across the country, forming groups in Ottawa, Montreal, British Columbia, and the Prairies between 1981 and the early 1990s. To unify these groups, the association created a national coordinating committee, and then a committee on professional standards; subsequently, committees on membership, technology, newsletter, mediation, and long-range planning were formed, along with other, ad hoc committees. A broader governance structure, led by an elected executive composed of a president, a past-president, vice-presidents, and numerous committee and branch chairs, followed. In 1994, the Freelance Editors' Association of Canada extended membership to in-house editors, resulting in a controversial name change – to the Editors' Association of Canada. The two-tier membership structure of the Freelance Editors' Association of Canada was retained after the adoption of the new name: associate membership for junior editors with insufficient hours to qualify for voting, and voting membership for editors (in-house and freelance) who have performed a minimum of 500 hours of editorial work in the twelve months preceding membership application.[13]

Functioning largely as a professional association, the EAC/ACR has produced several publications, including *Editing Canadian English* and *Meeting Editorial Standards*, and it publishes a bi-monthly newsletter, *Active Voice*. The association also hosts workshops on professional development and provides four job-hunting aids; namely, a hotline that matches clients with editors registered with the EAC/ACR, networking at meetings,[14] a national directory, and work exchanges among members. It also moderates electronic discussion groups, provides standard contracts and fee scales to its membership, and offers group insurance as well as mediation services. The EAC/ACR membership – which stood at approximately 1,600 in summer 2001, still predominantly women – is increasingly concerned with professional standards, editorial process and technique, and formalizing the relationship between editors and other actors in the publishing cycle (Upton Reed 1999, 7).[15] Along with pursuing legal certification under the SAA on behalf freelance editors, beginning in the mid-1990s, the association worked on developing an accreditation system for editors, both member and non-member. Despite its certification as the representative bargaining agent for a narrow group of freelance editors under the SAA, the EAC/ACR's priorities as a membership-based organization continue to reflect editors' struggle for recognition as professionals. In addition to the fundamental obstacles confronting any group of independent contractors seeking collective representation under the law, this struggle affects their pursuit of collective bargaining with federal producers.

2. INDEPENDENT CONTRACTORS AND PROFESSIONALS?: AMBIGUITY AND UNCERTAINTY UNDER CANADA'S FEDERAL REGIME OF COLLECTIVE BARGAINING

Freelance editors are independent contractors who typically deal with multiple employers or clients on a project-by-project basis. The nature of their employment situation thus places them outside of two threshold definitions tied to workers' ability to organize and bargain collectively in the federal jurisdiction: the definitions of *employee* and *dependent contractor*. The definition of *professional* under the *Canada Labour Code* and corresponding provincial legislation also affects freelance editors, since the SAA derives its own definition of the term from such legislation.

The *Canada Labour Code* defines *employee* as "any person employed by an employer and includes a dependent contractor and a private constable, but does not include a person who performs management functions or is employed in a confidential capacity in matters relating to industrial relations."[16] As outlined in the introduction to this book, various tests – including the fourfold test, the business integration or organization test, and the economic realities test – are used to determine employee status. Yet the fourfold test dominates to the present. Its components are: whether the individual in question controls the performance of his or her work, owns his or her tools, has a chance of profit, and has a risk of loss (Arthurs 1965; England, Christie, and Christie 1998). Affirmative answers to these questions identify the worker as an independent contractor and negative ones as an employee. The weight of the fourfold test nevertheless rests on a notion of control, defined as personal subordination of one person to another at a given work site (Fudge 1999b, Fudge and Vosko 2001a, Ocran 1997). Under this type of interpretation, freelance editors, like many home workers, salespeople, craftspeople, or professionals, fall outside the definition of *employee*; since they own their own tools and since there is no evidence of personal subordination at a single work site, the control test is answered in the negative.

In the same legislation, *dependent contractor* is defined to include owner-drivers, fishers involved in joint ventures, and, more broadly, "any other person who, whether or not employed under a contract of employment, performs work or services for another person on such terms and conditions that they are, in relation to that other person, in a position of economic dependence on, and under an obligation to perform duties for that person."[17] Since the notion of economic dependence was introduced in the *Canada Labour Code*, the Canada Industrial Relations Board (CIRB) has examined numerous factors in determining dependent contractor status, largely finding a worker to be a dependent contractor when he or she is in a relationship of considerable economic dependence and subordination.

The emphasis on economic dependence in the definition of *dependent contractor* excludes freelance editors, given that they have multiple employers and work on a project-by-project basis. Freelance editors resemble most closely the own-account self-employed, who may have ongoing relationships with a number of clients in the same sector, and who make a living bidding sequentially on various types of work. Prior to the introduction of the SAA, labour board decisions (federal and provincial) over the status of freelance artists as a group were mixed, but freelance artists were mainly found to fall outside the scope of federal collective bargaining law.[18] Since the introduction of the SAA, most decisions pertinent to certification reflect either the finding that artists are employees or independent contractors rather than dependent contractors, because the act does not require artists selling products or performing services to be dependent contractors or to have only one predominant employer.

A third threshold definition relevant to freelance editors is *professional employee*, since the SAA extends coverage to professional artists and defines *professional* in accordance with federal and related provincial legislation. In the *Canada Labour Code*, a *professional employee* is defined as an employee who is, in the course of employment, engaged in the application of specialized knowledge ordinarily acquired by a course of instruction and study resulting in graduation from a university or similar institution; and who is, or is eligible to be, a member of a professional organization that is authorized by statute to establish the qualifications for its membership.

Collective bargaining law treats professionals in an ambivalent manner partly because of questions of loyalty and confidentiality and partly because their human capital (that is, specialized knowledge and skill) may be perceived to take them out of the labour market. In the former case, groups such as Crown attorneys may simply be excluded from coverage under collective bargaining legislation. Other groups may be excluded from the definition of *employee* under federal and/or provincial legislation yet still be permitted to engage in collective bargaining under different legislation. In such instances, while the treatment of specialized or skilled groups of professionals varies from jurisdiction to jurisdiction, exclusions are justified on the basis of concerns over anti-competition or factors such as a group's desire for exclusion due to professional ethics. For example, legislation in Ontario and Alberta contains specific exclusions for registered members of the professions of architecture, dentistry, medicine, and law.

Artists are not listed among excluded categories of professional employees in any jurisdiction in Canada. Where they are employees or dependent contractors, therefore, artists under the federal jurisdiction should benefit from collective bargaining rights extended under the *Canada Labour Code*. However, an artist's work may technically be undertaken in his or her role as a professional or otherwise and as an employee, a dependent contractor, or an independent contractor. In Canada, many artists are independent contractors. This employment status conventionally raises concerns over anti-competition, especially in light of the conspiracy provisions of the *Competition Act* and the potentially anti-competitive aspects of peer-group control mechanisms.[19] Concern over anti-competition is the primary obstacle to extending collective bargaining rights to professionals who are also independent contractors. This impediment exists for artists, many of whom create and sell artistic works rather than provide services. However, it is questionable whether concerns about the combination of artists are warranted as a matter of public policy, since artists' products are unique, making it virtually impossible for them to create even partial product markets by acting in concert.

The precarious situation of artists falling outside the definitions of *employee* and *dependent contractor* contributed to the enactment of special federal collective bargaining legislation. By targeting professional artists who are independent contractors, principally those who produce artistic works rather than perform personal services, the consequent SAA expands the scope of federal collective bargaining law. Indeed, it introduces an alternative regime. Still, this new legislation is narrow – applying mainly to artists defined in terms of their product rather than their labour – and it is complicated by the requirement that artists demonstrate that they are professionals.

3. THE *STATUS OF THE ARTIST ACT*: EXPANDING CANADA'S COLLECTIVE BARGAINING REGIME

In 1992, Canada became the first country in the world to enact special legislation extending collective bargaining rights to freelance or self-employed professional artists. The *Status of the Artist Act* permits professional artists who are independent contractors to form associations and bargain collectively with federal producers. It introduces a collective bargaining regime that centres on the production of artistic works rather than the performance of personal service. How did this special collective bargaining legislation emerge, and why were independent professional artists thought to require it? How did their employment situation affect the shape of the act, and how does this legislative framework differ from other legislative models (for example, Quebec's legislation)?

A. History and Origins

A complex set of international, national, and provincial developments led independent professional artists to be singled out as requiring special collective bargaining legislation. At the international level, the origins of the SAA date to 1980, when the UNESCO General Conference in Belgrade adopted the *Recommendation on the Status of the Artist*. The Belgrade Recommendation declares that "artists must have the right to be recognized as a professional category and to constitute trade unions or professional organizations," and it invites states to "encourage the free establishment of such organizations in disciplines where they do not yet exist."[20] At the national level, a number of voluntary recognition arrangements between producers' and artists' associations predated the Belgrade Recommendation. By 1980, for example, the Union des artistes, the Alliance of Canadian Cinema, Television and Radio Artists, the Canadian Actors' Equity Association, and the American Federation of Musicians of the United States and Canada had been successful in concluding scale agreements with some producers – both individual producers and collectivities of producers. However, producers were not compelled by law to negotiate with these associations. The significance of the Belgrade Recommendation was its role in hastening a range of regulatory initiatives, which would force producers to recognize artists in a similar fashion to employees under the Canadian variant of the Wagner model of industrial relations. Indeed, in response to this international development, the federal government undertook several studies on the socio-economic status of professional artists, beginning with a federal cultural policy review in 1983, followed by the 1986 Task Force on the Status of the Artist, headed by Paul Siren and Gratien Gélinas.

Against the backdrop of the lobbying efforts of artists' groups with histories of voluntary collective bargaining with producers, the Siren-Gélinas Task Force confirmed the precarious economic situation of artists and called for special legislation granting self-employed artists collective bargaining rights equivalent to those of employees.[21] The task force's report offered a blueprint for extending collective bargaining to artists who are independent contractors operating in the public and private sectors. It advanced proposals for professional recognition, the extension of economic and social rights, and a framework for collective bargaining for the arts. In a skilful move designed to preempt jurisdictional conflict, the task force also recommended that "If there shall exist any conflict between the provisions of this Act and any other Act of Parliament of Canada, including but not limited to, any one or more of the *Criminal Code of Canada*, the *Copyright Act*, the *Combines Act*, the *Workplace Hazardous Materials Information System Act* and the *Canada Labour Code*, the provisions of this Act shall prevail."[22] Although the federal government was slow to respond to the recommendations of the task force, one province – Quebec – responded quickly and decisively.

The Quebec legislature passed two statutes to address the status of the artist within the provincial jurisdiction, in 1987 and 1988. The first establishes a process for recognizing artists' associations representing creators and performers in theatre, opera, music, dance, variety entertainment, film, sound recording, dubbing, and the recording of commercial advertisements; this legislation entitles recognized artists' associations to negotiate group agreements, which must include a model contract for the performance of services.[23] The second statute provides for the recognition of artists in the fields of visual arts, arts and crafts, and literature, but it places greater emphasis on individual contracts between artists and producers/promoters:[24] it permits "group agreements, containing minimum conditions for the circulation of works and model contracts" (MacPherson 1999, 359). The Quebec legislation requires producers to form associations, and it introduces first-contract arbitration one year after an artists' association serves notice of its intention to bargain with a producer. This legislation shares several features with Quebec's *Collective Agreement Extension Act*, as it provides a way for artists to extend key employment-related standards throughout a specified artistic sector. While they cover self-employed artists producing artistic works, both statutes focus on persons who offer their services as creators, performers, or visual artists rather than on creating a collective bargaining regime that centres on the production of artistic works (that is, products). Quebec thus avoided potential jurisdictional conflicts surrounding intellectual property and competition. Other provinces, however, were not as quick as Quebec to respond with legislation.[25]

After Quebec enacted the legislation, the House of Commons Standing Committee on Communications and Culture recommended that legislation be developed to extend collective bargaining legislation to self-employed artists in the federal jurisdiction.[26] As a result, Bill C-96 was introduced in December 1990, and although it died on the order paper, it was reintroduced as Bill 7 in the next session of Parliament. The SAA received royal assent in June 1992 and came into force in May 1995.

B. Artists' Precarious Status and the Shape of the Status of the Artist Act

The SAA advances a collective bargaining regime for independent professional artists dealing with federal producers (excluding subcontractors to federal producers), although it is weaker than the Siren-Gélinas Task Force proposed it should be, since it does not supersede the *Canada Labour Code*, the *Public Service Staff Relations Act*,[27] the *Copyright Act*,[28] and the *Competition Act*.[29] This creates a potential for conflict between several legal regimes within the federal government's legislative authority,[30] and it narrows the scope for collective bargaining in the arts.[31] Four features of the act overcome the two central obstacles to collective bargaining typically confronted by this group: namely, that individuals must establish that they are controlled (that is, employees) and/or economically dependent on a single employer (that is, dependent contractors) in order to secure collective bargaining rights. First, the act extends collective bargaining rights to self-employed professional artists, overcoming the requirement that individuals demonstrate that they are employees to acquire these rights. Second, it defines self-employed artists belonging to artists' associations as *combinations of employees* under the *Competition Act*, exempting them from liability under that act for acting in concert. Third, by embedding collective bargaining law certification principles in the act itself, it introduces a regime managed by a tribunal (the CAPPRT) and characterized by a novel approach to representation. Fourth, it constructs a collective bargaining regime centred on the producers of artistic works and built around agreements of minimum terms – known as scale agreements – which ensure that minimum terms cannot be imposed on an artist who may be in a stronger bargaining position vis-à-vis a given producer.

Extending Collective Bargaining Rights to Independent Professional Artists   The SAA applies to professional independent contractors who are authors of artistic, dramatic, literary, or musical works within the meaning of the *Copyright Act* or to directors responsible for the overall direction of audiovisual works, performers, and those who "contribute to the creation of any production in the performing arts, music, dance and variety entertainment, film, radio and television, video, sound-recording, dubbing or the recording of commercials, arts and crafts, or visual arts, and fall within a professional category prescribed by regulation."[32] The act thus distinguishes professional artists from hobbyists and identifies groups of artists that it deems to be professionals based on three issues: whether the artist is paid for a display or presentation and is recognized as an artist by other artists; is in the process of becoming an artist according to the practice of the artistic community; and is a member of an artists' association that adheres to a set of by-laws pertaining to membership.[33] The act allows the government to include, by regulation, additional groups of artists contributing to the creation of a production.

Under the act, the term *artist* means "independent contractor," and the statute recognizes that "for tax purposes, an independent contractor may be incorporated, or may deal with those who engage his or her services through other arms' length arrangements."[34] Yet the statute does not define *independent contractor*.

Artists' Associations as Combinations of Employees under the Competition Act The SAA requires professional artists to be independent contractors in order to be covered by the legislation. To enable artists falling into this category (that is, artists with multiple employers) to bargain collectively, section 9(2) deems professional artists' associations to be "combinations of employees" for the purpose of the *Competition Act*. This provision "relieves certified artists' associations from the threat of prosecution as a conspiracy in restraint of trade," since the *Competition Act* precludes independent entrepreneurs from limiting the supply of products (MacPherson 1999, 361). Section 9(2) prevents the Canadian Competition Tribunal from intruding on the jurisdiction of the CAPPRT and vice versa. The CAPPRT has not yet decided a case concerning the *Competition Act*.[35] It is intent on following the letter and the spirit of that act, although several potential complications may emerge. Specifically, while section 4(1)(a) of the *Competition Act* states that the act does not apply to "combinations or activities of workmen or employees for their own reasonable protection such as workmen or employees," section 4(2) specifies that this exemption does not extend "to a contract, agreement or arrangement entered into by an employer to withhold any product from any person, or to refrain from acquiring from any person any product other than the services of workmen or employees,"[36] distinguishing sharply between agreements governing the supply of labour power and products. There is no reported case law interpreting section 4(2); thus, while it is important to mention this section of the *Competition Act*, its significance for scale agreements negotiated under the SAA remains unclear.

The most prominent concern pertaining to anti-competition raised thus far relates to the issue of whether copyright can be a subject of scale agreements. Copyright is related to collective bargaining under the SAA for two reasons: the act designates who is an artist in section 6(2)(b)(i) on the basis of how *author* is defined in the *Copyright Act*;[37] and artists' groups receiving certification under that section could conceivably negotiate terms pertaining to copyright with producers and include them in scale agreements. Under section 6(2)b(i), artists are defined as authors within the meaning of the *Copyright Act*. In the *Copyright Act*, section 13(3), there is a presumption that the copyright in works created by employees in the course of their employment belong to the employer, yet works created by self-employed professional artists can be subject to negotiation.

Early decisions of the CAPPRT suggest that it "envisioned a scale agreement could contain provisions related to copyright in works that a producer commissioned from an artist" (MacPherson 1999, 374). While noting the tribunal's awareness that transactions involving intellectual property are normally subject to the *Copyright Act*, a lawyer employed by the tribunal described the relationship of anti-competition policy and copyright under the SAA in this way: "Given the nature of artistic services and their relation to commerce and competitive markets, it is unlikely that a refusal to license copyright to a producer would be seen as an anti-competitive act. The very economics of arts and culture would make this difficult. In fact, it is a challenge to imagine a scenario involving the Tribunal, artists or producers which would in fact invite the Competition Bureau to act."[38] To date, CAPPRT has tried to reconcile the many forms of remuneration artists receive for the use of their works, suggesting that the choice be left to the artists' associations.[39]

The CAPPRT and the New Collective Bargaining Regime for Independent Professional Artists and Producers Designed to overcome barriers to collective representation among self-employed professional artists, the collective bargaining regime introduced under the act is novel in several respects. It is administered by a tribunal composed of members with expertise in the arts.[40] The tribunal can certify organizations that are representative of artists in a sector that is found to be suitable for bargaining. It can also provide remedies in cases where it finds that there has been a failure to bargain in good faith in the negotiation of a scale agreement. Although there was considerable debate over whether a separate board from the CIRB was necessary, legislators opted for a special board to deal with self-employed professionals in recognition of the unique features of labour relations in the artistic community. During the hearings of the Standing Committee on Communications and Culture, artists' groups argued that labour relations in the arts are less adversarial than those in industrial sectors, since "producers and artists alike are involved in the creative process and, to some extent, they can change hats," necessitating the creation of a separate board (Farkas 1999, 93).

By detailing various procedures, however, the SAA vests less discretion in the CAPPRT than most labour codes vest in labour boards. The justification for designing the statute in this way is that artists' groups are relatively new as bargaining agents, whereas trade unions were well established when collective bargaining was introduced. While other collective bargaining legislation is silent on the content of trade union constitutions, relying instead on labour relations boards to set out central features of union constitutions (for example, provisions that ensure union democracy) through their jurisprudence, section 23(1) of the SAA sets out several prerequisites for certification. The constitution of an association must include bylaws that establish membership requirements for artists, give regular members the right to participate and vote in the meetings of the association and in a ratification of any scale agreement affecting them, and provide members with access to a certified financial statement attesting to the affairs of the association. These prerequisites resemble what labour boards require of unions before they will certify them as representative bargaining agents. Once a given agent fulfils these criteria, certification proceeds in two stages. These resemble procedures under Quebec's now dramatically restructured *Collective Agreements Extension Act* and Ontario's recently repealed *Industrial Standards Act*, although neither statute provided for collective bargaining but rather for the extension of key terms through a sector.[41] The CAPPRT first decides on the appropriate sector for collective bargaining and then determines which applicant organization is the "most representative" of artists in the sector.[42] The process of sector designation under the act allows artists' associations to apply for certification in one or more sectors.[43] Although the tribunal has discretion in defining a sector, including the power to decide whether a group of artists constitutes a sector suitable for bargaining,[44] it prefers large craft units spanning the country. Regardless, in making a determination, it must consider the common interests of the artists for whom the application is being made, the history of professional relations among the artists and the applicant association, and any relevant geographic criteria.[45] After identifying the sector suitable for collective bargaining, the CAPPRT determines whether the applicant association is most representative.[46] Only artists have the right to intervene on this issue; producers must seek the permission of the tribunal if they wish to question the representativity of an artists' association.[47] Under most collective bargaining regimes in Canada, the test for representativity is fifty plus one, but under the SAA, an association must only establish that it is the most representative. Certifications are treated as fixed-term renewable licenses (typically, the term is three years) to ensure that associations remain representative over time. The act allows for non-renewal when an application for revocation or replacement of the certified artists' association has been filed.[48]

The Scale Agreement   With certification, artists' associations gain the right to bargain on behalf of all artists in the sector. Yet, in contrast to most other collective bargaining regimes, under this statute artists' associations negotiate scale agreements with producers. These agreements set minimum terms and conditions for the provision of artists' services and other related matters.[49] They allow individual artists to negotiate contracts, but they prevent producers from paying any less than the amount provided in a scale agreement to a professional artist working in a sector in which an artists' association has been certified. This is an attempt to minimize precarious work relationships in the arts, and it initiates a form of collective agreement with roots only in the sports and entertainment sector[50] and industrial standards agreements. The agreements also allow artists and producers to engage in pressure tactics with due notice (thirty days after scale agreements expire).

The framework for encouraging artists' and producers' associations to negotiate scale agreements is novel in many respects, yet it contains a profound structural weakness. Unlike Quebec legislation, federal legislation does not compel producers to form associations for the purpose of collective bargaining.[51] It merely encourages their formation through relatively informal recognition procedures: to obtain recognition under the act, a producers' association need only file a copy of its membership list with the tribunal. Few producers' associations have formed to date, making it difficult and costly for artists' associations to negotiate agreements applicable to artists in a given sector, since they must serve notice to bargain and negotiate with producers individually. Artists' associations are attempting to respond to this obstacle by developing model agreements.[52] Despite these shortcomings, the virtue of scale agreements is still their capacity to enable independent professional artists who are neither controlled (that is, employees) nor economically dependent on a single employer (that is, dependent contractors) to attain minimum terms. Combined with the other three central features of the statute, they are pivotal to collective bargaining between artists and producers in the federal jurisdiction, even though they mainly benefit artists creating artistic works.

4. "THE MOUSE THAT ROARED": FREELANCE EDITORS' STRUGGLE FOR COLLECTIVE BARGAINING RIGHTS UNDER THE *STATUS OF THE ARTIST ACT*

The EAC/ACR was among the first of the artists' associations to apply to be certified as the representative bargaining agent for its sector under the SAA and the twentieth of twenty-seven associations to receive certifications as of January 2004, permitting it to negotiate scale agreements with producers in the federal jurisdiction.[53] The EAC/ACR case is important for several reasons. Albeit highly creative, the association's pursuit of collective bargaining under the SAA reveals the profound limits of the statute due to its focus on product rather than the performance of personal service and its narrow application to artists as defined by the *Copyright Act*. In making its first application, in February 1996, the EAC/ACR initially sought to represent a sector "composed of freelance and in-house editors of books, periodicals, government documents and other printed materials in both official languages,"[54] but it quickly encountered the limits of the new statute. It recognized that in order for it to win certification, freelance editors would have to assert authorship (or possibly claim to be "directors" of artistic works) and thereby initiate an intricate legal battle over copyright. Upon discovering that the category "editors of literary works" was not on the list of professional artist categories falling under section 6(2)(b)(iii) of the SAA – the main segment of the act that includes independent professional artists who perform rather than create artistic works – the EAC/ACR was compelled to amend the sector that it sought to represent.[55] Consequently, on 20 June 2000, when the regulations were finally in place, it applied for certification as the representative bargaining agent for a sector composed of all professional freelance editors engaged by a producer subject to the SAA to prepare original works in the form of compilations or collective works within the meaning of the *Copyright Act*; or to prepare original works of joint authorship, for which the editor's contribution constitutes the work of a joint author in either French or English.[56]

From 20 June 2000 to 1 November 2002, the EAC/ACR's application for certification moved through several stages. In advancing the case for certification, because of the limited list of professional categories falling under the act, the EAC/ACR's initial aims were to illustrate that freelance editors are professionals and to secure greater legitimacy for the association. When it became apparent that it had to demonstrate that editors are authors in order to gain certification, the EAC/ACR stepped up its efforts to prove that freelance editors are authors within the meaning of the SAA (and hence the *Copyright Act*), while judiciously noting that they are authors who rarely assert copyright due to the nature of their profession. Describing the ethic of invisibility in editing, the EAC/ACR challenged the tribunal to "fashion its own definitions [of authorship] for the purposes of the *Status of the Artist Act*," since the *Copyright Act* does not define the word *author* – a complex undertaking for the EAC/ACR, given how narrow the aperture *artist* is under the act.[57] In advancing this challenge, the EAC/ACR confronted opposition from interveners, especially the Writers' Union of Canada (TWUC).[58] While supporting editors' right to certify, TWUC objected to the route that the tribunal compelled editors to use to gain access to the SAA, arguing that it threatened writers' moral rights and copyrights. Ultimately, the CAPPRT responded somewhat favourably to the EAC/ACR's struggle to certify. Yet, as the EAC/ACR case proceeded through various stages – including a request for reconsideration filed by TWUC, along with an application for judicial review in the Federal Court of Appeal based on claims that the tribunal had erred in law and in fact in its initial decision – the scope of the certification grew narrower and narrower.

A. Towards Certification: The EAC/ACR's Initial Arguments and TWUC's Response

The EAC/ACR first made formal arguments and offered evidence in favour of certification on 17 January 2001. Its manager, Connie John, began by describing the history of the EAC/ACR, the size and geographic scope of its membership, and its governance structure. She then indicated that editors in the proposed sector are involved in trade publishing, which accounts for approximately 20 to 30 per cent of their work, but 70 to 80 per cent of it is editing academic materials, advertising copy, cookbooks, computer manuals, databases, and the like, a dimension of the publishing industry that TWUC's certification does not cover. Against this backdrop, the EAC/ACR introduced evidence to show that editors fall under the act. The first step was to demonstrate that editors are skilled professionals.

To establish editors' professional status in accordance with section 18(b) of the act, the EAC/ACR described the many different forms of editing, which often proceed sequentially yet are distinct processes unto themselves. In so doing, it devoted particular attention to developmental editing, structural and substantive editing, line editing, copyediting, and proofreading.[59] In describing the forms of editing, the EAC/ACR drew on evidence provided by two freelance editors as well as an MA thesis prepared by Rhonda Bailey entitled "The Editor as Merlin: A Case Study of the Editing Process for *Zigzag: A Life on the Move* by James Houston" (1998), which it submitted to the tribunal along with other evidence.

The EAC/ACR made it clear that writers are always entitled to accept or reject editorial suggestions, "subject to any agreement to the contrary with the publisher."[60] Yet, while acknowledging that the writer has the final say, it also noted that "there may be cases where a publisher and writer may agree that the editor will have certain prerogatives and will be able to override the writer's wishes in certain areas."[61] In describing the work of editors, freelance editor Rick Archbold emphasized that in some cases the quality of the final work depends on the editor's ability as a writer. Archbold described "the situation of individuals who write on subjects in respect of which they have specialized expertise but who do not have any particular facility for writing," and he noted that in such instances, "an editor takes a hands-on role and can actually become a co-author, albeit an invisible one."[62]

This testimony set the stage for a larger claim that some forms of editing constitute invisible co- or joint authorship. In the hearings, the EAC/ACR described the ethic of invisibility as follows: "It manifests itself primarily in two ways. First, any changes made to a manuscript are invisible to the reader: to accomplish this, the editor must ensure that his or her suggestions reflect the original style and voice of the writer. Second, the editor must not attempt to lay claim to the moral rights or the copyright in the finished work: the writer must retain the sole right to be associated with the work as its author, and as its author, is normally the first owner of the copyright in the work. Editors are normally satisfied with an acknowledgment by the writer ... An editor who does not respect this custom will soon find himself or herself without work."[63]

The EAC/ACR used the ethic of invisibility to establish the weight of editors' contributions to many manuscripts, pointing to their written contributions, while deciding not to make a formal claim regarding authorship at that point. After providing this description, Connie John noted that "the work of editors described above attracts copyright and moral rights,"[64] but it is customary for editors to waive these rights. Jim Lyons, another editor testifying on behalf of the EAC/ACR, added that some editing calls for extensive written contributions (for example, textbooks), but other editing does not demand this type of creative input (for example, government work). On this basis, the EAC/ACR argued that editors may fall under several parts of the act – sections 6(2)(b)(i) and (ii) – depending upon the nature and level of their contribution. The association also made a clear distinction between writers and editors and noted that editors are excluded from TWUC's constitution.

TWUC, the only intervener appearing before the tribunal, did not contest the EAC/ACR's claim to professional status or its description of the tasks involved in editing. However, to forestall the claim that some forms of editing constitute authorship, it argued that the EAC/ACR overstated the role of editors, especially their artistic contribution. From the outset, the source of TWUC's opposition to the EAC/ACR's application was its reluctant (albeit necessary) claim to authorship to secure certification. On behalf of TWUC, Bill Freedman, a freelance writer, testified that he did not view editors as co-authors, characterizing the editor's contribution as "negligible" and the copy-editing process as "mechanical."[65] To develop the case that editors are not authors, Christopher Moore, a writer and historian, also described his experience as a co-author and compared it to working with an editor, suggesting that experienced editors rarely make extensive rewrites, especially without consulting the writer.[66]

To preserve the integrity of its own certification, TWUC also invited witnesses to comment on its perceived jurisdiction. Its executive director, Penny Dickens, argued first that TWUC's members are not restricted to trade publishing – they write textbooks and academic materials as well.[67] She asserted further that TWUC did not intend to limit its negotiation of scale agreements to the area of trade publishing but "to negotiate in relation to writing of any books over 44 pages."[68] Still, on cross-examination, Dickens confirmed that a writer must have written at least one trade book to become a member of TWUC, substantiating the EAC/ACR's claim that editors cannot be members of TWUC.[69]

Based on the initial testimony from the EAC/ACR and TWUC, the tribunal established that the application raised questions concerning several sections of the *SAA* and the *Competition Act*.[70] Yet it summarized the four central issues raised by the certification as follows: whether editors are artists within the meaning of the *SAA*; the suitability, for bargaining purposes, of the sector proposed by the EAC/ACR; whether the EAC/ACR is representative of the artists in the sector; and whether the EAC/ACR's bylaws comply with subsection 23(1) of the *SAA*.[71]

In the first stage of deliberations, the EAC/ACR satisfied the tribunal that editors are independent contractors and professionals as defined by act. However, the association failed to convince the tribunal that the group of editors it sought to represent was composed of authors. The summary of issues, however, suggests that the EAC/ACR needed to satisfy the tribunal that editors are authors in order to receive certification.

B. Responding to the Tribunal: The EAC/ACR's Call for an Expansive Conception of Authorship and TWUC's Opposition

In the second stage of deliberations, the tribunal invited the EAC/ACR and TWUC to respond to the four core issues in the case. Realizing that it would only receive certification by convincing the tribunal that editors are authors, the association submitted that editors are authors on two grounds: first, they are authors of literary works within the meaning of the *Copyright Act* and therefore fall under section 6(2)(b)(i) of the *SAA*; second, they are directors of literary works under section 6(2)(b)(ii). To support its argument for characterizing editors as authors, the EAC/ACR noted that the *Copyright Act* fails to define the word *author*, leaving it to the tribunal to shape its own definition.[72] It further contended that "editors are authors of compilations, collective works and works of joint authorship," given their roles in writing indexes, glossaries, tables of contents, and bibliographies, and, in particular, in compiling the works of others, such as short stories and poems.[73] It also argued that editors are joint authors in their creative involvement with writers: "The EAC/ACR submits that all types of editing, from developmental editing to copy editing, constitute the work of a joint author. The EAC/ACR argues that, in writer-editor relationships, the contribution of one author (the writer) is not distinct from that of the other author (the editor). An equal contribution by joint authors is not necessary, provided that both have made a significant contribution ... editors do make a significant contribution, sufficient to meet the test for joint authorship."[74] The EAC/ACR called for defining editors as authors on the basis that there are at least two types of authors: writers and editors. The difference between these two types of authors, it argued, is that "editors typically waive copyright and moral rights."[75]

To advance its argument that editors are independent professional artists who direct literary works, the association relied on a tribunal decision in *Canadian Actors' Equity*, in which it was determined that stage managers are artists even though they primarily coordinate productions. Since editors are part of the process of developing and refining literary works, it argued, they should be covered under section 6(2)(b)(ii) of the act.[76] The EAC/ACR submitted that it sought to represent a sector of editors, many of whom are also authors but whose multiple artistic roles do not overlap in the creation of a single work, while TWUC's certification only gave it the right to represent "writers who are authors."[77] It also reiterated that its membership of 1,200 constituted more than half of the estimated total number of artists in this sector.[78]

TWUC did not contest the EAC/ACR's arguments regarding its representativity, but it rejected the association's contention that editors could be authors under the act and the appropriateness of the sector in its submission.[79] TWUC had initially agreed that editors could be authors of compilations or collective works under the *Copyright Act*. However, it shifted course in the second round, opposing the claim that editors are joint authors within the meaning of the *Copyright Act*[80] and asserting that "the only area of agreement [between the EAC/ACR and TWUC] was that editors could be authors of compilations."[81] TWUC argued further that editors do not "direct, in any manner, a literary work," maintaining that editors should properly be subject to the SAA professional category regulations. As the hearings proceeded, TWUC expressed the view that editors should have the right to negotiate scale agreements, but not as authors; where editors are considered joint authors or authors of literary works, they fall within its jurisdiction. TWUC opposed certifying the EAC/ACR to represent author-editors.[82]

In its final rebuttal, the EAC/ACR argued that reducing the sector to editors who are authors of compilations "would make a mockery of the work of editors."[83] Refuting TWUC's claim that editors fail to make creative contributions and are therefore not entitled to copyright, it contended that copyright law has no creativity requirement. Yet it noted, once again, that editors have no desire to assert copyright, and that they have no interest in doing so, given the ethic of invisibility. The EAC/ACR asserted that it was pursuing certification for one purpose only: to enable editors to benefit from scale agreements and collective bargaining more broadly.

C. Certification: The Tribunal Navigates Its Narrow Jurisdiction

In the second round of deliberations, the CAPPRT decided the EAC/ACR application on the basis of whether editors were authors within the meaning of the SAA, whether the sector proposed by the EAC/ACR was suitable for bargaining, whether the EAC/ACR was representative of artists in the sector, and whether the EAC/ACR's bylaws complied with the act. While the tribunal was easily convinced that freelance editors are independent skilled professionals, it was unwilling to certify the EAC/ACR as the representative bargaining agent for its entire constituency of freelance editors because it was not persuaded that editors are artists (that is, authors). At this stage, narrowing considerably the sector that the EAC/ACR sought to represent, the tribunal found that only two types of editing constitute authorship: editing compilations or collective works, and joint authorship. In setting the parameters for these two types of editing, it established that compilations and collective works include, but are not limited to, the preparation of indexes, glossaries, tables of contents, bibliographies, and compilations of the works of others, such as anthologies of short stories or poems.[84] It also made the proviso that editors' contributions must meet the relatively low threshold of originality required for authorship.[85] In the case of joint authorship, it established that two or more authors must collaborate, citing an expert on the subject: "frequently, this will involve engaging in the production of a work by joint labour in the implementation of a preconcerted joint design."[86] Yet contributions need not be equal in quantity or quality, provided that they are considerable and original.[87]

In establishing that editors must either edit compilations or collective works or serve as joint authors to be deemed artists, the tribunal addressed the fact that many editors neither assert copyright nor purport to have it. Its principal finding was that the ethic of invisibility has no bearing on the presence or absence of copyright: "an editor who otherwise meets the criteria for an author does not lose that status merely because he or she does not assert copyright."[88] It also found that editors are not "professionals who direct, in any manner, literary works," and therefore they do not fall under section 6(2)(b)(ii), as it relates solely to performances.[89] The effect of this dimension of the tribunal's decision is highly significant. Without coverage under section 6(2)(b)(ii) or the professional category regulations, freelance editors had just one option: to pursue their claim to authorship even more vigorously.

The issue of whether professional freelance editors are a suitable sector for collective bargaining was less controversial. The tribunal found that editors display common interests and conform to the relevant geographic and linguistic criteria set out in the statute.[90] The only issue that the tribunal was compelled to address was TWUC's claim that author-editors of works of joint authorship or collective works fall within its certification. Its conclusion was simple: "TWUC ... stated that it does not wish to represent editors. Having considered the evidence and arguments, the Tribunal is satisfied that the sector for which TWUC was certified is intended to be a sector composed of 'writers who are authors of literary works' notwithstanding that the certificate only mentions 'authors of literary works.' By making this finding, the Tribunal is not affecting a revocation or partial revocation of TWUC's certification; it is merely interpreting the intended scope of the certification."[91]

The issue of representativity was similarly straightforward for the tribunal. The EAC/ACR's total membership constituted more than half of all independent professional editors in the federal jurisdiction, and no other artists' association indicated an interest in representing editors.[92] The only remaining issue for the tribunal was the requirement that the EAC/ACR change its bylaws to formally extend to its regular members the right to participate in a ratification vote on any scale agreement and the right to access a copy of its financial statements.[93] Thus, on 28 February 2001, when the tribunal delivered its first analysis and conclusions, it ordered that the application for certification be stayed until the EAC/ACR had altered its bylaws.

On 27 September 2001, after the EAC/ACR had changed its bylaws, the CAPPRT formally granted the association's application for certification, making just a few minor modifications.[94] The tribunal held that editors who are authors of original works in the form of compilations or collective works, and authors of works of joint authorship in English or French, are artists in the meaning of the act. It held further that professional freelance editors represent a suitable sector for bargaining, and that the EAC/ACR is the association most representative of artists in this sector. In rendering this decision, the tribunal attempted to avoid potential jurisdictional conflicts by ensuring that the certification only covered freelance editors, and by reassuring itself that the group of editors that the EAC/ACR proposed to represent was composed of professionals. Rather than extending coverage to editors under sections 6(2)(b)(ii) or (iii), it opted to extend coverage only to editors who are authors within the meaning of the *Copyright Act*; this not only trod a fine line where overlap with the federal copyright regime is concerned, but it also limited access to collective bargaining to editors deemed to be creators of artistic works (that is, products) – specifically, to authors of literary works.

D. The EAC/ACR Certification in Question

The certification of the EAC/ACR as the representative bargaining agent for editors who are authors of original literary works in the form of compilations or collective works and authors of literary works of joint authorship represented an important victory for the EAC/ACR. Yet the association's capacity to construct a collective bargaining regime around the creation of artistic works – in this case, literary works – through the negotiation of scale agreements with federal producers was short-lived. On 29 October 2001, TWUC made application for judicial review of the CAPPRT's decision and filed a request that the tribunal reconsider its two previous decisions. On the surface, the debate generated by TWUC's application for judicial review and its request for reconsideration pivoted on the question of where editing ends and authorship begins. But fundamental problems with the narrow scope of the act – expressed primarily as pressure for an expansive definition of *authorship* from some workers and resistance to an expansive definition from others, and also as sharp objections to the limited list of professional categories of artists falling under the act – lay at its root. In making application for judicial review,[95] TWUC used the strongest means at its disposal to force a reversal of the tribunal decision: the claim that it had exceeded the jurisdiction of the SAA in certifying the EAC/ACR.

In its application for judicial review, TWUC claimed that the tribunal had "acted without jurisdiction, beyond its jurisdiction or failed to exercise its proper jurisdiction" in the EAC/ACR certification.[96] The application rested on several issues. First, TWUC claimed that the tribunal incorrectly interpreted the *Copyright Act* definition of *work of joint authorship* and hence erroneously determined the meaning of *authors of literary works* in the EAC/ACR case.⁹⁷ Second, it contended that the tribunal had neglected to consider properly the suitability of the sector for bargaining "by failing to consider whether a sector with an indeterminate membership whose application can only be determined on a case by case basis has the requisite suitability."⁹⁸ Third, TWUC suggested that in granting the certification, the tribunal effectively amended or partially revoked or rescinded its certification for not covering "all authors of literary works" but "writers who are authors" to avoid conflict with the new sector of "editors who are authors." Fourth, it argued that the tribunal had designated a sector that overlaps with previous certifications of other writers' organizations, "despite the purported exclusion of authors covered by certifications of these organizations."⁹⁹

TWUC also claimed that the tribunal had erred in law, arguing that it had incorrectly determined the meaning of *joint authorship* under the *Copyright Act*. The Writers' Union suggested that there cannot be a valid distinction in copyright law and under the SAA between writers who are authors and editors who are authors.¹⁰⁰ It contended that the CAPPRT had intruded into the jurisdiction of the *Copyright Act* – and stretched its definition of *authorship* – as well as designated a sector that overlapped with other sectors, and thus interfered with the jurisdictions of various writers' associations. Despite the EAC/ACR's repeated emphasis that editors are not interested in asserting copyright or moral rights, TWUC's constituency opposed the expansive notion of authorship adopted by the CAPPRT to compensate for the narrow scope of this alternative collective bargaining regime.

The request for reconsideration that TWUC filed with the CAPPRT rested on the same issues as its application for judicial review. On 17 January 2002, the tribunal decided to reconsider the previous panel's interpretation of the meaning of *joint authorship* under the *Copyright Act* – specifically, the criteria of mutual intent/common design and the ability of the writer to accept or reject an editor's suggestions and its significance – and to address the question of the partial revocation of existing certification orders, such as those accorded to TWUC, the Periodical Writers' Association of Canada (PWAC), the Société des auteurs de radio, télévision et cinéma (SARTEC), the Union des écrivaines et écrivains québécois (UNEQ), the Playwrights' Union of Canada (PUC), and the Writers' Guild of Canada (WGC).¹⁰¹ In the hearings that took place on 9–10 May 2002, the CAPPRT heard evidence from TWUC and received submissions from TWUC and other writers' associations and responses from the EAC/ACR on these issues.

TWUC presented seven editors as witnesses, and they expressed the common sentiment that they "never considered themselves to be joint authors with the writer of the work, even when their contributions as an editor were very significant."[102] They also claimed that the writer can always refuse or accept the editor's suggestions.[103] TWUC's aim was to challenge the CAPPRT's interpretation of the meaning of *joint authorship*, make clear that writers have the last word on the final product, and illustrate that certifying the EAC/ACR as the appropriate representative of freelance editors who are joint authors entailed a partial revocation of its certification.

In response to this testimony, the EAC/ACR presented several witnesses in defense of its certification. It wanted to ensure that editors of compilations or collective works and editor-authors of literary works of joint authorship continued to be defined as artists. One of the association's witnesses, Rosemary Shipton, the coordinator of Ryerson University's publishing program, gave testimony akin to that of TWUC's witnesses, claiming that her work as "publisher's editor" entails contributing to authors' projects, but, as an editor, she merely assists the author.[104] Still, in support of the claim that some editors are authors, she highlighted the "dual definition" of the word *editor*, making a distinction between the "organizing editor" and the "publisher's editor." For Shipton, the organizing editor contributes to the concept or, in her words, "provides some shape to the work,"[105] and, by implication, is an author.[106]

TWUC then made the following claims on the issue of the criteria of mutual intent/common design: first, it argued that the term *author* only applies to the creator of the work, and that "the editor is not the creator of the work and therefore not entitled to protection under the *Copyright Act* as joint author."[107] It admitted, however, that the threshold for creativity in a work is unsettled in Canadian law. Second, TWUC argued that a finding of joint authorship requires mutual intent and a common design – a claim that the PUC elevated in its submission – and it suggested that the tribunal erred in law in failing to consider this requirement. TWUC also claimed that the writer's acceptance or rejection of the editor's suggestions is the norm: the writer's vision and design is always paramount.[108] On the issue of the partial revocation of existing sectors, all the writers' associations present (that is, TWUC, the PUC, and the WGC) argued that the sector granted to the EAC/ACR overlapped with TWUC's sector because TWUC's certification did not exclude joint authors or authors of collective works and compilations.[109]

Before addressing the three main issues, the EAC/ACR made several preliminary submissions. It reasserted that the definition of *author* in the *Copyright Act* is not confined to writers, and that "because editors contributed to the fixed written form of the work, they too can be included in the statutory definition of author."[110] On the issue of mutual intent/common design, it claimed that copyright law does not contain a requirement of mutual intent, but rather, "it is the nature of the work that determines the issue of joint authorship."[111] The EAC/ACR's reaction was that common design is an element of joint authorship; the significance of the editor's collaboration makes the editor a joint author, although editor-authors subscribe to the ethic of invisibility.[112] The EAC/ACR dealt with the argument that its certification amounted to a partial revocation of that of TWUC by arguing that the tribunal's 27 September 2001 decision (number 36) merely clarifies it. Furthermore, the number of compilations or collective works prepared by professional editors is far greater than the number prepared by members of TWUC, so the EAC/ACR would be the most representative bargaining agent for these professional editor-authors.

The three central issues raised by the submissions of the writers' associations and the EAC/ACR were: whether the original panel employed the appropriate test for determining joint authorship within the meaning of the *Copyright Act*; whether the original panel erred in determining that certain editors are joint authors of a literary work within the meaning of that act; and whether editors can be authors of original literary works in the form of compilations and collective works. In addressing the question of the appropriate test for determining joint authorship within the meaning of the *Copyright Act*, the CAPPRT found that the definition of *work of joint authorship* has two elements: collaboration and contribution. It held that "the issue of whether professional freelance editors are joint authors cannot be determined on the basis of the intent of the parties alone."[113] Rather, "an editor must contribute significant original expression and collaborate with the other author in a pre-concerted joint design in order to be a joint author."[114] In dealing with what it labelled "the crux of the issue" – the question of whether the original panel erred in determining that certain editors are joint authors of a literary work within the meaning of the *Copyright Act* (and therefore artists in the meaning of the SAA) – the tribunal found that substantive and developmental editing are significant, as the original panel had emphasized, but joint authorship also requires collaboration, and the previous panel had overlooked this essential element.[115] Evidence presented on whether editors can be authors of original literary works in the form of compilations or collective works provoked a divided response from the CAPPRT. Here, it found that "a sector composed of professional freelance editors who are the authors of compilations of data which include indexes, glossaries, tables of contents and bibliographies ... is an appropriate sector to be certified."[116] Yet it rejected the original conclusion that editors may be authors of collective works in the absence of evidence that editors are involved in the general conception, design, arrangement, and coordination of the separate parts of collective works.[117]

The CAPPRT recognized that editors are "essential to the literary world."[118] But, in a rare acknowledgment of the limits of the SAA, it found that "as the legislation is now drafted, professional freelance editors who provide services in the nature of developmental and substantive editing do not fall under the jurisdiction of the Act."[119] Consequently, the tribunal rescinded its two decisions in the case, numbers 33 and 36, and named the sector suitable for bargaining as that "composed of professional freelance editors who are engaged by a producer subject to the *Status of the Artist Act* to prepare original works in the form of compilations of data, including but not limited to original indexes, glossaries, tables of contents and bibliographies," excluding authors covered by the certifications granted to TWUC, the PWAC, the SARTEC, the UNEQ, the PUC, and the WGC, and retained the EAC/ACR as the representative artists' association.[120] On 1 November 2002, the sector certification grew more limited; the EAC/ACR became the representative bargaining agent for an even narrower group of professional freelance editors. Satisfied with the decision, TWUC withdrew its application for judicial review once the thirty-day period in which any party may file a request for reconsideration had passed.

E. Freelance Editors' Limited Victory

The struggle of the EAC/ACR to gain certification to represent professional freelance editors under the SAA and the narrow parameters of the CAPPRT's final decision offer important lessons about the limits and possibilities of new federal legislation extending collective bargaining rights to independent professional artists. Two outcomes of the EAC/ACR certification highlighting the weakness of the SAA as an alternative regime merit special emphasis: the impracticable scope of the collective bargaining provided for under the final EAC/ACR certification, and the jurisdictional tensions between editors' and writers' associations aggravated by the EAC/ACR's pursuit of certification. These outcomes reveal the extent to which the tribunal is constrained by section 6(2)(b)(i), which ensures that the statute centres on the production of artistic works rather than the performance of service, and by the limited group of professional artists included by regulation, a group to which professional freelance editors arguably belong. In its attempts to avoid intruding on the territory of other federal statutes by carefully defining *professionals* and *authors*, the CAPPRT's final ruling in the EAC/ACR case reflects its effort to navigate an impossibly narrow legal regime whose central flaw is its application to *professional artists* only – a term defined so rigidly that it not only excludes a range of cultural workers but also constrains the range of artists and the number of potential sectors falling under the new legislation.

Owing to the restrictive character of the legal regime, the scope of the EAC/ACR certification is exceedingly limited. To collectively bargain with federal producers under the act, freelance editors must not only satisfy the tribunal that they are independent contractors and professionals falling under the EAC/ACR's jurisdiction, but also that they are authors of original works in the form of compilations of data. Only a minute group of professional freelance editors is now able to call upon the SAA, due to the product that they provide (that is, an original contribution to written work amounting to authorship) rather than the service that they perform (that is, editing). The CAPPRT's ruling has thus resulted in the exclusion of many professional freelance editors. While they are independent contractors falling under the EAC/ACR's jurisdiction and professionals under the statute, many freelance editors, including those involved in structural and substantive editing, fail to conform to the definition of *professional artist*, according to which editing must equal authorship. Still, for the EAC/ACR, the decision represents a victory: any scale agreement successfully negotiated, even if it applies to a small segment of its membership, could be used by editors as a precedent to secure better terms and conditions for other editing work with federal and non-federal producers. In this optimistic view, the EAC/ACR certification could foster more and better voluntary agreements over a wide range of terms and conditions, including minimum rates, income protection plans, disability insurance, pension benefits, and hours of work, organized around the creation of artistic works.

The process of attaining the EAC/ACR certification nevertheless created tensions between cultural workers (and between their associations) who had otherwise enjoyed harmonious relations. Indeed, the conflict between editors and authors is an artifact of the scheme. On the one hand, the SAA instructs the CAPPRT to ensure that artists' associations do not overlap in their scope and membership. On the other hand, the statute should, in theory, allow individual independent professional artists to wear a range of hats and belong to more than one artists' association. A distinctive feature of the act is its recognition that an artist's work and derivative works may be created in different media and fall under different copyright or performance categories. In the EAC/ACR case, the tribunal rendered the decision that professional freelance editors had to be authors under the *Copyright Act* in order to be covered by the SAA. Its ultimate decision is more palatable to TWUC than its two earlier decisions, but it still aggravates tensions between the EAC/ACR and writers' associations by its reliance on authorship – particularly its distinction between "writers who are authors" and "editors who are authors." The decision also calls into question other principles underlying the statute, specifically the notion that independent professional artists who wear several hats can benefit from representation by various associations on a task or project-by-project basis. The CAPPRT made its decision on authorship out of necessity, but its certification of the EAC/ACR overlooks an overriding sentiment behind the SAA: that industrial relations in the arts should reflect the unique character of the arts and be inclusive of the many activities tied to the creative process (Farkas 1999, 93).

The results of the tribunal's decision are the designation of a sector composed of professional freelance editors who are authors and a certification for the EAC/ACR. Yet this case highlights the profound limits of the SAA model. While the statute is an important alternative regime, it fails to draw many groups under its auspices, including a large group of professional freelance editors with multiple clients, who could never make standard collective bargaining work for them.

5. REREGULATING THE PRECARIOUS WORK RELATIONSHIP: EVALUATING THE *STATUS OF THE ARTIST ACT* MODEL

The beauty of the SAA is, on the one hand, that associations of independent professional artists are deemed to be "combinations of employees" for the purposes of the *Competition Act*, relieving certified artists' associations of the threat of prosecution for being a "conspiracy in restraint of trade" and, on the other hand, its introduction of scale agreements is a means of extending collective bargaining rights to independent contractors who sell their products to multiple parties. However, the SAA's application to artists rather than to all cultural workers, its narrow conception of *professional artist*, and its focus on the creation of artistic works pose significant challenges.

These features of the act are unlikely to change in the near future. Rather than recognizing the fundamental flaws in the SAA itself, the federal government responded to a formal evaluation of the legislation, conducted in 2002, by asserting that the main obstacle to collective bargaining in the arts is federalism: "the legislation's impacts are limited by its scope, as the act applies only to labour relations within federal jurisdiction, while the majority of artistic activity actually falls within provincial jurisdiction. However, with the exception of Quebec, and more recently some enabling legislation in Saskatchewan, none of the provinces have enacted legislation aimed at improving the socio-economic situation of self-employed artists ... federal legislation by itself is insufficient to bring about significant change in the socio-economic circumstances of artists."[121] If the freelance editors' struggle to attain collective bargaining rights signifies what is to come, then the SAA is facilitating the extension of a regime of professional self-regulation to a small number of independent professional artists and their associations; it is advancing a flawed model of regulation for the provinces and territories to follow.

Although it has yet to be tested, the provision that artists' associations are combinations of employees technically protects those receiving certification from the threat of prosecution under the *Competition Act*. The existence of this provision makes it highly unlikely that professional artists acting in concert will be accused of engaging in anticompetitive practices, especially given the vehicle for extending collective bargaining rights to professional artists. Under the SAA, certified artists' associations are entitled to negotiate scale agreements of minimum terms, enabling individual artists to bargain upwards and thereby only curtailing competition at the bottom of the labour market. If the negotiation of scale agreements proceeds smoothly for the EAC/ACR, these agreements may result in the extension of a range of benefits to a small group of freelance editors in need of social protection. In this case, the power of a given scale agreement is its potential to raise the bottom of the labour market for freelance editors (largely women) who are isolated and who frequently work from home. Agreements of minimum terms between producers and associations of dispersed workers in precarious situations pose limited risks of reprisal from producers due to the anonymity of, for example, freelance editors. Scale agreements also suit the needs of independent contractors since they are designed on the basis of a multi-employer model.

As the case of freelance editors demonstrates, the organization of a collective bargaining regime around the creation of artistic works (that is, products) is also an innovative dimension of this regime. The dominant framework for collective bargaining in Canada, even among workers covered under special legislation, assumes the performance of personal service under conditions of economic dependence; this framework takes a bilateral employment relationship as its norm. The precarious socio-economic status of many artists in Canada and their relations with multiple producers motivated the enactment of special legislation. The result is a regime that does not link the right to organize and bargain collectively with performance of personal service, nor does it place significant weight on economic dependence per se, let alone dependence on a single employer. Rather, it focuses on the situation of independent professional artists involved in the creation of artistic products and engaged by multiple producers. Freelance editors coming under the act are able to organize because of what they produce and because they are professionals. The SAA thus contributes to filling a gap in Canada's collective bargaining regime by enabling some independent professionals (albeit a limited number) to set scale agreements on the basis of the creation of artistic works, so long as their representative organizations adhere to a clear set of guidelines setting out appropriate structures of representation.

There are obvious merits to the new federal collective bargaining legislation geared to freelance professional artists. Still, the narrow category "independent professional artist" leads to numerous exclusions. In the EAC/ACR case, the CAPPRT ruled that only certain professional freelance editors fall under the SAA, even though editing work is positioned squarely in the arts. The EAC/ACR case thus illustrates that the category "independent professional artist" is a default grouping, fashioned to fill the space surrounding the *Canada Labour Code*, the *Public Service Staff Relations Act*, the *Competition Act*, and the *Copyright Act*, and this small group is gaining collective bargaining rights through new legislation designed to supplement rather than transform the regime of collective bargaining dominant since World War II.

One reason that the EAC/ACR gained certification despite editors' marginal status and the controversy over authorship is its self-identification as a professional association. Its testimony satisfied the tribunal that it is an association of professional editors concerned with developing professional standards, formalizing the relationship between editors and other actors in the publishing cycle, and using certification as a means of attaining recognition for the editing profession. There is every indication that the EAC/ACR is seeking legitimacy as a professional association. Yet, even in this seemingly benign pursuit, the EAC/ACR encountered obstacles in attaining certification on behalf of editor-authors, let alone for all professional freelance editors, suggesting the need to broaden the scope of the SAA to extend collective bargaining rights to other groups of independent contractors in the arts and culture sector who perform personal service or labour for multiple producers. Profound tensions are at work here. The strength of the SAA, and its most innovative design feature, is that it covers independent contractors, exempts their collective activities from the *Competition Act*, and provides for a flexible form of scale agreement. Yet this regime is limited by its organization around artistic product rather than service or labour, its application to professional artists only, and its failure to compel producers to form associations.

Conclusion: What Have We Learned?

Self-employed workers organize in order to improve their working conditions and remuneration. The case studies in this book illustrate how such diverse groups of self-employed workers as newspaper carriers, rural route mail couriers, personal-care workers, and freelance editors have attempted to obtain some form of collective representation and bargaining. Their stories make it abundantly clear that the dominant model of labour organization – industrial unionism – which is premised on the organization of all workers of a particular employer at a particular work site, is not a suitable vehicle for organizing the many groups of self-employed workers who work for several different employers at different locations and who face a particularly high risk of having their work contracted out, even if they successfully organize at one of their work sites. The case studies also amply demonstrate how great the challenge is to redesign labour law to meet the diverse needs of self-employed workers in today's rapidly changing labour market.

In this conclusion, we want to reflect upon the lessons that we have learned from studying the attempts of these four groups of workers to organize. But before turning to what the case studies have taught us about the limitations of the prevailing collective bargaining model, we must first address an underlying normative and economic issue: whether self-employed workers should be entitled to enjoy access to some form of collective representation and bargaining. This question is crucial, because unless it is possible to justify allowing self-employed workers to organize and bargain collectively, it is unlikely that any legislative and institutional reforms designed to promote this action will be adopted.

Thus, we begin our conclusion by examining whether providing legislative and institutional support for self-employed workers to bargain collectively can be justified within the framework of liberal democracy. We focus on how the principles of freedom of association and freedom of competition shape the laws and policies regarding self-employed workers, and we argue that legal and institutional support for collective representation and bargaining by self-employed workers is justified. We then turn from the normative to the institutional dimension of self-employed workers' organization and identify what we have learned from the case studies about what kinds of laws, policies, and institutions must be developed in order to provide self-employed workers with real access to appropriate forms of collective representation and bargaining. The case studies are used to illustrate the limitations in the prevailing collective bargaining model that make it very difficult for self-employed workers to benefit from it. In the final section, we move beyond the limitations in the existing model to suggest a range of models that would promote collective representation and bargaining for the self-employed. We begin by identifying two principles of institutional design, parity, and plurality, which, we argue, should shape any approach to collective representation and bargaining by self-employed workers, and we sketch a range of different models that could be adopted. We conclude by considering the politics necessary to achieve these reforms. Without a concerted political movement to extend these mechanisms to the self-employed, it is unlikely that any reform will occur. Employers will likely resist change, since they seek greater freedom of action without union constraint. Politicians who have accepted the neo-liberal agenda, with its emphasis on individualism and competitiveness, are unlikely to embrace policies that promote collectivism. Building a more inclusive labour movement and creating a set of institutions that can accommodate the diverse interests of workers in today's labour market will require a major political commitment by trade unions and social justice groups as well as a transformation of the terms of political discourse.

I. COLLECTIVE REPRESENTATION AND BARGAINING FOR SELF-EMPLOYED WORKERS: THE PRINCIPLE OF FREEDOM OF ASSOCIATION

To answer the question of whether self-employed workers ought to have access to collective representation and bargaining we must start from first principles. The starting point for discussions of collective action to influence the labour market in liberal-democratic societies ought to be the principle of freedom of association. In the labour context, this principle has three components: liberty of association, right of association, and effective means of association. These components are not as deeply rooted in some liberal-democratic societies as in others, but they gained widespread acceptance in Canada through the hard-fought struggles of workers in the nineteenth and twentieth centuries. In Canada, the *Trade Union Act* of 1872 firmly entrenched the liberty of workers to associate in order to improve the terms and conditions of their work.[1] This meant that workers could not be prosecuted for combining to improve their conditions. Provincial statutes first established in the 1930s a right to associate, stipulating that employers and the state were prohibited from interfering with, or retaliating against, workers who chose to associate. This right was considered to be of such fundamental importance that it was protected by an amendment to the *Criminal Code* in 1939 (Fudge and Tucker 2001). These rights and freedoms were institutionalized as cornerstones of private sector post–World War II labour relations regimes through the creation of administrative mechanisms for their enforcement. As well, post-war labour relations laws provided an effective means of establishing collective representation and bargaining by workers by requiring that employers recognize and bargain with trade unions that had obtained the support of a majority of workers in a constituency known as the "bargaining unit." This third component of the principle of freedom of association was extended to workers in the public sector in the early 1960s. Since then, public policy across Canada and Quebec has continued to endorse the three components of the freedom of association in its collective bargaining legislation, notwithstanding the growing predominance of neo-liberal ideology.

The principles of freedom of association are not just a matter of ordinary domestic law. The liberty and rights dimensions of this fundamental principle have long been part of international law and more recently were entrenched in Canadian constitutional law. The International Labour Organization (ILO) passed Convention 87, *Freedom of Association and Protection of the Right to Organize*, in 1948, and Canada ratified it in 1972. Article 2 stipulates: "Workers and employers, *without distinction whatsoever*, shall have the right to establish and, subject only to the rules of the organisation concerned, to join organisations of their own choosing without previous authorization."[2] In 1993, Canada entered into the North American Agreement on Labour Cooperation

(NAALC), pursuant to which it committed itself to promote eleven labour principles. The first is "freedom of association and protection of the right to organize."[3]

Canada also constitutionally entrenched freedom of association in article 2(d) of the *Charter of Rights and Freedoms*.[4] In a recent Supreme Court of Canada decision interpreting the meaning of freedom of association in the labour context, Mr Justice Lebel stated: "The guarantee of freedom of association stands in a special place within the Canadian Constitution ... The affirmation by the Canadian Constitution of a right of association confirms the importance ascribed to the societal phenomenon of association within Canadian society."[5] In another recent decision, the Supreme Court of Canada recognized that in some circumstances, the charter's guarantee of freedom of association required the state to take affirmative steps to protect vulnerable workers who attempted to exercise their freedom from retaliation by employers and to give the workers an opportunity to make collective representations to their employers.[6] But like all rights and freedoms, freedom of association is not absolute. It must be balanced against other fundamental rights and the public interest. However, given its importance in liberal democracies, the burden of justifying limits on it ought to lie, as it does in Canadian constitutional law, on those who wish to impose the limits.

Within labour relations law, policy, and practice, there have been two major justifications offered for denying workers access to collective bargaining legislation: conflict of interest and competition policy. The conflict of interest justification is the basis for the exclusion of management personnel and those employed in a confidential labour relations capacity from collective bargaining legislation. Prevailing public policy in Canada considers that the potential conflicts that collective bargaining might create for managers who owe their employers loyalty are of sufficient importance to override these workers' freedom of association. Still, competition concerns form the basis for the exclusion of certain classes of professionals – including doctors, lawyers, and dentists – from such legislation. These workers are considered to be more like entrepreneurs than employees, and in some jurisdictions, Ontario for example, they are simply deemed by statute not to be employees for the purposes of collective bargaining legislation.

The scope of these exclusions, however, is often controversial. For example, the managerial exclusion is problematic because of doubts about the salience of the conflict of interest rationale in a mature system of collective bargaining and because the implementation of less hierarchical management structures makes it unclear who is caught by the exclusion.[7] As well, the anti-competition rationale for professionals has in part succumbed to political pressure, most notably for doctors who have access to alternative forms of collective representation and bargaining, often accompanied by a commitment to submit disputes to binding arbitration.[8]

The contested nature of the principles for limiting workers' freedom of association suggests that the wholesale exclusion of self-employed workers from effective mechanisms of collective bargaining should also be open to challenge and reexamination, even given the assumptions and operating principles that inform the current collective bargaining regime. Does either of these principles justify the exclusion of self-employed workers as a group from laws, institutions, and policies designed to support collective bargaining? Clearly, the conflict of interest principle does not justify the exclusion of all self-employed workers from access to collective bargaining mechanisms. Any self-employed workers who exercise managerial functions or who are employed in a confidential labour relations capacity would be covered by the existing specific exclusions.

The question of whether the wholesale exclusion of self-employed workers is justified on competition grounds is more difficult. Like freedom of association, free competition is of relatively recent vintage, and it has always been subject to significant exceptions. With the rise of neo-liberal orthodoxy, the trend has been towards greater dependence on competitive markets, less scope for workers' collective action, and a reduction in government regulation. Despite this trend, unlike freedom of association, free competition is not entrenched in the Canadian Constitution, although international competition is certainly protected through free trade agreements (Schneiderman 1996). Historically, regulated labour and product markets were the norm until the early nineteenth century, and it was not until the last decade of that century that the House of Lords established the modern common law on restraint of trade (Crysler 1967; Hay and Rogers 1997). But even then the principle of free competition was never absolute. Anti-combines legislation only applied to arrangements that unduly lessened or prevented competition,[9] and so it was always open to argument that some forms of combination or limitations on competition were legally justified because they were in the public interest. Apart from making administrative and judicial decisions interpreting the extent of the prohibition on collective action, governments also made political judgments regarding the public interest in restricting competition. One prominent reason for allowing collective action was to encourage the construction of a countervailing power to redress situations marked by unequal power relations between private actors (Arthurs 1965). This is the basis for exempting "combinations or activities of workmen or employees for their own reasonable protection as workmen or employees" from the application of the *Competition Act* and for the promotion of collective bargaining.[10]

Against this background, we can begin to address the question of whether self-employed workers should be subject to the regime of competition or to a regime of collective representation and bargaining. As we argued in the introduction, and as the case studies illustrate, it is simply not tenable as a general rule to equate self-employment with entrepreneurship. A large portion of the self-employed are in very precarious economic situations, receiving low remuneration and enjoying little in the way of employment security or employment-related benefits. This is certainly true of the self-employed workers featured in the case studies. *Toronto Star* carriers own little business capital beyond a car, exercise little control over distribution beyond deciding the order in which they will deliver their newspapers, and do not accumulate capital. Their contracts provide little security, and the work is not well paid. They are disproportionately drawn from new immigrant populations and racialized groups. Rural route mail couriers are in a similar situation, although they work in a predominantly rural labour market and the majority of them are women. Personal-care workers can hardly be said to conform to the image of the self-employed entrepreneur in business for herself. Besides, perhaps, a car, they do not own any significant productive assets. The work is low-paid and insecure, its intermittent nature results in part-time and split-shift schedules, and it is mostly performed by immigrant women from racialized groups. Finally, freelance editors own little by way of business assets besides a computer; and although they are not directly supervised, they exercise little real control over their work activity and have almost no capacity to expand their business. The work is sporadic, and their annual incomes are generally low.

The case studies in this book, along with studies of other groups of self-employed workers (Clement 1986; Rainbird 1991), indicate that it is inappropriate to treat all self-employed contractors like entrepreneurs. If the quantitative data discussed in the introduction and the qualitative studies detailed in the preceding chapters are correct, then the situation of self-employed workers resembles that of employees more closely than that of entrepreneurs. For this reason, they should not be subjected to a regime of competition. Thus, a sweeping exclusion of independent contractors from a statutory scheme of collective representation and bargaining based on competition concerns is unwarranted.

The case studies also reveal the inequality that pervades relations between self-employed workers and the persons and entities with whom they contract, and thus the public interest in promoting opportunities for the construction of countervailing power should override competition concerns. Particular groups of self-employed workers who would be unduly advantaged by their ability to reduce competition could be specifically excluded; public policy and labour legislation already deals with such concerns. Not only is this position consistent with that of the Freedom of Association Committee of the ILO governing body, which recently affirmed that self-employed workers should enjoy the right to organize and that the existence of an employment contract should not determine whether a person has access to this right,[11] but it is also consistent with the legislative approach adopted by Manitoba and Saskatchewan.[12]

2. LIMITATIONS IN THE PREVAILING COLLECTIVE BARGAINING MODEL

It is one thing to establish the principle that a group of workers ought to be covered by a statutory collective bargaining scheme; it is quite another to design one that will both meet the group's needs and protect legitimate public concerns in relation to collective action. The case studies in this book demonstrate that the dominant collective bargaining regime in Canada simply does not work for many groups of self-employed workers. In particular, the studies point to four related problem areas that have prevented these workers from accessing the general collective bargaining regime: getting in, staying in, bargaining structure, and dispute resolution.

A. Getting In

Workers seeking to get into the collective bargaining regime must overcome several hurdles. These include establishing employee status; organizing a majority of employees in an administratively defined bargaining unit; coming to terms with employer property and contract rights that limit where, when, and how organizing activities occur; and dealing with the fact that remedies for unfair labour practices are limited. While all workers face these hurdles, they are particularly difficult – although not necessarily insurmountable – for self-employed workers seeking to establish collective bargaining relationships.

In its drive to organize the *Star* carriers, the Communications, Energy and Paperworkers Union of Canada (CEP) was able to overcome the isolation often associated with self-employment because the distribution system required workers to gather at distribution points, where they were often forced to wait because of production delays. CEP was also able to convince the Labour Relations Board that the carriers were dependent contractors eligible to participate in the collective bargaining scheme. However, the lengthy process, which was riddled with administrative delays, enabled the *Star* to contract out the carriers' work. The delays also posed a serious challenge to the union's ability to keep the carriers organized while the certification application was in limbo.

Because it knew that the legal status of the rural route couriers was in dispute, the Canadian Union of Postal Workers (CUPW) anticipated a very long and expensive campaign to organize these workers. For several years, CUPW supported an independent organization for the couriers before it mounted a traditional membership sign-up campaign. The requirement that a union obtain the membership of a majority of the workers in a bargaining unit within a six-month period imposed enormous costs in this case, since the workers were dispersed across the country. Few unions have the resources to organize workers who are geographically dispersed.

The personal-care workers employed by a non-profit agency successfully organized under the auspices of the Canadian Auto Workers union (CAW). Their success was due, in part, to the strong worker networks that exist between workplaces in the sector. Most personal attendants work for multiple agencies, and the resulting networks helped recently unionized workers to organize at their second job or in other workplaces in the sector. The success of this strategy depends on a centralized model of service delivery, yet such a model is not necessarily optimal from the perspective of clients or workers. At the same time, workers under the new direct funding model will have difficulties establishing employee status.

Finally, collective representation and bargaining for freelance editors did not depend on establishing employment status. The editors never claimed that they were employees. Instead, their ability to bargain collectively depended on their being categorized as independent professional artists covered by special federation legislation. Their narrow victory not only demonstrates the possibility of designing an alternative approach to "getting in" that does not depend on employee status or even on obtaining majority support from a dispersed group of workers, but it also reveals the problems that arise when collective bargaining is extended to self-employed workers on a piecemeal basis.

B. Staying In

It is one thing for workers to organize and gain representation rights; it is another for them to establish and sustain collective bargaining relationships over time. Despite the constant churning of businesses that is characteristic of liberal market (capitalist) economies – especially during periods when competition is intense and the number of small and medium-sized enterprises is growing – employers and governments are actively restructuring to reduce costs and gain greater control over the production process. Since unions are often viewed as obstacles to the success of such measures, employers are becoming more aggressive in resisting unions in the first place and in ridding themselves of unions once they have become established.

Workers who are marginal to the core business of their employers – which almost always includes the precarious self-employed – are particularly vulnerable. The *Star*'s decision to contract out home delivery after the CEP gained majority support from its carriers is the most egregious example of this phenomenon that we encountered in the case studies. However, each of these groups of workers is vulnerable to restructuring and contracting out. The employment status of personal-care workers (and hence their ability to remain within the collective bargaining regime) is insecure because of several challenges. These are based on the site of their employment (that is, private homes), ongoing debate over whether the work is controlled by the agency or the client, and efforts by the Ontario government to alter funding arrangements in a way that would make the client the direct employer. Postal workers also face insecurity due to Canada Post's strategy of contracting out parts of its operations. And many freelance editors are self-employed because publishers contract out editing work rather than give it to in-house staff (Stanworth and Stanworth 1995).[13] Despite this transformation in their employment status, these workers were still able to engage in collective bargaining, since the *Status of the Artist Act* does not require them to be employees. Thus, the freelance editors' case illustrates how collective bargaining systems not based on employee status may mitigate the negative impacts of subcontracting on workers. This is an important lesson in light of the general trend towards the restructuring of business enterprises from vertical integration to corporate networks.

C. Bargaining Structure

Collective bargaining in Canada is characterized by its decentralized nature and by exclusive bargaining agency. The standard bargaining unit consists of the employees of a single employer at a particular work site who share a community of interest. This narrow conception of workers' common interests produces a preponderance of small bargaining units with limited bargaining leverage and high servicing costs (Forrest 1986; Fudge 1993; MacDonald 1998). Moreover, to win the right to bargain, a union must gain majority support from the workers deemed to be an appropriate bargaining unit. While these structural features of Canadian collective bargaining law affect all workers, they pose a particular challenge for many self-employed workers whose work arrangements, as we discussed earlier, are often geographically diffuse, who are at high risk of having their work contracted out, and who often work for several employers. Freelance editors escaped some of these structural limitations because they were able to access the *Status of the Artist Act*, but because the act does not require producers to form associations, collective bargaining can be time-consuming and expensive. The overwhelming majority of self-employed workers are not even this lucky.

The *Star* carriers, for example, were placed in a separate bargaining unit from other unionized employees because of their dependent contractor status and because of the customary division of the newspaper industry labour market between editorial, production, and distribution workers. This structure allowed the *Star* to contract out distribution with less disruption to its relations with core production and editorial workers. As well, the absence of a broader-based bargaining structure made contracting out financially attractive, since a new employer would not be bound by the collective bargaining agreement and could rehire the carriers on individual contracts at terms less favourable than those offered by the *Star*. The role of bargaining unit structure in the organization of the rural route mail couriers is rather more complex, reflecting the unique circumstances of Canada Post and the problem that exclusive representation causes when rival unions vie for the same group of workers.

Personal-care workers faced the fewest obstacles in establishing bargaining units. They also made significant gains by, for example, bringing part-time and full-time workers together in one bargaining unit, challenging the classic tendency to organize units based on the single work site, and defying norms about appropriate vehicles for organizing. Once they had argued successfully that the non-profit agency matching workers with people with disabilities was their employer and that the living spaces of people with disabilities were the work sites of personal-care workers, establishing the right to bargain was relatively straightforward. These workers organized themselves into units on the basis of combining independent living facilities containing multiple living units and outreach personal-care work coordinated by an agency. Although they amalgamate the work sites of a single employer, the largest work sites in this sector have between fifteen and twenty employees, and the smallest has only one. Moreover, there are multiple employers in this sector. Multi-employer bargaining would significantly increase the bargaining power of personal-care workers, but there is no prospect of this. Indeed, any changes that occur are likely to be of the opposite nature. Direct funding threatens to undermine the ability of personal-care workers to organize and bargain collectively.

D. Dispute Resolution

The traditional mechanism for resolving collective bargaining disputes in Canada – industrial action such as strikes and lockouts – is not particularly appropriate for the groups of workers we have studied here. When workers can inflict significant economic harm on their employers by withdrawing their labour power together, then the strike can be a potent weapon. But most workers, most of the time, are not in a position to take such action; neither are self employed workers, especially given how bargaining units are structured. Achieving first collective agreements has proven particularly difficult for unions, and for this reason some jurisdictions have made first-contract arbitration available in at least some circumstances.

The cases of personal-care workers, *Star* carriers, and rural route mail couriers illustrate the problems with using the strike as the primary mechanism for resolving disputes. Even though personal-care workers are not essential workers and are legally entitled to strike, is it not a useful form of dispute resolution for them, since people with disabilities depend on them, and strike action often yields fierce opposition from the general public. As a result, Local 40 modified its tactics of dispute resolution. To minimize conflicts between personal-care workers and the people they serve, Local 40 emphasized the links between the precarious economic situation of workers and deteriorating personal-care services; it also made proposals for the redistribution of public funds to allow workers a greater proportion of those funds relative to management. These tactics stretched the industrial model and made the strike instrument somewhat less blunt, although many people with disabilities still oppose the strike tactic. The case of personal-care workers employed by non-profit agencies highlights the limits of the legal forms of dispute resolution associated with industrial unionism. There is a pressing need for forms wherein clients, personal-care workers, and their unions negotiate together with the funding body, which has been absent from the negotiating table.

The *Star* carriers' case provides another example, in a very different context, of the need for alternative forms of dispute resolution. By the time the Labour Board finally determined that these workers were dependent contractors, the carriers had limited bargaining leverage because during the long delay, solidarity within the bargaining unit had deteriorated, and, more importantly, the *Star* had made arrangements to contract out the work. In these circumstances, the carriers' strike had a limited effect, and they were left with few options except to negotiate a severance package with the *Star*. First-contract arbitration was simply not an option for them because the Conservative government had narrowed access to this dispute resolution mechanism in the mid-1990s.[14]

Rural route mail carriers faced somewhat different problems with respect to dispute resolution, because, as independent contractors, they are barred from using typical dispute resolution mechanisms. Instead, they adopted innovative tactics to pressure the federal government to provide them with access to collective bargaining, including a complaint under the labour-side agreement attached to the North American Free Trade Agreement. However, in the end, it was CUPW's traditional economic power that enabled it to obtain voluntary recognition as the couriers' representative and employment status for these workers.

Although our case study of freelance editors does not reach the point of dispute resolution, it is notable that Quebec's legislation not only requires producers to form associations, but it also mandates first-contract arbitration one year after an artists' association serves notice of its intent to bargain with a producer. In contrast, the framework for the negotiation of scale agreements in the federal *Status of the Artist Act* neither compels producers to form associations nor provides for first-contract arbitration. Relatively few producers' associations have formed to date, making it challenging for groups like the Editors' Association of Canada to negotiate scale agreements applicable to workers in their sector, since they must serve notice to bargain and negotiate with producers individually. These structural impediments affect artists' capacity to secure scale agreements and resolve disputes.

3. REALIZING FREEDOM OF ASSOCIATION AND COLLECTIVE BARGAINING FOR SELF-EMPLOYED WORKERS: PRINCIPLES AND POLICIES

A. Principles for Legal and Institutional Reform: Parity and Plurality of Representational Forms

To end this book, we want to draw upon our discussion of the justification for providing self-employed workers with access to effective mechanisms for collective representation and bargaining. We also want to look at what the case studies have taught us about the limitations in the prevailing collective bargaining model in order to suggest principles that should inform public policy and to sketch a range of different institutional mechanisms that conform to these principles. Our starting point, which is obvious from the case studies, is the fact that self-employed workers want to organize in order to improve the terms and conditions of their work. We have argued that there is no principled reason within a liberal-democratic society to deny all self-employed workers the freedom to associate and bargain collectively. The statistical data about self-employed workers in Canada demonstrate that only a minority of the self-employed – mostly self-employed employers – could realistically be classified as entrepreneurs who control the risks of the production process or accumulate capital. The majority of the self-employed are subject to the same risks as employees. Similarly, the case studies demonstrate the erroneous equation of self-employment with entrepreneurship and how some self-employed are more like workers than entrepreneurs. Thus, we endorse the position of the ILO that all workers, regardless of their specific employment status, are entitled to fundamental rights and freedoms at work, including the freedom of association (Benjamin 2002; Hepple 1995; Sen 2000). We call this principle of equal treatment the parity principle, and it entails allowing self-employed workers the same rights and freedoms as employees.

In applying this principle, however, we should not ignore differences in social location and economic condition either between the self-employed and employees or among the self-employed. The case studies show that self-employed workers cannot gain effective access to collective bargaining simply by ensuring that the definition of *employee* in labour relations statutes is expanded to include them. Instead, it is necessary to provide legislative support for alternative institutional arrangements to accommodate a diversity of employment situations and the changing boundaries of employment. We call this the principle of plurality of representational forms. These situations range from that of the self-employed – such as freelance editors, fishers, and trucker drivers, who are not dependent upon a particular employer but who nevertheless require collective bargaining to mitigate their precarious economic status – to that of the so-called independent contractors – such as newspaper carriers and route salespeople who work for contractors who provide a retail sales network for large cable and telecommunications firms. The range also includes the situation of employees – such as personal-care providers, who are employed by small agencies and are rarely permitted to bargain directly with the government that provides the funds, and rural route mail couriers and domestic and farm workers, who are simply excluded from collective bargaining legislation. Thus, the parity principle must be supplemented by a principled commitment to a plurality of representational forms.

The latter principle addresses the fact that the law must support a variety of collective representation and bargaining schemes because no single mechanism can possibly respond to the diverse needs of the self-employed. Currently, most workers have no legally supported options aside from traditional statutory collective bargaining schemes, yet it is clear that legal and institutional diversity is neither impossible nor impractical. Although often quite limited in scope, a number of alternative mechanisms already exist. In this book, we encountered the federal *Status of the Artist Act*, which provides for collective representation without majority support and for multi-employer bargaining. Other groups have also had specialized schemes created for them. For example, construction industry provisions in collective bargaining statutes require multi-employer bargaining in some sectors, and in Quebec, union membership is mandatory. Another example is collective agreement extension statutes allowing the terms of an agreement to be extended across an industry in a particular geographic region (Minsky 2001; Valée and Charest 2001). Finally, doctors in Ontario are subject to a statutory collective bargaining scheme cobbled together from several pieces of legislation; it makes the Ontario Medical Association (OMA) the exclusive bargaining agent for doctors in the province, compels doctors to pay dues to the OMA, and imposes a duty to bargain on the Ministry of Health.[15] In short, when the political will is present, legislators have shown themselves to be remarkably adept at creating a diversity of schemes to facilitate collective action by groups that are either excluded from conventional labour laws or do not fit the mould for which those dominant schemes were designed.

The achievement of the principles of parity and plurality in freedom of association would require at least three related changes from existing collective bargaining laws. First, workers themselves must be entitled to determine with whom they will associate. Under the prevailing collective bargaining legislation, it is up to the labour tribunal – which considers the wishes of the workers as only one factor – to determine which workers can join together in a bargaining unit. Workers, not tribunals, should have the right, subject only to restrictions that are supported by compelling public policies (such as prohibitions against discrimination), to determine their own community of interest and to identify those with whom they will associate for the purpose of collective bargaining. Second, a union or workers' association must not be required to command majority support from an administratively defined bargaining unit in order to win the right to represent and bargain on behalf of its members. The principles of majority support and exclusive representation that are currently embedded in Canadian collective bargaining law and policy need to give way to accommodate a more expansive model of freedom of association that will better meet the needs of self-employed workers. And third, any reforms must include bargaining structures that will facilitate meaningful collective bargaining for self-employed workers. It is no longer possible to maintain a regime that, with few exceptions, only requires bargaining to take place between a single employer and a group of its employees. A significant number of self-employed persons have contractual relations with several employers, and the current model of collective bargaining does not work for them. Moreover, employers can simply contract out work to other entities and thereby rid themselves of both unions and collective agreements. Thus, it is important to develop mechanisms that allow for the negotiation of multi-employer or industry-wide agreements.

Such mechanisms have been devised and implemented at various times and places for particular groups of workers. It is time to look at these other models to see if they can be revised and expanded to meet the needs of the wide range of self-employed workers.

B. Laws, Policies, and Institutions: Organizations of Self-Employed Workers and Collective Bargaining Models

Two ideas – labour market unionism and community unionism – have been identified as the core collective bargaining innovations responsive to today's labour market (Fine 1998). Labour market unionism addresses the need to move beyond the traditional industrial model of workplace organizing and bargaining. Community unionism addresses the need to expand the narrow focus of business unionism beyond traditional topics of bargaining, such as terms and conditions of employment, to include matters relating to service and standards. As well, it expands the group of those who have the right to participate in collective bargaining beyond employees and employers to include clients and consumers and other relevant constituencies (Cranford and Ladd 2003; Fudge 1994; Tufts 1998). It also draws our attention to transitional union structures that can help to define future models of collective representation (Middleton 1996; Vosko 2000; Wial 1993). In this section, we assess the relevance of labour market and community unionism for the workers profiled in this book in order to suggest options for reform. These models are suitable for a very wide variety of self-employed workers, and they comprise a broad range of mechanisms for achieving collective bargaining. We do not present the models as a comprehensive list of all possible reform options; rather, our goal is to use them to illustrate the diversity of institutions, laws, and policies that conform to the principles of freedom of association, parity, and pluralism in representational forms and to stimulate further thinking on how to meet the challenge of institutional redesign.

As a starting point, facilitating labour market unionism among the groups of workers that are the subjects of this book requires that collective bargaining institutions, laws, and policies be available to self-employed workers. It is thus first necessary to address the key justification for denying collective bargaining rights to self-employed contractors: anti-competitive behaviour. The case of the freelance editors illustrates that a collective bargaining regime can be developed for independent contractors who contract with multiple employers that deals with concerns about anti-competitive behaviour. Two key measures of the *Status of the Artist Act* serve as checks on anti-competitive practices: the treatment of certifications as renewable fixed-term licenses, and the introduction of scale agreements. Renewable licenses allow for a review to ensure that unacceptable anti-competitive practices have not become institutionalized, while scale agreements only set minimum terms and conditions while permitting individuals to negotiate higher rates.

The next step is to design legislation that lets self-employed workers who are mobile across work sites and who have multiple employers or contracts bargain collectively. Craft and sectoral-based models – such as those developed for some parts of the construction industry (MacDonald 1998),[16] and for artists and performers (Fudge and Vosko 2001b; Langille and Davidov 1999; MacPherson 1999) – merit consideration for self-employed workers who lack a single work site and who work for multiple clients, or who are employed in segments of the labour market dominated by small business, which presents a challenge and disincentive to union organizing.

In Canada, there are several legislative models that allow for regional multi-employer agreements to limit competition in a given sector, defined geographically and/or by industry. One is the craft model of collective bargaining, which allows workers to organize by trade or occupation rather than workplace, enterprise, or industry.[17] Unlike industrial unionism, craft unionism is based on employment security in a labour market rather than job security with a given employer. Craft unions seek to provide their members with employment security by controlling the supply of labour and establishing a monopoly over skills (Cobble 1991; Fine 1998). Craft unionism was the dominant form of unionism in North America before the emergence of mass production. Historically, it took the form of territorial organizing in metropolitan labour markets (Fine 1998; Gordon 1999). Today, it operates primarily among skilled construction trades and related occupations at the sectoral and (often) provincial levels (MacDonald 1998).

The craft model may well hold potential for the newspaper carriers outsourced by the *Star* and the personal-care workers employed under the contract model of a government-funded agency, as well as other workers, because when it is broad-based it takes into consideration subcontracting relationships in highly competitive industries (Gordon 1999, 565).[18] Contemporary legislation in provinces such as Ontario, Quebec, and British Columbia allow for a broader-based craft model in the construction industry (MacDonald 1998). In Ontario, for example, legislation permits province-wide certification in the industrial, commercial, and institutional sectors of the construction industry. The minister of labour designates employer and employee bargaining agencies vested with exclusive authority to negotiate a province-wide agreement for each trade or craft. Outside of those sectors, unions are certified on a geographic basis and negotiate individual collective agreements with each employer. There is, however, a provision for accreditation of an employers' organization as the exclusive bargaining agent for all employers in that geographic region, and any collective agreement that is negotiated would be binding for all existing and future employers. In these circumstances, individual collective agreements are invalid (Minsky 2001).[19] The construction unions are able to unionize within this situation not only because of the legislation but also because of their economic power, which results from their monopoly over their skills and high union density in the industry – two conditions that are not present among newspaper carriers or personal-care workers. To be meaningful for self-employed workers, this model would have to include legislation that deems functionally dependent subcontractors as related employers of the entities upon which they are dependent (for example, garment retailers, newspaper corporations, and governments).[20]

The focus on employment security characteristic of craft unionism rather than job security with a single employer provides insights for developing a model of representation suitable to personal-care workers. Dorothy Sue Cobble uses the broader term "occupational unionism" to emphasize that key elements of the craft union model were also used by groups such as waitresses, food servers, agricultural workers, janitors, and longshoremen in order to provide security for their casual and mobile members (1991, 420–1). Occupational unionism as practised by these groups was characterized by an emphasis on occupational identity; control over the labour supply in the occupation; rights and benefits through occupational membership rather than work site affiliation; and peer control over occupational performance standards. Like craft unionism, occupational unionism is based on organizing and bargaining across a metropolitan labour market. The emphasis on occupational identity and peer control over performance standards is particularly relevant for personal-care workers. Occupational unionism is capable of incorporating the value that most health-care and social services workers place on care work (Armstrong 1993). Moreover, government outsourcing of the provision of services and the move towards individualized funding programs make it essential to delink security, rights, and benefits from a particular job or client/consumer, as occupational unionism does. However, exclusive union and worker control over hiring based on seniority in the occupation does not fit well with personal-care work; the intimate nature of this work indicates that clients/consumers should have control over who provides the services.

Another way of overcoming the problem of multiple employers or the threat of contracting out is geographical unionism. Bargaining between employers and workers in related occupations and sectors would allow unions to establish uniform wages and benefits in a given geographical area. Geography has been key to unions' organizational strategies historically, and attention to geography remains essential with the globalization of production (Gordon 1999; Herod 1998; Wilton and Cranford 2002). However, general geographical unionism – organizing along a completely horizontal basis without regard to occupation or industry – would be difficult to institutionalize. Workers today, such as janitors in the United States, have been able to raise wages and standards in urban labour markets by combining geographical unionism and occupational unionism, but they have not been able to secure these protections in legislation (Cranford 2001; Wial 1993).

In Canada, several models either exist or have been proposed that allow for regional multi-employer agreements to limit competition in a given sector defined by a combination of geographical area and similar enterprises within that area. One model proposed in British Columbia would have permitted unions at small enterprises, such as fast-food outlets in a specific territory, to combine their bargaining units and bargain jointly with their employers. The proposal called for legislation that would oblige multiple employers to bargain together with the certified union representing their employees; however, additional workplaces would not be added to the collective agreement unless majority support at those workplaces was demonstrated (MacDonald 1998).[21] This requirement of majority employee support before new workplaces are covered by the sectoral collective agreement would limit the applicability of this model to the many self-employed workers who move between workplaces in a given sector where it is nearly impossible to organize a union based on a majority vote (Fudge and Vosko 2001b, 343).

Another, broader-based bargaining model is the Quebec decree system. Based on the European model of juridical extension of labour relations and standards, the decree legislation allows for the extension of the terms of a collective agreement across a sector to cover both unionized and non-unionized workers. The decree system is an important model to examine because it does not require a demonstration of majority support in order to win bargaining rights before negotiations take place. However, the decrees do not regulate a system of representation for workers.[22] Nor do they provide a structure for democratic accountability. As well, the discourse of international competitiveness has been used to justify statutory changes, resulting in a decline in the number of decrees (Valée and Charest 2001). The decree system once covered several highly competitive industries made up of small workplaces, such as the garment and furniture industries, but it now covers only a small percentage of Quebec workers (Grant 2004).

These forms of labour market unionism demonstrate the need to address, once again, labour supply issues. Indeed, the *Status of the Artist Act*, by giving freelance editors, as self-employed contractors, the ability to bargain collectively, essentially transformed the Editors' Association of Canada into a union. The focus on the supply of labour, characteristic of craft and occupational unionism, should be key to new models of representation, yet the case of personal-care workers illustrates that in occupations that provide social services to human beings, new models must also incorporate the voice and participation of clients/consumers as well as workers (Boileau 2002; Corriveau 2002).

Community unionism can also be an important vehicle for advancing the interests of self-employed workers, because it focuses on organizing workers who may not be able to participate in statutory collective bargaining schemes and on linking workers' struggles with those of other groups to pursue common concerns. As well, it can allow for building networks of social and political solidarity, which are vital for successfully mobilizing around working-class issues. For example, the achievement of any of the reforms discussed earlier requires legislation. But such legislation will only be enacted through campaigns that publicize the unequal bargaining power of workers and employers and disclose the limits of the dominant regime. This strategy was pursued by CUPW in its drive to organize the rural route mail couriers. Because the couriers were deprived of employee status, CUPW focused on developing the couriers' self-organizing capacities and embarrassing the Canadian government internationally. The union adopted a political strategy of uniting workers around issues of unfairness and social injustice, a common strategy among public sector and other social service workers (Armstrong 1993), as well as artists and other professionals.

As the case studies illustrate, workers' associations have the capacity to facilitate mutual assistance among workers and engage their members in a politics of collective struggle that can provide the basis for forming a union and establishing collective bargaining. However, this need not be their goal. Indeed, in many instances, workers' associations are defined as being distinct from unions precisely because they seek to raise standards in an occupation or sector without recourse to collective bargaining or charging dues.[23] Some workers' associations do not engage in collective bargaining because they are geared more towards professionalization than unionism, which they regard as too conflictual (Heckscher 1988). By contrast, other such associations aspire to be unions but are either unable to achieve collective bargaining under the current legislation or reject the structural limitations of collective bargaining laws and policies and the attendant practices of traditional unions. Workers' associations illustrate the need for collective representation that transcends the employment relationship in order to bring income and employment security to mobile workers with multiple employers (Middleton 1996; Vosko 2000; Wial 1993).

To be successful, however, community unionism must not only obtain community support for workplace issues but also bring community concerns into the workplace. In California, for example, legislation enacted in 1999 requires counties to set up "public authorities" that combine multiple employers into one employer of record. This entity bargains with the union, trains home-care workers, provides a registry to match workers with clients and consumers, and maintains state and federal funding (Delp and Quan 2002, 9); it must have a majority of consumer representatives on its advisory board. In exchange, the union must agree not to use the strike as a method of dispute resolution, and, significantly, the union contract must give consumers the right to hire and fire workers with or without just cause. Recognizing the possibility for conflicts between workers who feel they are unjustly terminated and clients/consumers who want to terminate workers for whatever reason, the union registry allows the workers to be placed with other clients/consumers (Delp and Quan 2002, 13).

One way to expand the employment security of workers and still allow for client/consumer discretion in hiring and firing would be to expand the scope of certification and bargaining beyond personal care to related fields and activities. A federated structure that combined elements of craft and industrial unionism once existed in North America. Craft unions in related fields, such as food and hotel services, came together to bargain collectively but retained their autonomy in other areas, such as the running of hiring halls, seniority rules, and training and apprenticeships (Vosko 2000; Wial 1993). The reintroduction of this sort of system would allow personal-care workers to take the particularities of care work into consideration regarding hiring and firing decisions while increasing the number of occupations within which they could be placed. This model would also allow for the fact that some workers do not see their work as a profession or trade and thus may move frequently between occupations.

Perhaps community unionism will become the political face of labour market unionism (Fine 1998). A different, more political orientation in the labour movement is required if self-employed workers are ever to enjoy freedom of association and collective bargaining. The case studies in this book demonstrate that self-employed workers have adopted a range of strategies and organizational forms in order to obtain greater power to bargain the terms and conditions of their employment. The studies also illustrate the need to provide institutional and legal support for these forms of collective representation and bargaining. The open question is whether self-employed workers will be able to develop the alliances within the labour movement, community organizations, and other social movements that can give them the political strength to access policies and laws that support instead of undermine their right to associate freely, thereby improving their living standards and working lives.

Notes

INTRODUCTION

1 For a discussion of the value of case studies as a research method, see Gomm, Hammersley, and Foster (2000); Mitchell (1983); Scholz and Tietje (2002); Travers (2001); Yin (1994).
2 Organization for Economic Co-operation and Development, "Partial Renaissance of Self-Employment," OECD *Employment Outlook*, 2000 [OECD].
3 Ibid. at p. 187.
4 While classical sociologists identify three classes, contemporary sociologists have developed more sophisticated maps of social relations. See Baxter and Western (2001); Clement and Myles (1994); Grusky (2001); Wright (1997).
5 International Labour Organization, International Labour Office, "Income Security and Social Protection in a Changing World," *World Labour Report*, 2000 [ILO 1]; International Labour Organization, International Labour Office, "Meeting of Experts on Workers in Situations Needing Protection," *Employment Relationship: Scope, Basic Technical Document*, 2000 [ILO 2]; OECD, supra note 2.
6 International Labour Organization, "Resolution Concerning the Promotion of Self-Employment," International Labour Conference, 77th session, *Provisional Report* 34, 1990 [ILO].
7 OECD, supra note 2.
8 Ibid.; ILO, supra note 6.

9 Organization for Economic Co-operation and Development, "Recent Developments in Self-Employment," OECD *Employment Outlook*, 1992, p. 155.
10 About 35 per cent of business owners had employees in 2000, down from 45 per cent in 1989. See Statistics Canada, *Labour Force Historical Review*, CD-ROM, 2001; Statistics Canada, Labour Force Survey, public use microdata custom tabulation [Labour Force Survey]; Satistics Canada, Survey of Self-Employment, public use microdata 2002 custom tabulation; Delage (2002). Data do not include unpaid family workers.
11 Labour Force Survey, supra note 10.
12 Statistics Canada, Survey of Labour and Income Dynamics, public use microdata, special run, 1999, 2000 [SLID].
13 Ibid.
14 Ibid.
15 Obtained from Statistics Canada, the data in this paragraph refer to net income. Income is defined as wages and salaries + CPP/QPP benefits + EI benefits + workers' compensation benefits + retirement pensions + other income + investment income + old-age security and GIS/SA + social assistance + child tax benefits + GIS/SA credit + provincial/territorial tax credits. Data on earnings are not available for the self-employed. Statisticians routinely argue that for the self-employed, income is a better indicator of economic status than earnings, since they derive a range of benefits from their employment status invisible in earnings data (SLID, supra note 12).
16 SLID, supra note 12.
17 These findings support a recent report by Graham Lowe and Grant Schellenberg, which found that 41 per cent of the self-employed (51 per cent in the own-account category) had fewer than five clients in 2000 (2001, table 4.2).
18 *Competition Act*, RSC 1985, c. C-34 (as amended), s. 4(1)(a).
19 Courts can review tribunal decisions, but in recent years they have adopted a deferential stance (Charney and Brady 1997, ch. 5).
20 *Re Lunenburg Sea Products*, [1947] 3 DLR 195 (NSCA).
21 British Columbia *Labour Relations Code*, RSBC 1996, c. 244, s. 1(1); Ontario *Labour Relations Act*, SO 1995, c. 1, Sched. A, s. 1(1) [OLRA].
22 *Canada Labour Code*, RSC 1985, c. L-2, s. 3(1).
23 Despite the similarity in the statutory definitions in the British Columbia and Ontario legislation, the approaches initially taken by the labour tribunals in the two jurisdictions were quite different; British Columbia's was much broader. Now their approaches are quite similar (Adams 1995, 6–4).

24 For example, in CLC, *Local 1689 v. Algonquin Tavern*, [1981] OLRB Rep. 1057, the Ontario Labour Relations Board listed eleven factors, including evidence of entrepreneurial activity and economic mobility, to be considered.
25 Manitoba and Saskatchewan have opted for this solution. The statutes in both jurisdictions state that the concept of "employee" is not relevant to determining the scope of collective bargaining legislation and that the important question is whether collective bargaining is appropriate (Manitoba *Labour Relations Act*, RSM 1987, c. L-10, s. 1). The different approach adopted in the Saskatchewan collective bargaining statute illustrates how significant the specific terms of the statutory discretion and the institutional orientation of the tribunal are for determining the success of this technique in expanding coverage. The Saskatchewan Board interpreted s. 2(f) (iii) of the *Trade Union Act* (RSS 1978, c. T-17 [as amended]), which includes within the definition of *employee*, "any person designated by the board as an employee for the purposes of this Act notwithstanding that for the purpose of determining whether or not the person to whom he provides services is vicariously liable for his acts or omissions, he may be held to be an independent contractor," as calling for the four-fold test as traditionally applied (*RWDSU. v. Sherwood Cooperative Association*, [1988] 88 CLLC 16,052). Saskatchewan's *Trade Union Act* was amended to provide that *employee* includes "a person engaged by another to perform services if, in the opinion of the board, the relationship between those persons is such that the terms of the contract between them can be the subject of collective bargaining" (at s. 2[f] [i.1]). According to Langille and Davidov (1999, 27), this subsection was enacted in 1972 (c. 137, s. 2), repealed in 1983 (c. 81, s. 3), and reinstated in 1994 (c. 47, s. 3).
26 In British Columbia, the labour tribunal has attempted to quantify the degree of economic dependence necessary for coverage under collective bargaining legislation, setting the receipt of 80 per cent of income from "the employer" as the bright line for determining employee status (Adams 1995, 6–7). See *Ridge Gravel and Paving Ltd and Teamsters, Local 213*, [1988] 88 CLLC 16,040 (BCIRC), application for reconsideration refused, 89 CLLC 16,030 (BCIRC). In Ontario, board jurisprudence is very clear: economic dependence is to be interpreted in relation to a particular employer and not to an industry (Sack, Mitchell, and Price 1997, para. 285).
27 The British Columbia tribunal is more inclined than its Ontario counterpart to find in favour of such status. The federal tribunal is also willing to attribute dependent contractor status in situations in which the worker occasionally employs other workers as assistants (Adams 1995, 6–7; Labour

Law Casebook Group 1998, 218; Langille and Davidov 1999, 28). Langille and Davidov also note that simply because a person occasionally hires another person to assist with the work, it does not mean that the first person is not an employee according to the common-law definition (Langille and Davidov 1999, 28, footnote 65, referring to *Head v. Inter Tan Canada Inc.*, [1991] 38 CCEL [2d] 159 [OCGD]).

28 *Canada Post Corporation Act*, RSC 1985, c. C-10, s. 13(5).
29 *OLRA*, supra note 21 at s. 3(a).
30 The Ontario Labour Relations Board had this remedial authority, but the Conservative government revoked it after the board exercised it in certifying a bargaining unit at a Walmart store in Windsor (SO 1998, c. 8). In some jurisdictions, the federal and Nova Scotia, for example, a union may be certified even though it does not have majority support in order to remedy an unfair labour practice (Carter et al. 2002, 244).
31 *OLRA*, supra note 21 at s. 9(5). In British Columbia and the federal jurisdiction, dependent contractors are included in units with employees. However, the distinction between dependent contractors and employees is still relevant in British Columbia, as the tribunal has refused to exercise its discretion to amalgamate dependent contractors into existing units of employees. See discussions of dependent contractors and bargaining units in Bendel (1982, 401) and Labour Law Casebook Group (1998, 218).
32 In Ontario, from 1992 to 2000, 67.3 per cent of newly certified units reached first collective agreements. Between 1992 and 1995, largely under an NDP government, the percentage was 78.6. Under the Progressive Conservative government, from 1996 to 2000, the percentage dropped to 53.4. (Information provided on request by the Ontario Ministry of Labour, Office of Collective Bargaining Information, July 2001.)
33 *Crown Employees Collective Bargaining Act, 1993*, SO 1993, c. 38, s. 10.
34 *Status of the Artist Act* SC 1992, c. 33 (as amended).

CHAPTER ONE

1 The Southern Ontario Newspaper Guild was affiliated with an international union, the Newspaper Guild, until 1994, when, after failing to negotiate greater autonomy, it voted to affiliate with the all-Canadian CEP.
2 *Toronto Star Newspapers Ltd*, [1999] OLRB Rep. 352.
3 *Labour Relations Act*, SO 1995, c. 1, Sched. A [*OLRA*].
4 *Toronto Star Newspapers Limited*, [2001] OLRB Rep. 168 [*Toronto Star 2001*].

5 *National Labor Relations Act*, c. 372, 49 Stat. 449 (1935).
6 For example, *Re Telegram Publishing Co. Ltd and William Amm and Others*, [1973] 3 LAC (2d) 175 [*Telegram Publishing*] (newspaper circulation managers held to be employees for the purposes of the Ontario *Employee Standards Act*).
7 As a result of changes in the occupational codes used by Statistics Canada, it is impossible to construct a time series beyond 1991 on this group's demographics. As well, because of the part-time nature of the work, many people engaged in newspaper distribution may not report it as their main occupation. Keeping these limitations in mind, between 1981 and 1991, the percentage of young carriers (between the ages of 15 and 21) and vendors decreased from 70 per cent to 53 per cent, while the percentage of women increased from 17 per cent to 23 per cent (Statistics Canada, "Newspaper Carriers and Vendors [SOC 5143] within Experienced Labour Force, 1981–1991 Censuses," special run).
8 For descriptions of these campaigns, see *Re Semiahmoo Management Ltd*, BCLRB No. 12/98 [*Semiahmoo*]; *Re Winnipeg Free Press*, [1999] MLBD No. 3 [*Winnipeg Free Press 1999*].
9 *National Labor Relations Board v. Hearst Publications Inc.*, 322 US 111 (1945).
10 Ibid., at 126.
11 *Buffalo Courier-Express, Inc. and American Newspaper Guild, Local 206*, 129 NLRB 932 (1960).
12 *Evening News*, 308 NLRB 82 (1992); *Times Herald Record*, 334 NLRB 48 (2001).
13 *Telegram Publishing*, supra note 6, aff'd 94 DLR (2d) 103 (OCA).
14 *Montreal v. Montreal Locomotive Works Ltd*, [1947] 1 DLR 161 (PC).
15 *Telegram Publishing*, supra note 6 at 188.
16 *Roltek Holdings Inc.*, [1993] OESAD No. 198.
17 BC Reg. 396/95; BC Reg. 5/98; *British Columbia Employment Standards Act and Regulations Interpretation Guidelines Bulletin*, <http://www.labour.gov.bc.ca/esb/igm/>; *Semiahmoo*, supra note 8 at paras 27–31; Graeme Moore, policy advisor, BC Employment Standards Branch, personal communication with the author, 4 December 2001.
18 *Thomson Canada Ltd (Winnipeg Free Press) v. Canada (Minister of National Revenue)*, [2001] TCJ No. 374 [*Thomson*].
19 Ibid., at paras 49–63.
20 *Vulcain Alarme Inc. v. M.N.R.*, [1999] 249 NR 1 cited ibid., at para. 10.
21 *Thomson*, supra note 18 at paras 105–6.
22 Ibid., at para. 92.

23 *Workplace Safety and Insurance Act, 1997,* SO 1997, c. 16, Sched. A, ss. 11–12.
24 Workers' Compensation Board, *Operational Policy Manual*, document No. 01-02-03.
25 Ontario Workers' Compensation Appeal Tribunal, Dec. No. 590/89; Annette Zekusic, account manager, WSIB, letter to the author, 14 November 2001; *Toronto Star 2001,* supra note 4 at para. 69.
26 In Ontario, the dependent contractor provision was originally enacted in 1975 (SO 1975, c. 76).
27 *Ottawa Citizen,* [1985] OLRB Rep. 819 [*Citizen*]; *Journal Le Droit,* [1985] OLRB Rep. 1372 [*Journal*]. Both cite *Algonquin Tavern,* [1981] OLRB Rep. 1057. Sue Tacon was the presiding vice-chair in both proceedings.
28 *Ajax Pickering News Advertiser,* [1993] OLRB Rep. 473 [*Ajax*]; *Kitchener-Waterloo Record,* [1997] OLRD No. 432 [*Kitchener*].
29 In one case, *Pacific Press,* BCLRB No. 142/74, drivers were found not to be dependent contractors. In *Flyer Force,* BCIRC No. C113/89 [*Flyer Force*], area supervisors were found to be employees; and in *Kamloops News Inc.,* BCIRC C215/90 (aff'd BCLRB Dec. No. C72/91) [*Kamloops*], *Alberni Valley Times Ltd,* BCIRC No. C130/92 [*Alberni*], and *Prince George Citizen,* BCLRB Letter Decision No. B282/94 [*Prince George*] drivers were found to be dependent contractors.
30 *Winnipeg Free Press 1999,* supra note 8 at para. 89.
31 *Semiahmoo,* supra note 8 at para. 88.
32 Ibid.
33 *Winnipeg Free Press 1999,* supra note 8 at para. 91; SM 1984–85, c. 21, s. 5 (repealing the dependent contractor provision and replacing it with the power to designate); SS 1972, c. 137, s. 2(f).
34 *Winnipeg Free Press 1999,* supra note 8 at paras 97–106.
35 *Toronto Star 2001,* supra note 4 at para. 22.
36 Ibid., at paras 78–103, quote at para. 90.
37 *Hollinger Canadian Newspapers, LP (c.o.b. Saskatoon Star Phoenix Newspaper),* [2000] SLRBD No. 73.
38 Ontario examples include: *Journal,* supra note 27 (drivers – Syndicat québécois de l'imprimerie et des communications); *Citizen,* supra note 27 (drivers – guild); *Ajax,* supra note 28 (drivers – RWDSU); and *Kitchener,* supra note 28 (drivers – teamsters' union). British Columbia cases include: *Flyer Force,* supra note 29 (area supervisors – guild); *Kamloops,* supra note 29 (drivers – CWA); *Alberni,* supra note 29 (collators, drivers, and office staff – Graphic Communications International Union); and *Prince George,* supra note 29 (drivers – CEP).

39 *Toronto Sun*, [1999] OLRB Rep. 104, para. 30.
40 In *Winnipeg Free Press 1999* (supra note 8), carriers who did not have designated routes or who did only relief work were excluded, while in *Toronto Star 2001* (supra note 4), a dispute arose over the inclusion of youth carriers and the carriers of a free weekend publication. Both groups were included.
41 OLRA, supra note 3 at s. 9(5).
42 *Caressant Care Nursing Home of Canada Ltd*, [1996] OLRB Rep. 748 at 755.
43 *Metroland Printing, Publishing and Distributing Ltd*, [1995] OLRB Rep. 986 (combining press and mailroom employees); *Windsor Star*, [1995] OLRB Rep. 714 (combining press, maintenance, and truck-driver employees); *The Spectator, A Division of Southam Inc.*, [1995] OLRB Rep. 559 (combining full-time editorial and part-time mailroom employees); *North Bay Nugget*, [1994] OLRB Rep. 1137 (combining full-time editorial and part-time mailroom employees); OLRA, supra note 3 at s. 114(1).
44 *Kamloops News Inc.*, BCIRC No. C72/91, reconsidering No. C215/90; *Alberni Valley* supra note 29; *Labour Relations Code*, RSBC 1996, c. 244, ss. 28, 142.
45 *Semiahmoo*, supra note 8. The board left it to the parties to devise a remedy, retaining jurisdiction to reconvene in the event agreement could not be reached. *Viking Logistics*, BCLRB No. 33/99 (holding that continuous and regular extraprovincial delivery brings the operation under federal jurisdiction).
46 The account of the *Star* organizing is derived from *Toronto Star 2001* (supra note 4); Howard Law and Brad Drake, guild representatives, interview by author, 26 June 2001. The absence of waiting-time payments has been identified as a major grievance of carriers (Schiller 2001). The Manitoba Labour Relations Board rejected a claim that the involvement of district managers in organizing while off duty was an unfair labour practice, although they left open the possibility that the newspaper might be able to pursue a remedy for breach of employment obligations in another forum (*Winnipeg Free Press 1999*, supra note 8 at paras 109–10).
47 Law and Drake, supra note 46. On the challenge of organizing immigrants, see generally Bronfenbrenner, Seeber, and Oswald (1997); Milkman (2000).
48 First-contract arbitration was introduced in Ontario in 1986. The NDP labour law expanded its availability in 1993, but the 1995 PC revisions restored the more restrictive 1986 approach.
49 *Pacific Press*, BCLRB No. B117/94. The case was peculiar in that the employer wanted the transfer to be classified as a sale of a business to prevent the displaced employees from conducting a strike against it. Moreover, the

acquirer was a federally regulated employer who would not be bound by the province's successor rights provisions.

50 *Pacific Press*, BCLRB No. B52/95, paras 60–89 [*Pacific Press*].
51 *Pacific Press*, BCLRB No. 374/96, paras 10–12, 132–77 [*Pacific Press 1996*].
52 *Pacific Press*, supra note 50 at paras 24–59. In the carrier supervision case, the board found that timely notice had not been given as required by the act and a provision in the collective agreement, but it left it to the parties to devise a remedy while retaining jurisdiction to resolve the matter in the absence of an agreement.
53 For the former, see *Pacific Press 1996*, supra note 51 at paras 34–59; *Toronto Star and Southern Ontario Newspaper Guild*, [1990] 18 LAC (4th) 49 (the work jurisdiction provision does not apply where work is assigned to an independent contractor). For the latter, see *Winnipeg Free Press*, [2000] MGAD No. 45.
54 This background is discussed in *Deverell v. Toronto Star Newspapers Ltd*, [2001] OJ No. 945 [*Deverell*].
55 For 1999–2000, the median time for disposition of non-construction certification cases from time of application was twenty-six days. Only twenty-eight cases took longer than six months. This case took over two years. See the 1999–2000 *Annual Report* of the Ontario Labour Relations Board, p. 29.
56 It was necessary to turn to the courts, because the 1995 labour law reforms severely limited the power of the board to grant interim relief.
57 *Deverell*, supra note 54.
58 Law and Drake, supra note 46.
59 J. Deverell, "Star Carrier Campaign Evaluation Report," unpublished report, 2001.
60 "Home Delivery Carriers Agreement between CEP Local 87-M and *Toronto Star* Newspapers," effective 14 April 2001–1 June 2004; "Carriers Ratify Terms of Surrender to the *Toronto Star*," *Guild Bulletin*, 14 April 2001.
61 See Acharya 2001a on the cost of privatization; 2001b on the strike cost.

CHAPTER TWO

1 This unsigned poem, attributed to Charles Maguire, appeared in the first issue of the newsletter of the Association of Rural Route Mail Couriers (ARRMC); the newsletter is undated, but it was published in the early fall of 1985.
2 Canada Post Corporation, "Newsroom/Fast Facts/Overview," <http://www.canadapost.ca/b ... /abut/newsroom/fast-facts/default-e.asp>; Canada

Post Corporation, *Annual Report*, 2001, <http:www.canadapost.ca/about/ annual_report/ vision.html>.

3 *Canada Labour Code*, RSC 1984, c. C-39 [*CLC*]. Subsection 13(5) of the *Canada Post Corporation Act*, RSC 1985, c. C-10 [*CPCA*], specifically excludes mail contractors from the definition of *employee* for the purposes of part 1 of the *Canada Labour Code* – the part that governs collective bargaining. They are not specifically excluded from either part 2, which governs occupational health, or part 3, which provides for minimum labour standards. However, in these parts, the definition of *employee* does not include dependent contractor and, thus, their scope is considered narrower than part 1, which governs collective bargaining. Despite this, it is not a foregone conclusion that rural route mail contractors who actually deliver the mail would not be employees for the purposes of parts 2 and 3, for there is case law that establishes that couriers who operate their own vehicles are employees. See *Dynamex Canada Inc. v. Morgan*, [2002] CLAD No. 147.

4 The ARRMC estimated that the majority of couriers were women. However, it is hard to tell, because in many cases a man might hold the contract but a woman would perform the work (Gibson 1990; Hannant 1987; Popaleni 1988; Smillie 1988).

5 *Canada Post Corp. v. Assn. of Rural Route Mail Couriers*, [1987] 87 CLLC 16029 at para. 14229 (CLRB) [*Canada Post*].

6 There is little data publicly available about the value of contracts and the work involved. Mavis Wiebe – a rural route mail contractor for twenty-five years who was involved in the ARRMC in the mid-1980s and who was a member of the ORRMC executive since the mid-1990s – has come to exemplify the typical rural mail contractor. In 1978, Canada Post paid her $1,000 a month, out of which she had to pay expenses incurred as she delivered mail to 326 points of call along her twenty-six-kilometre, predominantly suburban route outside Surrey, BC. In 1999, she received $1,900 a month to make slightly fewer than 1,000 calls. Calculating the cost of operating her vehicle (depreciation, gas, repairs, and insurance) at $1,000 month, she estimated that for a route that took between twelve and fourteen hours a day to cover, her pay averaged out at $6.84 per hour (Lynda Sabourin and Mavis Wiebe, rural route mail couriers, submission to the Canada Post Mandate Review, 10 February 1996; Pearson 1999). Barbara Spinney, who was a Canada Post courier for over twelve years, quit after trying, unsuccessfully, to negotiate for more money. Her monthly income was $1,900, but after accounting for rising fuel costs, part-time help, and

auto insurance, she was left with an hourly rate lower than the minimum wage (Duffy 1989). See also Sue Eybel, president of the ARRMC, submission to the Canada Post Mandate Review, 14 February 1996.

7 While some part of the difference in compensation and benefits for rural carriers likely stems from the difference in general wage rates between the two countries and the much larger size of the USPS, employment status and the right to bargain collectively also contribute to the gap. Moreover, it is difficult to compare wage rates across national boundaries due to factors such as labour market differences and exchange rate fluctuations. For this reason, the wages of rural couriers in relation to the minimum wage is used (Union Net International, "Continental Divide: Collective Bargaining Rights and Rural Letter Carriers' Compensation in the United States and Canada," 2001, <http://laboris.uqam.ca/toronto/documentation.htm.>.

8 CPCA, supra note 3.

9 Outside the public service and the broad public sector, it is rare to find specific provisions in legislation otherwise not related to labour relations that exempt a group of workers from general labour legislation. Members of the armed forces, RCMP officers, CSIS agents, Crown lawyers, and judges are excluded from federal collective bargaining legislation on the ground that conflicts of interest could result if they were allowed to bargain collectively (Woods 1968, 139–40; Beth Bilson, "Which Side Are You On? Loyalty and Conflict of Interest as Criteria in Determining Employee Status," 2001, <http://laboris.uqam.ca/toronto/documentation.htm>). These groups of government employees are regarded as owing the Crown a special loyalty that trumps their right to bargain collectively. Rural route mail couriers do not enjoy this special status. In Ontario, agricultural and domestic workers are excluded from collective bargaining legislation, and the exclusion of these groups has been justified on the ground that they work at sites – family farms or family homes – that are unsuitable for collective bargaining. The Supreme Court of Canada decided in December 2001 that the Ontario government's denial of legislative protection of agricultural workers' right to join and participate in trade unions violates their charter-protected freedom of association. The court ordered the government to introduce a scheme of protection. The legislation enacted by the Ontario government simply provides unfair labour practice protection for individual workers; it does not provide assistance for collective bargaining, which, according to the Supreme Court of Canada, is not constitutionally protected. See *Dunmore v. Ontario (AG)*, [2001] 207 DLR 193, SCC 94 [*Dunmore*]; *Agricultural Employees Protection Act*, SO 2002, c. C-16.

10 *Post Office Act*, RS 1970, c. 212.
11 Ibid., at ss. 2(1), 22-30, 31.
12 *House of Commons Debates*, 029 (24 October 1980) at 4087 (Hon. Bill Vankoughnet).
13 See the remarks of Shirley Carr, president of the CLC, to the Standing Committee on Miscellaneous Estimates ("Minutes of Proceedings and Evidence of the Standing Committee on Miscellaneous Estimates/Procès-verbaux et témoignages du Comité permanent des prévisions budgétaires en général," 1980, 37:40, 11-12-1980) [Minutes].
14 See the seminal discussion of the concept "dependent contractor" by Harry Arthurs (1965).
15 André Ouellet, postmaster general, to the Standing Committee on Miscellaneous Estimates, Minutes, supra note 13 at 41:53-4, 18-12-1980.
16 Ibid., at 18-12-1980.
17 Saturday rural delivery was maintained in Prince Edward Island until 1990.
18 Sue Eybel, interview by author, 11 October 1990. Eybel and Charles Maguire attended the convention of the Country Mail Association of Canada, which was held from 31 August to 2 September 1985.
19 Dan Coldwell, director of transportation contracting services for Huron Division, letter to all Huron Division land transportation contractors, 19 December 1985.
20 Canada Post, "Planning the Future of Rural Route Services," 21 April 1986 (document for the cross-Canada meetings with rural route couriers).
21 Dan Coldwell, letter to all Huron Division land transportation contractors, 2 October 1986. In this letter, Coldwell announces that as of 1 April 1987, all rural route contracts with Canada Post Corporation will go to public tender at the end of their term.
22 These changes included the amalgamation of rural routes and the substitution of super-mailboxes for existing lot-line delivery in low-density areas. Canada Post, "Summary of the 1986/87 to 1991/92 Corporate Plan," 1986.
23 Some companies began to bid on, and win, rural route contracts. On occasion, they hired former rural mail contractors who had lost their contracts to deliver the mail on their old routes for less money than the couriers had received when they held the contracts.
24 Canada Post, "Summary of the 1987/88 to 1991/92 Corporate Plan," 1986, p. 9.
25 For a compelling discussion of Rural Dignity's origins and its battle with Canada Post, see Campbell (1990).

26 Standing Committee on Government Operations, "Minority Report Re: The Standing Committee on Government Operations Examining the 1986/87 to 1990/91 Canada Post Corporate Plan," 1986, 7:3, 4. The committee was persuaded that it was unnecessary for Canada Post to retrench lot-line delivery for 100,000 rural residents, and Canada Post later modified this aspect of its plan.
27 Eybel, supra note 18.
28 Ibid.
29 Ibid.
30 *Canada Post*, supra note 5.
31 Eybel, supra note 18.
32 Ibid.
33 *Canada Post*, supra note 5.
34 *U.A. v. Société Radio-Canada /Canadian Broadcasting Corp.*, [1982] 1 CLRBR (NS) 129, para. 149, citing Arthurs 1965.
35 CLC, supra note 3 at s. 21(c).
36 *Canada Post*, supra note 5 at para. 14235.
37 Ibid., at para. 14236.
38 Ibid., at para. 14238.
39 Ibid., at para. 14245.
40 Ibid.
41 Ibid.
42 Ibid., at paras 14245-6. First, the board stated that the wording discussed during committee deliberation was not that which was ultimately adopted, and second, relying on Supreme Court of Canada jurisprudence on the use of extrinsic evidence such as parliamentary debates for the purpose of statutory interpretation, it decided that the minister's statement could not be adduced as evidence of legislative intent.
43 Noting that it was necessary first to find that couriers were mail contractors in order to trigger section 13(5), the board said that it had to determine two things: whether the couriers were involved in the transmission of mail; and, referring to the French version of the definition of *mail contract*, whether the couriers performed contracts *for* service ("contrats d'entreprise") rather than contracts *of* service ("contrats de louage de services"). After scouring the *Canada Post Corporation Act* for the term *transmission* and its cognates, the board decided that the word *transmit* was discrete from *collecting* and *delivering*, since *transmission* referred to the movement of mail between locations and not between individuals and businesses. While couriers were involved in the collection and delivery of mail, they were not engaged in the "transmission" of mail, and thus they were not mail contractors. The issue

raised by the French version of the definition of *mail contractor* was essentially the same issue the board dealt with in the first part of its decision. The distinction between a contract *for* service and one *of* service is basically equivalent to the distinction between an independent contractor and an employee. Accordingly, the board decided that its earlier findings supported the conclusion that the couriers were not under a contract for service and thus not mail contractors as defined in the French version.

44 Canadian Press Wire Service, 26 May 1988, quoting Villeneuve's earlier remarks.
45 Polins (1987), quoting Mike Rapsey on behalf of Canada Post.
46 Ibid.
47 *Canada Post Corp. v. Assn. of Rural Route Mail Couriers*, [1987] 88 CLLC 14006 (FCA). In a short concurring decision, Desjardins agreed with Hugessen that the issue of the application of 13(5) was jurisdictional in nature. Marceau, who agreed with Hugessen in the result, disagreed with his characterization of the issue as jurisdictional. However, he said that although the standard of review was the higher standard of "patently unreasonable," the board's decision was patently unreasonable.
48 Hugessen stated: "I confess I have little difficulty in concluding that the board was wrong in deciding that couriers were not mail contractors within the meaning of the *Canada Post Corporation Act*" (ibid., at para. 12026). Noting that the board purported to find ambiguity in the definition of *mail contractor* through an examination of the meaning of the term *transmission*, Hugessen declared, "The ambiguity escapes me. The couriers convey mail from place to place. They do so under contract. Therefore they are mail contractors. It is difficult to imagine how Parliament might have expressed itself in clearer terms." And he was just as dismissive of the board's attempt to rely on the definition of *mail contractor* in the French version to avoid the application of section 13(5). Characterizing the board's reasoning as circuitous, he complained that "the whole of s. 13(5) becomes useless surplusage if its only purpose is to declare not to be dependent contractors or employees persons who could never be so in any event."
49 Eybel was upset with this decision, but she said that as the LCUC paid the lawyer and called the shots, there was little she could do (supra note 18).
50 Rural Route Mail Couriers of Canada, CLC Local 1801, newsletter, 1 October 1990.
51 *Levine v. Canada Post Corp.*, [1987], 72 di 120 (CLRB).
52 Dougald Brown of Nelligan, Power, letter to Sue Eybel, 31 May 1989. Eybel agreed to Canada Post's request that she adjourn her complaint.

53 Rural Route Mail Carriers of Canada, statement of claim filed with the Federal Court, 23 March 1989.
54 *Rural Route Mail Carriers of Can., Local 1801 v. Canada (AG)*, [1989] 29 FTR 105.
55 *Rural Route Mail Carriers of Canada, Local 1801 v. Canada (AG)*, [1990] CarswellNat 1135 (FCTD).
56 Since the postal unions and the CLC were no longer subsidizing the local, it applied to the Charter Challenges Program for money to finance the legal action. However, in 1990, the application was rejected on the ground that the couriers' complaint was not a strong charter test case. According to the director of the Court Challenges Program, there was no conclusive evidence that the majority of couriers were women, and the residency aspect of the case was not sufficiently developed (Kathleen Ruff, director of the Court Challenges Program, letter to Dougald Brown of Nelligan, Power, 1 March 1990).
57 "Minutes of the Proceedings of the Turner Committee," 1990, 46:6–2 [Minutes].
58 Standing Committee on Consumer and Corporate Affairs and Government Operations, Postal Services in the 1990s. *Turner Committee Report*, 1990.
59 Minutes, supra note 57, Jean-Marc Robitaille, the member for Terrebonne (at 40:21), and Gaby Larrivée, the member for Joliette (at 40:22).
60 Bill C-346, *An Act to Amend the* Canada Post Corporation Act *(Mail Contractors)*, 34th Parliament, 2d Sess., 1990 (first reading, 12 December).
61 Deborah Bourque, interview by author, 28 August 2001, Ottawa.
62 Canada Post has an exclusive privilege, granted under the *Canada Post Corporation Act*, to deliver letters. In 2000, the huge private corporation United Parcel Service (UPS) announced that it intended to launch a challenge under NAFTA to Canada Post's exclusive privilege (Casey 2001). For a discussion of the challenges facing Canada Post and CUPW, see Scott Sinclair, "The GATS and Canadian Postal Services," published on the CUPW Web site: <http://www.cupw.ca>.
63 Bourque, supra note 61.
64 Ibid.
65 Ibid.
66 D.W. Tingley, national president of CUPW, letter to Sue Eybel, 24 July 1995; Bourque, supra note 61.
67 D.W. Tingley, letter to all rural route mail couriers, local presidents, and secretary treasurers, 27 July 1995; Deborah Bourque, third national vice-president of CUPW, letter to all CUPW locals, 16 November 1995 [letter];

Deborah Bourque, "Rural Rights, Not Wrongs," CUPW *Perspective*, 3 July 2000.
68 Tingley, supra note 67.
69 Gaston Nadeau of Trudel, Nadeau, Lesage, Lariviere and Associates, letter to Donald LaFleur of CUPW, 8 May 1995.
70 For a summary of the case law of the Supreme Court of Canada on these issues, see Fudge (2000). However, in a recent decision by a seven-to-one majority, the Supreme Court of Canada held that the government was under a positive obligation to provide legislative protection to vulnerable employees – in that case, agricultural workers – to protect their freedom to associate in unions (*Dunmore*, supra note 9). Only one member of the court (Madame Justice L'Heureux-Dubé) decided the equality issue, stating that occupational status could be a ground for an equality claim under the charter.
71 Bourque, letter, supra note 67.
72 ORRMC executive members Alice Boudreau, Ginette Laliberté, Mavis Wiebe, Denis Kohlman, Cheryl Coughlin, Cynthia Patterson (campaign coordinator), and Deborah Bourque (ex-officio), interview by author, 18 October 2001, Ottawa.
73 Sue Eybel, submission to the Canada Post Mandate Review, 14 February 1996; Rural Dignity of Canada, submission to the Canada Post Mandate Review, 15 February 1996; CUPW, "Towards a Modern Public Postal Service: Brief to the Canada Post Mandate Review," submission to the Canada Post Mandate Review, 15 February 1996.
74 Minister of Public Works and Government Services Canada, "The Future of Canada Post Corporation: Canada Post Mandate Review," 1996.
75 *Constitution of the Organization of Rural Route Mail Couriers*, amended March 2000. The close relationship between CUPW and the ORRMC was clear in the latter's constitution, which stated that CUPW was voluntarily helping couriers establish an organization that would work closely with it to achieve "justice and dignity for rural route mail couriers through a fair and equitable tendering process, the right to bargain working conditions and ... other attainable benefits" (<http.//www.cupw.ca/pages/ document_eng.php? Doc_ID=67>).
76 Canada Post Corporation, response to Public Communication US NAO-9804 (Rural Mail Couriers) before the US NAO under the NAALC.
77 Irasema Garza, secretary of the US NAO, letter to Deborah Bourque, third national vice-president of CUPW, February 1999.
78 Robert White, president of the CLC, letter to Irasema Garza, 8 March 1999.

79 Conference details and papers are available at <http://laboris.uqam.ca/toronto.htm>. It is interesting to note that the Supreme Court of Canada in *Dunmore*, supra note 9, subsequently found that Ontario legislation excluding agricultural workers from legal protection of their right to join and participate in unions violated their charter-protected freedom to associate.
80 See the ORRMC Web site; no longer independent, it has been incorporated into the CUPW site: <http://www.cupw.ca/pages/index-e.php>.
81 Both the NDP and the Bloc Québécois emphasized the law's basic unfairness in denying rural route couriers the right to bargain collectively. Martin emphasized that according to the *Canada Labour Code*, rural route couriers were dependent contractors and, thus, employees – they were not the independent entrepreneurs that the government and Canada Post claimed they were. He also made it very clear that his bill would not tie the rural route mail couriers to CUPW. In defence of the exclusion, the parliamentary secretary for the minister responsible for Canada Post asserted that only CUPW would benefit from the change, that the tendering process was fair, that rural contractors only worked part time, and that there would be grave implications for Canada Post if mail contractors were to be treated as employees. See *House of Commons Debates*, 019 (5 November 1999) at 1203 (Hon. Pat Martin); 058 (28 February 2000) at 4061 (Hon. Gary Lunn); 076 (31 March 2000) at 5541 (Hon. Joe Jordan).
82 ORRMC executive members, supra note 72. Canada Post and government officials refused repeated requests for interviews to discuss the situation of the rural and suburban mail couriers.
83 Ibid.; Canada Post, *Delivery Reference Manual*, November 2000.
84 Wendy Milne, transportation contracting officer, letter to Mavis Wiebe, 15 July 1999. The letter was an invitation to Wiebe to tender an agreement with Canada Post concerning Surrey Rural Route 8.
85 For a complete list of all the legal documents relating to the UPS complaint, see, under the heading "Dispute Settlement: NAFTA/Chapter 11/Investment; Cases Filed Against the Government of Canada," *United Parcel Service of America, Inc. ("UPS") v. Government of Canada*," <http://www.dfait-maeci.gc.ca/tna-nac/menu-en.asp>.
86 Canadian Union of Postal Workers, "Postal Workers and Allies Demand Fair Treatment for Rural Route and Suburban Mail Courier," 16 April 2002, <http://www.cupw.ca>.
87 Supra note 9.
88 George Floresco, third national vice-president of CUPW, interview by author, 14 March 2003, Ottawa.

89 Alice Boudreau, former president of the ORRMC and temporary technical assistant at CUPW, interview by author, 14 March 2003, Ottawa.
90 The CPAA and CUPW had very different political orientations and approaches to collective bargaining. Moreover, the CPAA feared that the larger union would swallow up its members. In 1999, Leroy Kuan, then–national president of CPAA, attended an ORRMC executive meeting, and friendly relations between the organizations continued throughout 2000. The CPAA wished the ORRMC and the couriers well, but it was not going to get involved in any attempt to organize couriers. Contact between the two organizations resumed in October 2001, when the ORRMC executive met with CPAA national directors (Boudreau, supra note 89).
91 Leslie Schous, president of the CPAA, letter to Alice Boudreau, 11 March 2002. On 18 March 2003, Boudreau wrote to Schous to remind her that the ORRMC had always been forthright in its intention to merge with CUPW. CPAA officials declined repeated request for interviews to discuss the rural and suburban mail couriers.
92 Floresco, supra note 88.
93 Alice Boudreau and Deborah Bourque, letter to rural and suburban mail couriers, 1 August 2003; Floresco, supra note 88; Boudreau, supra note 89.
94 Pat Fagan, national vice-president of the CPAA, "ORRMC," CPAA newsletter, April 2002.
95 Along with other members of CUPW, the rural route TTAs travelled across Canada in November and December, meeting with couriers to develop their demands and to update them on the progress of the representation campaign. They had forty-nine meetings with seven hundred couriers, and they developed a series of demands (Floresco, supra note 88).
96 Number 20 in CUPW's program of demands deals with the couriers and requires that Canada Post "Negotiate the inclusion of rural and suburban mail couriers into the collective agreement with separate classification and improved wages, benefits and protections for these workers" ("2003 Negotiation: CUPW Program of Demands," *CUPW Perspective* 30, no. 3 [2002], <http://www.cupw.ca/pdfs/eng/perspectiveoct2002eng.pdf>).
97 CUPW applied for the CIRB to review the bargaining units at Canada Post and place the couriers within the operations unit it represented. In the alternative, it argued that it should be certified as the bargaining agent for the couriers.
98 George Floresco, interview by author, 12 March 2003, Ottawa; CUPW, application for review under sections 18, 18.1, and 24 of the *Canada Labour Code*, CIRB file no. 23454-C, 10 January 2003.

99 In the matter of the *Canada Labour Code*, part 1, "Industrial Relations," "A Complaint of Bad Faith Bargaining and Unfair Labour Practices Pursuant to Sections 50(a), 98(a) and 97 Thereof by the Canada Post Corporation, Applicant Employer and the Canadian Union of Postal Workers, Respondent Union," 17 January 2003.

100 Canada Post, response, CIRB file no. 23454-C, 31 January 2003.

101 Sean T. McGee of Nelligan, O'Brien, Payne on behalf of CPAA, letter to Pierre Sioui-Thivierge, regional director registrar for CIRB, 28 January 2003, re CIRB file no. 24454-C.

102 Canadian Postmasters and Assistants' Association, "Survey of Rural Route Mail Contractors," *CPAA-ACMPA Bulletin* 8, no. 2 (2003).

103 Floresco, supra note 88.

104 Daryl Bean, the former president of the Public Service Alliance of Canada, was appointed mediator. The CLC disputes protocol is established under the CLC constitution, article IV, section 21, and it provides that the CLC president appoint someone to mediate the dispute; if there is no resolution, the mediator must report this to the president (Floresco, supra note 88; Daryl Bean, letter to Kenneth V. Georgetti, president of the CLC, 10 March 2003).

105 Kenneth V. Georgetti, letter to Deborah Bourque and Leslie Schous, 7 May 2003.

106 CPAA signed a collective agreement with Canada Post during the CLC mediation process, ensuring that CUPW would be prohibited by law from attempting to sign up CPAA members in retaliation for CPAA's attempt to represent rural couriers after CUPW had done all the work in organizing them ("Negotiations Update: Canada Postmasters and Assistants Association," April 2003, <http//:cpaa-acmpa.ca/news_e.htm>).

107 Geoff Bickerton, CUPW research director, interview by author, 14 March 2003, Ottawa.

108 The international arbitration tribunal dismissed the part of UPS's NAFTA complaint alleging that Canada Post engaged in unfair competition. See *United Parcel Service of America, Inc. ("UPS") v. Government of Canada* (2002), ch. 11 panel, "Award on Jurisdiction," on the Department of Foreign Affairs and International Trade Web site: <http://www.dfait-maeci.gc.ca/tna-nac/documents/ Jurisdiction%20Award.22Nov02.pdf>.

109 Ibid., "Amended Statement of Claim under the Arbitration Rules of the United Nations Commission on International Trade Law and the North American Free Trade Agreement" (30 November 2001): < http://www.dfait-maeci.gc.ca/tna-nac/documents/statement_claim.pdf>.

110 Ibid., "Statement of Defence of the Government of Canada" (7 February 2003): <http://www.dfait-maeci.gc.ca/tna-nac/documents/IntegratedStatement.pdf>.

111 CUPW, along with the Council of Canadians, has attempted to intervene in these proceedings, and it has been unsuccessful. See ibid., "Petition of the Canadian Union of Postal Workers and the Council of Canadians" (10 May 2001): <http://www.dfait-maeci.gc.ca/tna-nac/documents/petitiontothearbitraltribunal CUP.pdf>; ibid., "Decision of the Tribunal on Petitions for Intervention and Participation as *Amici Curiae*" (17 October 2001): <http://www.dfait-maeci.gc.ca/tna-nac/documents/IntVent_oct.pdf>.

112 "We have demonstrated that Canada's postal service can be profitable without privatization. We have set an enviable example that many other industrialized countries should follow. Sadly, public transportation, telecommunications and postal service in many Western countries have already been privatized" (André Ouellet, president of Canada Post Corporation, in *CUPW Perspective* 31, no. 1 [2003], <http://www.cupw.ca/pdfs/eng/perspective_apr03_eng.pdf>).

113 Bickerton, supra note 107.

114 Bill C-342, supra note 60; George Floresco, third national vice-president of CUPW, letter to local presidents, 29 November 2002 (political lobbying package).

115 Canadian Union of Postal Workers, "A Contract for the Future," 27 July 2003, <http://www.cupw.ca>.

116 Canadian Union of Postal Workers, "Ratification 2003: The Results Are In," 25 September 2003, <http://www.cupw.ca>.

117 Geoff Bickerton, CUPW research director, e-mail to the author, 27 November 2003.

118 There were a number of critical issues on the table during the 2003 negotiations – including the contracting in of the urban expedited parcel service and the recognition of rural couriers as Canada Post employees – that might not have been salvaged by CUPW in the event of a strike. Moreover, the success of a purely political campaign for recognition of the couriers' employee status was not a foregone conclusion; although Martin's private member's bill was only narrowly defeated in 1999, it was due only to luck that it won the lottery and survived first reading in the first place. Without the threat of a strike by the membership of CUPW's large operations unit over the issue of recognizing the couriers' employee status, Canada Post and the federal government could easily have waited until the couriers lost heart or CUPW decided it could not continue funding the couriers' organization.

119 For a summary of the key elements of the collective agreements, see Lynn Bue, "A Victory for Rural and Suburban Mail Carriers," 2003, <http://www.cupw.ca/pages/document_eng.php?Doc_ID=481>.

120 *Mail contractors* is a broad term covering agreements worth millions of dollars with Air Canada for air delivery, contracts for hundreds of thousands of dollars with trucking firms to haul mail across provincial borders, and rural route contracts valued at less than $10,000 a year.

121 Bickerton, supra note 107. Canada Post officials refused repeated requests to be interviewed.

CHAPTER THREE

1 In this chapter, I use the term *personal-care workers* to refer to all workers providing personal-care services under various employment relationships and models of care. When relevant, I employ the more specific terms used in a particular care model, such as *attendants* (those who provide services through agencies), or in a particular employment relationship, such as *domestic workers* (those who are employed directly by the recipient of their services).

2 Ontario *Labour Relations Act*, so 1995, c. 1, Sched. A [OLRA].

3 In-depth interviews were conducted on 25 October 2001 with Jenny Ahn, a former attendant worker and currently the president of Canadian Auto Workers (CAW) Local 40; on 14 March 2001 with an anonymous male worker who had been employed in several Social Support Living Units (SSLU) settings since the mid-1980s and was involved in organizing other workers; and on 22 March 2002 with an anonymous female worker who had worked for both an Outreach and an SSLU employer and was involved in organizing. These respondents are immigrants from groups that are well represented in the sector. Brief personal communications took place with another long-time CAW staff person and a Service Employees International Union (SEIU) staff person, both of whom will remain anonymous.

4 Many disability activists and government programs refer to people with disabilities as *consumers*. This term, in many ways, objectifies the workers who provide the services and gives the impression that people with disabilities have the knowledge and power to choose their care in a free market. In contrast, some organizations that provide services and some workers use the term *client*. Many disability activists reject this term, as it connotes a medicalized model of care. As a compromise, the term *client/consumer* is

used in this chapter to refer to the person with a disability to whom the worker provides services.

5 Ontario Advisory Council for Disabled Persons, *Integration, Independence and Interdependence for Physically Handicapped in Ontario: A Policy Focus for the Province*, 1976.

6 Ontario Ministry of Community and Social Services, Ministry of Health, Office for Senior Citizens' Affairs, Office for the Disabled, *Strategies for Change: Comprehensive Reform of Ontario's Long Term Care Services*, 1990.

7 Ontario Advisory Council for Disabled Persons, *Independent Living: The Time Is Now*, 1988.

8 Centre for Independent Living in Toronto, *Attendant Services Options for Consumers: A Directory*, 1997 (available from the CILT at: 205 Richmond Street West, suite 605, Toronto, ON, M5V 1V3) [*Attendant Services Options*].

9 *Ontarians with Disabilities Act* Committee, "Making Ontario Open for People with Disabilities: A Blueprint for a Strong and Effective *Ontarians with Disabilities Act*," 1998, <http:\www.odacommittee.net.brief9oa.html>.

10 *Individualized funding* is a broader term than *direct funding*, encompassing models in which funding is individualized but not directly given to the individual with a disability.

11 Ontario Advisory Council for Disabled Persons, *Annual Report*, 1989; Karen Yoshida et al., Centre for Independent Living in Toronto, *A Case Study Analysis of the Ontario Self-Managed Attendant Services Direct Funding Attendant Service Pilot: Independent Living in Action*, 2000. *Long-term care* is the term used by the Ontario government to refer to programs that provide services to people with chronic impairments and illnesses, and to senior citizens. It is common to distinguish between long-term institutional care and home care (Haiven and Haiven 2002, 12–13). While these site-based distinctions have historically been evident in most provinces, they are blurring now that many types of care are being offered in private homes. In this context, it is useful to define *home care* more broadly as the provision of services meant to prevent, delay, or substitute for those previously provided by long-term care institutions as well as by acute-care institutions. It is also important to note that home care increasingly occurs "at the intersection of Medicare and social service systems" (Flood 1999, 8–9). This study illustrates the blurring of the distinctions between long-term care and home care in Ontario.

12 Ministry of Health, Ministry of Community and Social Services, and Ministry of Citizenship, "Redirection of Long-Term Care and Support Services in Ontario: A Public Consultation Paper," 1991 ["Redirection"], "Building Partnerships in Long-Term Care: A Local Planning Framework," 1993, "Building Partnerships in Long-Term Care: A Policy Framework," 1993, "Building Partnerships in Long-Term Care: An Implementation Framework," 1993.
13 Ibid., "Redirection."
14 Bill 101, *An Act to Amend Certain Acts Concerning Long-Term Care*, Part IV, s. 2.3, 11.1(1), (2), 35th Legislature (Ontario), 3rd Sess. (first reading, 26 November 1991; second reading, 9 December 1992; third reading, 3 May 1993; royal assent, 1 June 1993).
15 Self-managed-care programs also exist in New Brunswick, Quebec, Manitoba, Saskatchewan, Alberta, and British Columbia.
16 Alix Goulet, "Vulnerable Employee, Vulnerable Employer: Self-Managed Attendant Service Direct Funding Pilot Project, An Examination of the Labour Issues," unpublished paper, 1994; see also Malhotra (2001).
17 Ontario Public Service Employees Union, "Services to the Developmentally Handicapped: A Five-Year Plan for Disaster; A Critique of the Five-Year Plan and Discussion of Alternatives," unpublished report, n.d.
18 Anonymous CAW staff person, interview by author, 6 November 2001.
19 Goulet, supra note 16.
20 Council of Canadians with Disabilities, "Self-Managed and Programmed Services: Threats and Opportunities," *CCD Health Inspector* 7 (1998), <http:\www.pcs.mb.ca/~cc/hitb2699.html>.
21 The definitions of *personal support services* and *homemaking services* are from the *Long-Term Care Act*, 1994 (SO 1994, c. C-26; O. Reg. 367/94), made under the *Ministry of Community and Social Services Act* (RSO 1990, c.M-20, as amended by 1993, c. 2, ss. 23, 24), which allowed for direct grants to persons with disabilities.
22 Jenny Ahn, interview by author, 25 October 2001.
23 Two anonymous attendant workers, interview by author.
24 Anonymous attendant worker, interview by author.
25 Ahn, supra note 22.
26 Data in this paragraph are based on analysis by the author of the public use microdata samples of the 2001 Labour Force Survey. Similar figures on status, form, and work arrangements are found for workers in the Toronto CMA (the metropolitan-area census).
27 Ibid.
28 Ahn, supra note 22; anonymous attendant worker, interview by author.

29 Analysis by the author of the public use microdata samples of the 1996 census for the Toronto CMA.
30 Anonymous attendant worker, interview by author.
31 The OLRB has argued that in cases where there is a question of whether a person is a dependent contractor, the board considers the type of economic dependence and the kind of business relationship existing between the person and the alleged employer. See *Huntsville District Memorial Hospital*, [1998] 47 CLRBR (2d) 109, para. 28 [*Huntsville 1*]; *Superior Sand, Gravel & Supplies Ltd*, [1978] OLRB Rep. Feb. 199, para. 20; Sack, Mitchell, and Price (1997), para. 2.82.
32 *OLRA*, supra note 2.
33 *Huntsville 1*, supra note 31; *Huntsville District Memorial Hospital*, [1998] OLRB Rep. Dec. 22 [*Huntsville 2*]. Similar OLRB rulings have been made for home child-care workers contracted to an agency. See *Ottawa Day Nursery Inc.*, [1987] OLRB Rep. Jan. 22 [*Ottawa Day*]; *Cradleship Creche of Metropolitan Toronto*, [1986] OLRB Rep. Feb. 21 [*Cradleship*]; *Andrew Fleck Childcare Centre*, [1987] OLRB Rep. Jan. 5 [*Andrew Fleck*]. See also the case brought before the New Brunswick Court of Appeal, *Canadian Red Cross Society v. United Steelworkers of America*, [1991] 115 NBR (2d)-115 RNB (2é) and 291 APR [*Red Cross*].
34 *Huntsville 1*, supra note 31. See also Human Resources Development Canada, "Visiting Homemakers, Housekeepers and Related Occupations, 6471" (<http://www.on.hrdc-drhc.gc.ca>), in which the government states that many visiting homemakers are self-employed.
35 *CLC, Local 1689 v. Algonquin Tavern*, [1981] 3 CLRBR 337 [*Algonquin*]. The factors are: use of substitutes; ownership of tools; evidence of entrepreneurial activity; selling one's services to the market generally; economic mobility or independence, including the freedom to reject job opportunities; evidence of some variation in the fees charged for the services rendered; integration into the employers' operations; degree of specialization, skill, expertise, or creativity required; control of manner and means of performing the work; contract amount, term, and manner of payment; similar conditions to employees.
36 *Huntsville 1*, supra note 31 at para. 41.
37 Ibid.
38 Ibid., at para. 42.
39 Ibid., at para. 44.
40 *Huntsville 2*, supra note 33.
41 Ibid., at para. 4.
42 Ibid., at para. 19.

43 Ibid., at para. 20.
44 *Nucleus Housing Inc.*, [1984] OLRB Rep. Jan. 64 [*Nucleus*]; *Sisters of St. Joseph of the Diocese of Peterborough*, [1991] OLRB Rep. Dec. 1406 [*Sisters*]. See also *Red Cross*, supra note 33.
45 *OLRA*, supra note 2 at s. 2(a).
46 *Nucleus*, supra note 44.
47 Ibid., at para. 9.
48 *Sisters*, supra note 44. The SEIU was certified as the bargaining agent for a full-time unit of lay employees of the Sisters of St. Joseph in 1988, and the parties had since negotiated two collective agreements. The dispute over employment status came up during the negotiation of the third collective agreement. When the SEIU sought to have the provisions of the *Hospital Labour Disputes Arbitration Act* (RSO 1990, c. H-14) apply to the full-time unit, the Sisters of St. Joseph argued that the workers were domestics employed in a private home and therefore not subject to the *OLRA* or to the act. The minister of labour referred the case to the Labour Relations Board to determine whether the workers were domestics, and thus whether they were excluded from the act. See also *Andrew Fleck*, supra note 33, in which the board ruled that the fact that funding for the services performed comes from an external source is not relevant to the determination of whether the individuals performing the services are dependent contractors.
49 *Sisters*, supra note 44 at paras 14–15.
50 *Nucleus*, supra note 44.
51 *Sisters*, supra note 44 at paras 22, 25.
52 Ibid., at para. 24.
53 In contrast, 70 per cent of nurse supervisors and registered nurses, 48 per cent of those with technical and related health occupations, and 50 per cent of those with health support occupations are covered by a union contract in Ontario. In the Toronto CMA, the equivalent figures are lower, at 63, 35, and 47 per cent, respectively (analysis of the public use microdata samples of the 2001 Labour Force Survey by the author).
54 Ahn, supra note 22.
55 Anonymous attendant worker, interview by author.
56 Ahn, supra note 22.
57 Anonymous attendant worker, interview by author.
58 Ibid.
59 Ahn, supra note 22.
60 Anonymous attendant worker, interview by author.
61 Ahn, supra note 22.

62 Ibid. Ahn suggested that the union and the agencies (employers) work together to lobby the government, and Local 40 worked with groups like the Canadian Health Coalition to lobby for more funding for long-term care. However, they have had little success in pressuring the Conservative government to increasing funding.
63 Anonymous attendant worker, interview by author.
64 Ahn, supra note 22.
65 ILGWU and INTERCEDE, "Meeting the Needs of Vulnerable Workers: Proposals for Improved Employment Legislation and Access to Collective Bargaining for Domestic Workers and Industrial Homeworkers," 1993.
66 Anonymous attendant worker, interview by author; Ahn, supra note 22.
67 Ahn, supra note 22.
68 Health Care Health and Safety Association of Ontario and the Workplace Safety and Insurance Board, "Health and Safety in the Home Care Environment," 2000, <http:// www.hchsa.on.ca> ["Health Care"].
69 *Occupational Health and Safety Act*, RSO 1990, c. O.1, s. 1(1) [OHSA]. See also Ontario Ministry of Labour, "A Guide to the *Occupational Health and Safety Act*," <http://www.gov.on.ca/LAB/ohs/g_ohse.htm>. However, in the case of an accident, inspectors cannot enter a home that is being used as a workplace unless they have the consent of the occupier. See "Health Care," supra note 68, p. 8.
70 OHSA, supra note 69, O. Reg. 67/93, amended to O. Reg. 142/99, Health Care and Residential Facilities.
71 Anonymous attendant worker, interview by author.
72 The Health Care Health and Safety Association of Ontario states that it is almost impossible to establish effective rules for maximum weights to be lifted, and it recommends that employers eliminate all manual lifting of people (see "How to Figure Out How Much You Can Lift," Fast Facts, <www.hchsa.on.ca>). However, some people with disabilities are critical of such agency-wide rules because they believe that they standardize individual care needs and fail to address the fact that being lifted can be life-threatening for people with some impairments. See Sarah Carpenter, "Lifts 'R Us!," *CILT Newsletter*, summer 2001, <http:\www.cilt.ca>.
73 Work refusals have also occurred because gloves were not supplied by the client/consumer or the agency. The title of the collective agreement, which covers the period of 1998 to 2001, will not be given here in order to protect the confidentiality of the workers in this bargaining unit.
74 The right to refuse work for persons employed in the operation of "a residential group home or other facility for persons with behavioural or emotional

problems or a physical, mental or developmental disability" does not apply when "the worker's refusal to work would directly endanger the life, health or safety of another person" (*OHSA*, supra note 69 at ss. 43[1] and 43[2]).
75 Anonymous attendant worker, interview by author.
76 Ahn, supra note 22.
77 Anonymous attendant worker, interview by author.
78 Ahn, supra note 22.
79 Ibid.; anonymous attendant worker, interview by author.
80 Two anonymous attendant workers, interview by author; Ahn, supra note 22.
81 Anonymous attendant worker, interview by author.
82 These issues are not unique to Ontario. In November of 1995, the Saskatchewan Human Rights Commission granted an exemption from the anti-discrimination (in employment) provisions of the Saskatchewan *Human Rights Code* to male residents of a special-care home in Melfort, allowing the residents to choose men to attend to their personal needs. The SEIU appealed this exemption, but the Court of Queen's Bench ruled on 17 January 1997 that the Human Rights Commission was right to grant an exemption (see *Service Employees International Union v. North Central Health District Board and the Saskatchewan Human Rights Commission,* [14 January 1997] Saskatoon No. 809 of 1996 [Sask. QBJ]).
83 Anonymous attendant worker, interview by author. Fourteen per cent of those employed by the two employers unionized in the 1980s were hired since 2000.
84 The amended *Ministry of Community and Social Services Act*, part of the *Act to Amend Certain Acts Concerning Long-Term Care*, Part IV, 2.3, 11.1-(1), allows for direct grants from the minister to people with disabilities. Part IV, 2.3, 11.1-(2) allows for a minister to give a grant to an agency or organization that will transfer the funds to individuals with disabilities.
85 See also *Application Guide, Self-Managed Care: Direct Funding* (available from the CILT).
86 This information is based on an analysis of the contract between the CILT and the Ontario government that guides the Direct Funding Program Pilot, which is found in Parker et al. (2000, appendix C). I was unable to secure a copy of the contract governing the final program. However, an analysis of the available material on the pilot and the final program suggests that few substantial changes were made in this area with the move from the Direct Funding Program Pilot to the Self-Managed Attendant Services: Direct Funding Program.
87 *Nucleus,* supra note 44.
88 *Huntsville 1,* supra note 31.

89 *Ottawa Day*, supra note 33; *Cradleship*, supra note 33; *Andrew Fleck*, supra note 33.
90 Self-manager cited in Parker et al. (2000, 11).
91 Ahn, supra note 22.
92 Self-managers have also gained functional flexibility, in that they receive tasks not available in unionized settings. The regulations allow the self-manager to hire one person as a housekeeper and personal attendant. However, there is an upper limit for housekeeping, set at four hours per week. The *Regulated Health Professions Act, 1991* (SO 1991, c. 18) significantly facilitates this task flexibility. When the act was first introduced, tasks such as catheterization were considered controlled acts. People with disabilities organized and won exceptions for certain controlled acts undertaken by workers assisting them with routine daily activities (see Roeher Institute 1993, p. 5).
93 O. Reg. 367/94, s. 2(1), Grants for Persons with Disabilities.
94 *Nucleus*, supra note 44; *Sisters*, supra note 44.
95 *Application Guide*, supra note 85.
96 See the CILT Web site: <http://www.cilt.ca>.
97 Ontario *Human Rights Code*, RSO 1990, c. H-19, s. 24(1)(c) (SO 1981, c. 53, s. 4[1]; SO 1986, c. 64, s. 18[5]). The code states that the right to equal treatment without discrimination is not infringed where "an individual person refuses to employ another for reasons of any prohibited ground of discrimination in section 5, where the primary duty of the employment is attending to the medical or *personal needs* of the person or of an ill child or an aged, infirm or ill spouse, same-sex partner or relative of the person. Section 5 gives every person the right to equal treatment with respect to employment without discrimination because of race, ancestry, place of origin, colour, ethnic origin, citizenship, creed, sex, sexual orientation, age, record of offences, marital status, family status or handicap."
98 <http://www.cilt.ca>.
99 *OHSA*, supra note 69 at s. 3(1). The act excludes all work performed by a servant to, in, or about a private residence. The term servant is not defined in the act, but according to an official with the Ontario Ministry of Labour, it refers to a person directly hired, paid, and supervised by an individual in his or her own home.
100 All workers in scheduled industries are covered, but only full-time "domestics" are included in the scheduled industries (*Workplace Safety and Insurance Act, 1997*, SO 1997; see Schedule 1, Class 1, "other services," 27, on full-time domestics).
101 The 2000 ESA appears better than the 1990 ESA for many domestic workers in that the latter distinguished between *domestic worker* and *domestic*

servant based on whether the worker lived in or out, and it set different levels of coverage for full-time and part-time (less than twenty-four hours a week) domestic workers. In contrast, the 2000 ESA defines one general category, *domestic workers*, without setting hour limits (Ministry of Labour, Employment Standards Fact Sheet for Domestic Workers for the 1990 ESA, <http://www.gov.on.ca/LAB/es/dom.htm>; for the 2000 ESA, <www.gov.on.ca/LAB/esa/esa_e/fa_domestcis_e.htm>.

102 O. Reg. 285/01, Exemptions, Special Rules and Establishment of Minimum Wage: Definitions (*Employment Standards Act, 2000*, RSO 2000, c. 41) [Exemptions].

103 *Dolega-Kamienski Estate*, [2003] OLRB Jan. 24 (OESAD No. 72., No. 1173–02-ES, Employment Practices Branch No. 41011116.

104 The regulations of the ESA define a *residential-care worker* as "a person who is employed to supervise and care for children or developmentally handicapped persons in a family-type residential dwelling or cottage and who resides in the dwelling or cottage during work period, but does not include a foster parent" (see Exemptions, supra note 102). The OLRB had to determine whether the employer/client/consumer was "developmentally handicapped" and whether his or her residence was a "family-type residential dwelling or cottage." The board decided that the employer/client/consumer was disabled but not *developmentally* disabled, and that the work site was a private household, not a "family-type residential dwelling or cottage," which it considered to be a group home. Following this logic, the OLRB argued that the worker was not a residential-care worker, but closer to a domestic worker.

105 Self-manager cited in Parker et al. (2000, 19).

106 Anonymous attendant worker, interview by author.

107 Furthermore, this survey likely underestimated the lower end of the range because the methodology centred on the self-managers who asked the two workers who worked the most hours to fill out the worker questionnaire (see Roeher Institute 1997, appendix 1).

108 *Application Guide*, supra note 85.

109 This is also the case for direct funding programs in other provinces (Morris et al. 1999).

110 Under the new *Employment Insurance Act* (SC 1996, c. 23), workers must have worked between 420 and 720 hours in the previous 52 weeks, which would average out to roughly 35 hours a week, and those reentering the system could need as many as 910 hours in the previous 52 weeks in order to qualify (Vosko 2003).

111 *Craftwood Construction Co. Ltd*, [1980] OLRB Rep. Nov. 1613, cited in Sack, Mitchell, and Price (1997, 2.88).

CHAPTER FOUR

1 The EAC/ACR certification applies only to professional freelance editors who are authors of original compilations of data, including, but not limited to, original indexes, glossaries, tables of contents, and bibliographies in French or English.
2 *Status of the Artist Act, 1992,* SC 1992, c. 33 [SAA].
3 TWUC made application for judicial review at the same time that it filed this request for reconsideration with the tribunal.
4 *Canada Labour Code,* RSC 1985, c. L-2 [CLC].
5 A survey of the EAC/ACR's membership reveals that most hold at least a BA, and many hold graduate degrees.
6 They also lack extended benefits typically attached to the full-time, full-year job; 29 per cent of freelance editors surveyed by the EAC/ACR in 1998 had no benefits, and 38 per cent had benefits through a spousal plan.
7 A UK-based study, involving a survey of 400 freelancers and 40 in-depth interviews, found that "what might constitute 35 hours of work in an in-house situation appeared to condense down to little more than 25 hours of freelancing" (Stanworth and Stanworth 1995, 222).
8 Anonymous freelance editor, interview by author, 26 June 2001 and 13 November 2001.
9 Publishers increasingly resort to subcontracting in an effort to reduce their fixed production costs, which account for fully one-third to a half of the total production costs in book publishing (International Labour Organization, *Symposium on Information Technologies in the Media and Entertainment Industries: Their Impact on Employment, Working Conditions and Labour-Management Relations, Report for Discussion,* 28 February-3 March 2000).
10 For a description of the editing process, see "Definitions of Terms" in the standard contract promoted by the EAC/ACR (Standard Freelance Editorial Agreement, Schedule A, <http://www.editors.ca/mmbr/guide.htm>).
11 Anonymous freelance editor, interview by author, 13 November 2001.
12 The ethic of invisibility is paradoxical. On the part of the editor, it entails the importance of remaining silent while obtaining payment and acknowledgment for one's work, thereby exercising one's moral right to remain anonymous and possibly waiving the right to assert copyright. Yet the editor stakes his or her career and professional reputation on being associated with successful manuscripts and/or imprints.
13 Voting membership is maintained by performing 500 hours of editing work every three years.

14 The EAC/ACR reports that 60 per cent of an editor's work comes from other editors.
15 EAC/ACR, *Members' Handbook*, 2000, p. 12.
16 CLC, supra note 4 at s. 3(1). This definition is broader than previous ones in the code – which defines *employee* as a person employed by an employer – in its addition of dependent contractors and constables, but narrower in its managerial exclusion.
17 Ibid.
18 For example, the board determined that a group of freelance journalists working for the CBC were employees due to their position of economic subordination (*Société Radio-Canada/Canadian Broadcasting Corporation*, [1982] 44 di 19, 1 CLRBR [NS] 129). In contrast, at the provincial level, the British Columbia Labour Relations Board found that freelance reviewers for two daily newspapers were dependent contractors. In *Pacific Press Ltd v. Vancouver-New Westminster Newspaper Guild Local 115*, it delivered its finding on the basis of integration between the reviewers and the papers, noting that "Their product ... is a central part of the cultural and entertainment section of the newspaper. It is required on nearly a daily basis. These reviewers must fit into the publication needs of the newspaper and accept assignments and direction of its editors. Out of these functional needs of both sides, a definite continuing relationship emerges between the newspaper and its freelance reviewers. These individuals work on a regular basis for the newspapers and in return earn a regular income, usually ranging upwards of 75 percent of their total earnings" (BCLRB No. 4/77, para. 37).
19 *Competition Act*, RSC 1985, c. C-34.
20 *Recommendation Concerning the Status of the Artist*, UNESCO, 21st Sess. (1980), s. 4(b).
21 *Status of the Artist: Report of the Task Force*, Supply and Services Canada, 1986, Recommendation 16a.
22 Ibid., Recommendation 47.
23 *An Act Respecting the Professional Status and Conditions of Engagement of Performing, Recording and Film Artists*, RSQ 1987, c. s. 32 [RSQ 1987].
24 *An Act Respecting the Professional Status of Artists in the Visual Arts, Arts and Crafts and Literature, and Their Contracts with Promoters*, RSQ 1988, c. s. 32.01.
25 For example, the Saskatchewan NDP government only recently passed legislation on the status of the artist, and it is much weaker than that of Quebec and the federal jurisdiction.
26 Standing Committee on Communications and Culture, *Second Report to the House: Status of the Artist, Minutes of Proceedings and Evidence of the*

Standing Committee on Communications and Culture, 34th Parliament, 2d Sess., 1989–90, No. 5.
27 *Public Service Staff Relations Act*, RSC 1985, c. P-35.
28 *Copyright Act*, RSC 1985, c. C-42 [*Copyright Act*].
29 In contrast, Quebec legislation dictates that a collective agreement must not be "contrary to public order or prohibited law" (RSQ 1987, supra note 23 at c. s. 32.1, s. 43).
30 For example, the definition of *artist* under section 6(2)(b) of the act refers to *authors* as defined by the *Copyright Act*. Among this statute, the *Canada Labour Code*, and the *Public Service Staff Relations Act*, conflicts could also arise over the distinction between *dependent* and *independent contractor*.
31 Regulations to the act introduced in 1999 further limit the scope of collective bargaining. While the CAPPRT recommended that "editing, research, continuity, library or archival work" be covered in 1995, after holding consultations during which various producers objected to the inclusion of editors, Human Resources Development Canada amended the regulations to exclude editors and several other groups. This compelled the EAC/ACR to base its argument for certification on behalf of freelance editors on section 6(2)b(i), arguing that certain editors are indeed authors (CAPPRT, letter to Minister Alfonso Gagliano, 29 April 1996 [on file with author]; Josée Dubois, executive director of the CAPPRT, interview by author, 6 December 2001).
32 Regulations pursuant to section 6(2)b(iii) extend coverage to independent contractors who contribute directly to the creative aspects of a production by carrying out activities in the following professional categories: camera work, lighting, and sound design; costumes, coiffure, and makeup design; set design; arranging and orchestrating; research for audiovisual productions, editing, and continuity.
33 *SAA*, supra note 2 at s. 18b. The act does not direct the tribunal to judge the quality of artistic work. It must simply concern itself with the presence (or absence) of the criteria set out in sections 18b(ii) and (iii) to determine whether an independent contractor is a professional for the purposes of section 6(2)(b) (Dubois, supra note 31).
34 *SAA*, supra note 2 at s. 9(2). MacPherson emphasizes that artists are not denied coverage under the act solely because they contract through an organization (1999, 361).
35 Since its inception, the only significant mention of competition in a CAPPRT decision involved *Re Periodical Writers Assn. of Canada* ([1996] CAPPRT No. 11, Dec. No. 014). In that case, the effects of new technologies on the

author-publisher relationship were raised, and the tribunal stated clearly that its ability to deal with this issue was limited by its jurisdiction (see para. 12).

36 To be clear, under the *Competition Act*, *product* is defined as including both articles and services. *Services*, in turn, is defined as all services "industrial, trade, professional or otherwise."

37 Drafters of the legislation needed a way to categorize artists falling within the federal jurisdiction that did not overlap with the Quebec legislation, and they determined that the *Copyright Act* provided the best mechanism for doing so. The EAC/ACR case is unique in its use of the *Copyright Act* to define authorship. Editors are the only group of artists compelled to make arguments on the basis of jurisprudence flowing from the SAA, since it was not obvious to the tribunal that they were artists within the meaning of the statute. Still, the claim that the tribunal has exceeded its jurisdiction, treading into the jurisdiction of the Copyright Board, was central to TWUC's application for judicial review. See *Re Writers' Union of Canada*, [1998] CAPPRT No. 4, Dec. No. 028 [*Writers' Union* 028].

38 Samatha Maislin-Dickson, personal communication with the author, 26 October 2001.

39 The tribunal refuses to arbitrarily limit the scope of collective bargaining. Yet it also assures concerned parties that negotiating copyright does not make the artists' association the agent of the artist for the purpose of granting licenses or assignments of copyright for those works. But the tribunal does seek to establish minimum terms and conditions that would apply when an artist decides to license or assign a particular copyright to a producer who is party to the scale agreement. See *Writers' Union* 028, supra note 37.

40 The tribunal is composed of a chair, a vice-chair, and up to four members appointed by the governor in council on the recommendation of the minister of labour in consultation with the minister of Canadian heritage. Since its inception, most members have come from the cultural community, and some have experience as government officials.

41 These two acts were in place when the SAA was first introduced.

42 SAA, supra note 2 at ss. 25, 26.

43 Since the tribunal is dealing with freelance artists, rather than requiring the employer to post a notice in the workplace, it must give public notice of every application for certification that it receives.

44 SAA, supra note 2 at s. 17.

45 Ibid., at s. 26(1).

46 Ibid., at s. 27 (1).

47 Ibid., at s. 26(2).
48 Ibid., at s. 28(3).
49 Ibid., at s. 5.
50 See *Canadian Wire Service Guild Local 213 v. CBC*, [1987] 70 di 26, CLRB Dec. No. 629.
51 SAA, supra note 2 at s. 24; RSQ 1987, supra note 23 at s. 32.1.
52 Dubois, supra note 31.
53 The inspiration for this section's subtitle comes from Connie John, manager of the EAC/ACR, who, in her summation at the CAPPRT hearings reconsidering the EAC certification on 9 May 2002, noted that opponents of freelance editors' certification under the SAA treated the EAC like "a mouse that roared." The first three artists' associations certified by the CAPPRT to represent a sector include the Société des auteurs de radio, télévision et cinéma, the Union des écrivaines et écrivains québécois, and the Canadian Actors' Equity Association. In the federal jurisdiction, producers range from Crown corporations (such as the CBC) to various government departments.
54 *Re Editors' Assn. of Canada*, [2001] CAPPRT Dec. No. 033, para. 2 [EAC 033].
55 The exemption of editors of literary works from regulations under this section made it necessary for the EAC/ACR to argue that freelance editors fall under section 6(2)(b)(i) and are therefore authors under the *Copyright Act* (Dubois, supra note 31).
56 EAC 033, supra note 54 at para. 3. To be clear, the EAC/ACR excluded in-house editors from the proposed sector because they are assumed to be employees, although practices vary in the publishing industry.
57 Ibid., at para. 33.
58 The following groups received intervener status "as of right": the Writers' Guild of Canada, the Société des auteurs de radio, télévision et cinéma, the Writers' Union of Canada (TWUC), and the Periodical Writers' Association of Canada. None of them appeared before the tribunal or presented written submissions except TWUC. The Canadian Newspaper Association (CNA) was also granted intervener status, but it merely submitted a letter to put itself on record as arguing that no decision of the tribunal in this case should have any affect upon newspapers, given the decision in *Periodical Writers' Association* (CAPPRT, [1996] Dec. No. 016). The EAC/ACR did not respond to the CNA's submission, and the tribunal deemed it inappropriate to rule on the issue.
59 The EAC/ACR defined *developmental editing* as a process whereby the "writer and editor jointly evolve a concept or story idea, [to] which either or both have contributed, into a strong outline or proposal." It characterized

structural and *substantive editing* as highly creative processes that involve the editor suggesting changes to the structure of the work. *Line* or *manuscript editing*, in contrast, was described as the line-by-line editing of the manuscript, "where the editor draws out the work of the author through his or her comments, queries and suggestions in the manuscript margins." The EAC/ACR also defined proofreading, which involves checking the final proof against the final manuscript version for typographical errors and deviations from the word-processing instructions (*EAC* 033, supra note 54 at para. 11).

60 Ibid., at para. 12.
61 Ibid., at para. 11.
62 Ibid., at para. 13.
63 Ibid., at para. 14.
64 Ibid., at para. 15.
65 He reported that "a novel usually takes nine months to write. An editor is involved at the end of the process and will take a few hours to read his manuscript and give verbal critique of a general nature" (Ibid., at para. 22).
66 On cross-examination, however, Moore confirmed that professional, experienced editors and writers are collaborators when the writer agrees that the editor should make extensive changes to the manuscript (Ibid., at paras 23 and 26).
67 Ibid., at para. 27.
68 Ibid.
69 Ibid., at para. 28.
70 In the case of the SAA, these provisions included: section 5, defining *artists* as "independent contractors"; section 6(2)(b)(i-iii), setting out the definition of *professional artist*; section 17(p)(i), enabling the tribunal to decide any question in the proceeding, including whether "a person is a producer or an artist"; section 23(1)(a-c), specifying bylaw requirements; section 25(1)(a-c), detailing procedures for application; section 26(1)(a-c), giving the tribunal the power to determine the sector or sectors that are suitable for bargaining; section 27(1), on determining representativity; and section 28, on final certification. In the case of the *Copyright Act*, the tribunal cited definitions of *book, collective work, compilation, literary work, performance, performer's performance,* and *work of joint authorship* under section 2, and the definition of copyright under section 3. It also cited section 12, establishing that "where a work is, or has been, prepared or published by or under the direction of Her Majesty or any government department," the copyright will belong to the Crown, subject to any agreement with the author, and, finally, section 14.1(1), referring to moral rights.
71 *EAC* 033, supra note 54 at para. 31.
72 Ibid., at para. 33.

73 Ibid., at para. 34.
74 Ibid., at para. 35.
75 The EAC/ACR acknowledged that while it did not have an example of a written waiver, a waiver may be implied (Ibid., at para. 36).
76 Ibid., at para. 37. See also *Re Canadian Actors' Equity Assn.*, [1996] CAPPRTD No. 7, Dec. No. 010.
77 The EAC/ACR referred to the certification of the PWAC, which characterizes its jurisdiction in a similar way, to defend its argument that TWUC certification only covers "writers who are authors" (EAC 033, supra note 54 at para. 38).
78 Ibid., at para. 39.
79 Ibid., at para. 41.
80 In taking this stance, TWUC raised the issue of originality, submitting that "editors do work of varying significance, but that no editing involves sufficient imagination or creative spark to meet the test for originality" demanded of authorship. Moreover, it contested the claim that the CAPPRT has the power to define the word *author*. To refute the EAC/ACR's claim that editors have copyright and moral rights in relation to the works that they edit, TWUC again noted that while editors suggest changes, writers ultimately decide whether to reject or accept them. According to TWUC, "only writers have moral rights in their works. Editors do not have such rights, not because they have waived them as the EAC/ACR suggests, but because moral rights simply do not arise with respect to editors. Nor does editing give rise to copyright. A finding to the contrary would literally turn the industry on its head" (Ibid., at para. 44).
81 Ibid., at para. 41.
82 Ibid., at para. 51.
83 Ibid., at para. 52.
84 Ibid., at para. 58.
85 The tribunal was clear that the editor must expend labour, skill, and judgment, but that a "creative spark" is not required as a test of originality, except in relation to the compilation of data (Ibid., at paras 59, 60).
86 Ibid., at para. 61.
87 The tribunal drew heavily on the EAC/ACR's description of the task of editing in defining *joint authorship* in its decision. It asserted that copy editing does not represent a significant enough contribution to make an editor a joint author, while "developmental editing and substantive and structural editing clearly involve significant contributions of original expression." The nature of the contribution of line editing, however, depends on the extent of an editor's efforts in a given case. The tribunal relied on Jim Lyons's testimony in constructing this continuum (Ibid., at paras 63–4).

88 The tribunal also noted that even when a person authors an original literary work under the direction of the Crown, that person nevertheless remains the author of the work (Ibid., at para. 66).
89 The tribunal supported its decision by referring to two other applications for certification (Ibid., at para. 68). See also *Re American Federation of Musicians of the United States and Canada*, [1997] CAPPRTD No. 1, Dec. No. 019, paras 31–4; *Re Guilde des musiciens du Québec*, [1997] CAPPRTD No. 2, Dec. No. 020, paras 30–2. In a rather shocking dismissal of TWUC's argument that editors could fall under section 6(2)(b)(iii), the tribunal also squarely rejected this suggestion, because editors are not named in the regulations (EAC 033, supra note 54 at para. 69).
90 Ibid., at paras 70–1.
91 Ibid., at para. 71. To clarify the boundaries of the EAC/ACR certification, the tribunal also excluded all authors covered by the certifications granted to PWAC, WGC, SARDEC, and TWUC (Ibid., at para.73).
92 Ibid., at paras 74–6.
93 Ibid., at paras 77–8.
94 To clarify the scope of the certification, it excluded authors covered by the Union des écrivaines et écrivains québécois (UNEQ), the Directors' Guild of Canada (DGC), and the Playwrights' Union of Canada (PUC), and it reinserted the term *literary* in the description of the sector. The EAC/ACR supported these amendments, since it was only seeking to represent editors of literary works, and since it respected the jurisdictions of these three artists' associations (*Re Editors' Assn. of Canada*, [2001] CAPPRTD No. 5, Dec. No. 036).
95 Application for judicial review is distinct from an appeal. It is restricted to legal questions that relate to the jurisdiction of the tribunal itself and given effect by the enabling legislation, in this instance, the SAA.
96 The Writers' Union of Canada and Editors' Association of Canada, Court File A-63201, Grounds for Application, A:4.
97 Ibid.
98 Ibid., at (iii), p. 4.
99 Ibid., at (iv).
100 It claimed, as well, that the tribunal had erred in law by failing to consider whether a sector with indeterminate membership is suitable for bargaining under section 26 of the statute, by failing to take account of the common interests and shared history of professional relations of editors who are joint authors and authors for whom TWUC and other writers' associations were already certified to represent, and by determining a sector for bargaining that conflicts with previous certifications.

101 *Re Writers' Union of Canada*, [2002] CAPPRTD No. 3, Dec. No. 039, at paras 14,16. The tribunal also deemed the relevant provisions of the SAA to be those related to the definition of *artist*, defined in accordance with the *Copyright Act*, and the tribunal's power to amend any determination, certification of an association, and sector designation as well as reassess representativity. In turn, it deemed the following provisions in the *Copyright Act* to be relevant: its definitions of *book, collected work, compilation, literary work, performance, performers, work of joint authorship*, and *copyright*; and its provisions related to authors' rights – specifically, the right to the integrity of the work, the right to be associated with the work, and the right to remain anonymous. (In examining issues surrounding copyright, it acknowledged that the Crown has control of any work prepared or published under the direction or control of Her Majesty or any government department.)
102 Ibid., at para. 20.
103 Ibid., at para. 26. One of its witnesses, writer Susan Crean, also gave evidence that "an editor of an anthology conceives of the concept of a book, gathers the material together and usually writes an introduction of some kind"; she maintained that such editors are really writers, and they should come under TWUC's jurisdiction.
104 Ibid., at para. 28.
105 Ibid., at para. 32.
106 Two of the EAC/ACR's witnesses also gave evidence that "it is not always the writer who has the final word on whether an editor's suggestions will or will not be incorporated into a work, particularly with respect to government work," and that substantive editing is always creative and collaborative, as is the work of the "overseeing editor" (Ibid., at paras 30, 32).
107 Ibid., at para. 33. The PUC and the WGC added to this claim by noting that the ethic of invisibility also illustrates that editors do not consider themselves authors (Ibid., at para. 41).
108 Ibid., at para. 34.
109 Ibid., at para. 45.
110 Ibid., at para. 49.
111 Ibid., at para. 52.
112 Ibid., at paras 54, 56. The EAC/ACR also asserted that the writer's ability to accept or reject changes is addressed in the contract. But, while in many cases writers can accept or reject changes, in government work the editor normally makes the final decision, and in such instances writers are the "scribes of editors" (Ibid., at paras 57–8).
113 Ibid., at para. 70.

114 Ibid., at para. 72.
115 The CAPPRT held, moreover, that an editor only collaborates in the sense that she or he assists the author in perfecting a work, and "the fact that the writer does not always retain the ability to accept or reject an editor's suggestions in the context of works commissioned by federal government departments does not alter the conclusion that editors are not joint authors in the works they edit" (Ibid., at para. 73). This rendering led the tribunal to set aside the question of whether editors who are joint authors were already covered by existing certifications – initially a defining question in this case – as it had determined that editors are not joint authors in the meaning of the *Copyright Act* (Ibid., at paras 77, 82).
116 Ibid., at para. 91.
117 Ibid., at para. 93.
118 Ibid., at para. 98.
119 Ibid.
120 Ibid., at paras 99–100.
121 In its lengthy report, however, the federal government acknowledged that "the Professional Category Regulations defining the categories of cultural workers eligible for coverage under the Status of the Artist Act should be reviewed" (Canadian Heritage, Corporate Review Branch, 2003, Recommendation 8, <http://www.pch.gc.ca/progs/em-cr/eval/2002/2002 25/6 e.cfm>).

CONCLUSION

1 *Trade Union Act*, SC 1872, c. 30.
2 International Labour Organization, *Freedom of Association: Digest of Decisions and Principles of the Freedom of Association Committee of the Governing Body of the ILO*, 4th rev. ed., 1996 (emphasis added) [ILO 1996].
3 NAALC, September 1993, Can.-Mex.-US, 32 ILM 1499 (1993). The NAALC only requires the signatory parties to enforce their existing labour laws and not to enact new laws. Moreover, the fundamental rights such as freedom of association, unlike the technical standards such as occupational health and safety standards, are not enforceable.
4 *Canadian Charter of Rights and Freedoms*, Part I of the *Constitution Act, 1982*, being Sched. B to the *Canada Act 1982* (UK), 1982, c. 11.
5 *R. v. Advance Cutting and Coring Ltd*, [2001] 3 SCR 209, at paras 170–1. By a narrow majority (five to four), the Supreme Court of Canada upheld

construction industry collective bargaining legislation in Quebec that required construction workers to join one of an enumerated list of unions against a claim brought by some workers, contractors, and real estate developers that the law violated their freedom from compelled association.

6 *Dunmore v. Ontario (Attorney General)*, [2001] 3 SCR 1016.
7 For a recent case in point, see *Children's Aid Society of Ottawa-Carleton*, [2001] OLRD No. 1234 (QL, OLRB).
8 Provincial Salary Agreement between the Government of the Province of British Columbia and the British Columbia Medical Association and the Medical Services Commission, 2002, British Columbia Ministry of Health Services, <http://www.healthservices.gov.bc.ca/msp/legislation/pdf/salary.pdf >.
9 Currently, *Competition Act*, RSC 1985, c. C-34, s. 45.
10 Ibid., s. 4(1)(a).
11 ILO 1996, supra note 2 at p. 51.
12 In both jurisdictions, the labour board is empowered to designate persons performing work to be employees when it is of the view that the contract between them can be the subject of a collective agreement or simply that it is appropriate (*Trade Union Act*, RSS 1978, c. T-17 [as amended]; *Labour Relations Act*, CCSM, c. L-10, s. 1).
13 International Labour Organization, *Symposium on Information Technologies in the Media and Entertainment Industries: Their Impact on Employment, Working Conditions and Labour-Management Relations, Report for Discussion*, 28 February-3 March 2000.
14 *Labour Relations Act*, SO 1995, c. 1, Sched. A, s. 43.
15 *Health Care Accessibility Act*, RSO 1990, c. H.3, ss. 3(1), (2); *Health Insurance Act*, RSO 1990, c. H.6, s. 27; *Ontario Medical Association Dues Act, 1991*, SO 1991, c. 51; *Physician Services Delivery Management Act, 1996*, SO 1996, c. 1, Sched. 1.
16 International Ladies' Garment Workers' Union (ILGWU) and INTERCEDE, "Meeting the Needs of Vulnerable Workers: Proposals for Improved Employment Legislation and Access to Collective Bargaining for Domestic Workers and Industrial Homeworkers," 1993 [ILGWU and INTERCEDE].
17 Ibid.
18 ILGWU and INTERCEDE, supra note 16.
19 Ibid., 51-4.
20 Ibid., 53-4. There is related-employer legislation in Ontario and elsewhere, yet it is very difficult to prove that two employers are related (Sack, Mitchell, and Price 1997, 6.88).

21 John Baigent, Vince Ready, and Tom Roper, *A Report to the Honourable Moe Sihota, Minister of Labour: Recommendations for Labour Law Reform*, 1992, British Columbia Ministry of Labour.
22 ILGWU and INTERCEDE, supra note 16 at p. 41.
23 Organizational forms are ideal types. Yet, as empirical and historical studies illustrate, associations, unions, and even cooperatives are not mutually exclusive forms with entirely different objectives in practice (Clement 1986; García 1994).

References

Abraham, Katharine G. 1990. "Restructuring the Employment Relationship: The Growth of Market Mediated Employment Relationships." In *New Developments in the Labor Market: Toward a New Institutional Paradigm*, edited by Katharine G. Abraham and Robert B. McKersie. Cambridge: MIT Press.
Acharya, Madhavi. 2001a. "Revenue, Operating Profits Rise at Torstar, But Special Charges Reduce Final Results." *Toronto Star*, 1 March.
– 2001b. "Torstar Reports Loss in Q1 of $92.7m." *Hamilton Spectator*, 3 May.
Adams, George. 1995. *Canadian Labour Law*. 2d ed. Aurora, ON: Canada Law Book.
Adams, Roy J. 1991. *Comparative Industrial Relations: Contemporary Research and Theory*. London: Harper Collins Academic.
Akyeampong, Ernest B., and Deborah Sussman. 2003. "Health-Related Insurance for the Self-Employed." *Perspectives on Labour and Income* 4, no. 5.
Arai, A. Bruce 2000. "Self-Employment As a Response to the Double Day for Women and Men in Canada." *Canadian Review of Sociology and Anthropology* 37, no. 2.
Armstrong, Hugh, Pat Armstrong, and M. Patricia Connelly. 1997. "Introduction: The Many Forms of Privatization." *Studies in Political Economy* 53.
Armstrong, Pat. 1993. "Professions, Unions, or What?: Learning from Nurses." In *Women Challenging Unions*, edited by Linda Briskin and Patricia McDermott. Toronto, Buffalo, and London: University of Toronto Press.

Armstrong, Pat, and Hugh Armstrong. 2002. *Thinking It Through: Women, Work and Caring in the New Millennium*. Halifax: Maritime Centre of Excellence for Women's Health.

– 2003. *Wasting Away: The Undermining of Canadian Health Care*. Don Mills, ON: Oxford University Press.

Aronson, Jane, and Sheila M. Neysmith. 2001. "Manufacturing Social Exclusion in the Home Care Market." *Canadian Public Policy* 27, no. 2.

Aronson, Robert L. 1991. *Self-Employment: A Labor Market Perspective*. Ithaca: Cornell University Press.

Arthurs, Harry W. 1965. "The Dependent Contractor: A Study of the Legal Problems of Countervailing Power." *University of Toronto Law Journal* 16, no. 1.

Bach, Michael, and Marcia Rioux. 1996. "Social Policy, Devolution and Disability: Back to Notions of the Worthy Poor?" In *Reflections on the Canada Health and Social Transfer (CHST)*. North York, ON: Roeher Institute.

Backhouse, Constance. 1976. "Labour Unions and Anti-combines Policy." *Osgoode Hall Law Journal* 14, no. 1.

Bakan, Abigail, and Daiva Stasiulis. 1995. "Making the Match: Domestic Placement Agencies and the Racialization of Women's Household Work." *Signs* 20, no. 2.

– eds. 1997. *Not One of the Family: Foreign Domestic Workers in Canada*. Toronto: University of Toronto Press.

Barnes, Colin, Geof Mercer, and Tom Shakespeare. 1999. *Exploring Disability: A Sociological Introduction*. Cambridge: Polity Press.

Baxter, Janeen, and Mark Western. 2001. *Reconfigurations of Class and Gender*. Stanford: Stanford University Press.

Bekken, Jon. 1995. "Newsboys: The Exploitation of 'Little Merchants' by the Newspaper Industry." In *Newsworkers*, edited by Hanno Hardt and Bonnie Brenen. Minneapolis: University of Minnesota Press.

Bendel, Michael. 1982. "The Dependent Contractor: An Unnecessary and Flawed Development in Canadian Labour Law." *University of Toronto Law Journal* 32, no. 4.

Benjamin, Paul. 2002. "Who Needs Labour Law? Defining the Scope of Labour Protection." In *Labour Law in an Era of Globalization: Transformative Practices and Possibilities*, edited by Joanne Conaghan, Michael Fischl, and Karl E. Klare. Oxford: Oxford University Press.

Bercusson, Brian. 1996. *European Labour Law*. London: Butterworths.

Bögenhold, Dieter, and Udo Staber. 1991. "The Decline and Rise of Self-Employment." *Work, Employment and Society* 5, no. 2.

Boileau, Josée. 2002. "Maintien à domicile: Quelques millions de plus pour adoucier la vie des handicapés." *Devoir*, 9 mai.

Broad, David, and Wayne Antony, eds. 1999. *Citizens or Consumers? Social Policy in a Market Society*. Halifax: Fernwood Publishing.

Brodie, Stewart, John Stanworth, and Thomas R. Wotruba. 2002. "Direct Sales Franchises in the UK: A Self-Employment Grey Area." *International Small Business Journal* 20, no. 1.

Bronfenbrenner, Kate, Ronald L. Seeber, and Rudolph A. Oswald, eds. 1997. *Organizing to Win: New Research on Union Strategies*. Ithaca, NY: ILR Press.

Bullen, John. 1986. "Hidden Workers: Child Labour and the Family Economy in Late Nineteenth-Century Urban Ontario." *Labour/Le Travail* 18.

Burr, Christina. 1999. *Spreading the Light: Work and Labour Reform in Late Nineteenth-Century Toronto*. Toronto: University of Toronto Press.

Buechtemann, Cristoph F., and Sigrid Quack. 1990. "How Precarious Is 'Nonstandard' Employment? Evidence for West Germany." *Cambridge Journal of Economics* 14, no. 3.

Campbell, Robert. 1990. "Postal Wars: Country Canada Takes on Corporatism." *Canadian Forum* 69.

– 1994. *The Politics of the Post: Canada's Postal Service from Public Service to Privatization*. Peterborough, ON: Broadview Press.

Canadian Postmasters. 1983. *The Canadian Postmasters, 1902–1982*. Ottawa: Canadian Postmasters and Assistants Association.

Canadian Press. 1987. "Mail Couriers Contract Workers, Court Rules." *Globe and Mail*, 23 December.

– 1988. "Union Bid Fails in Supreme Court." *Globe and Mail*, 27 May.

Carter, Donald D., et al. 2002. *Labour Law in Canada*. The Hague: Kluwer Law International.

Casey, Brian J. 2001. "Canadians Should Applaud UPS's Case against Canada Post." *Globe and Mail*, 15 February.

Charney, Richard J., and Thomas E.F. Brady. 1997. *Judicial Review in Labour Law* [looseleaf]. Aurora, ON: Canada Law Book.

Clement, Wallace. 1986. *The Struggle to Organize: Resistance in Canada's Fishery*. Toronto: McClelland and Stewart.

Clement, Wallace, and John Myles. 1994. *Relations of Ruling: Class and Gender in Postindustrial Societies*. Montreal and Kingston: McGill-Queen's University Press.

Cobble, Dorothy Sue. 1991. "Organizing the Postindustrial Work Force: Lessons from the History of Waitress Unionism." *Industrial and Labor Relations Review* 44, no. 3.

Compa, Lance. 1999. "NAFTA's Labour Side Agreement Five Years On: Progress and Prospects for the NAALC." *Canadian Labour and Employment Law Journal* 7, no. 1.
Corriveau, Jeanne. 2002. "Les handicaps réclament des états généraus." *Devoir* 15 février.
Cranford, Cynthia. 2001. "Gender, Labor and the Politics of Citizenship: Organizing 'Justice for Janitors' in Los Angeles." Ph.D diss., University of Southern California.
Cranford, Cynthia J., and Deena Ladd. 2003. "Community Unionism in Canada." *Just Labour: A Canadian Journal of Work and Society* 3.
Cranford, Cynthia, Leah F. Vosko, and Nancy Zukewich. 2003. "The Gender of Precarious Employment in Canada." *Relations industrielles/Industrial Relations* 58, no. 3.
Creighton, Breen 2001. "Freedom of Association." In *Comparative Labour Law and Industrial Relations in Industrialized Market Economies*, edited by Roger Blanpain and Chris Engels. 7th ed. The Hague: Kluwer Law International.
Crysler, Alfred Cosby. 1967. *Restraint of Trade and Labour.* Toronto: Butterworths.
Curran, James and Roger Burrows. 1986. "The Sociology of Petit Capitalism: A Trend Report." *Sociology* 20, no. 2.
Dale, Angela. 1986. "Social Class and the Self-Employed." *Sociology* 20, no. 3.
– 1991. "Self-Employment and Entrepreneurship: Notes on Two Problematic Concepts." In *Deciphering the Enterprise Culture: Entrepreneurship, Petty Capitalism and the Restructuring of Britain*, edited by Roger Burrows. London and New York: Routledge.
Daniels, Arlene. 1987. "Invisible Work." *Social Problems* 35, no. 5.
Davidov, Guy. 2002. "The Three Axes of Employment Relationships: A Characterization of Workers in Need of Protection." *University of Toronto Law Journal* 52.
Deakin, Simon. 2001. "The Contract of Employment: A Study in Legal Evolution." *Historical Studies in Industrial Relations* 11.
Dee, Garth, Nick McCombie, and Gary Newhouse. 1999. *Workers' Compensation in Ontario Handbook.* Toronto: Butterworths.
Delage, Benoit. 2002. *Results from the Survey of Self-Employment in Canada.* Hull, QC: Human Resources Development Canada.
Delp, Linda, and Katie Quan. 2002. "Homecare Workers Organizing in California: An Analysis of a Successful Strategy." *Labor Studies Journal* 27, no. 1.
Denton, Margaret A., et al. 1999. "Occupational Health Issues among Employees of Home Care Agencies." *Canadian Journal on Aging* 18, no. 2.

Donovan, Rebecca. 1989. "'We Care for the Most Important People in Your Life': Home Care Workers in New York City." *Women's Studies Quarterly* 1–2.

Drache, Daniel, and Harry Glasbeek. 1992. *The Changing Workplace*. Toronto: Lorimer.

Duffy, Andrew. 1989. "Postal Courier Quits over Pay Raise." *Toronto Star*, 3 January.

Dunn, Peter. 1999. *The Development of Government Independent Living Policies and Programs for Canadians with Disabilities*. Waterloo, ON: Centre for Social Welfare Studies.

du Rivage, Virginia L., François J. Carré, and Chris Tilly. 1998. "Making Labor Law Work for Part-Time and Contingent Workers." In *Contingent Work*, edited by Kathleen Barker and Kathleen Christensen. Ithaca: Cornell University Press.

Eardley Tony, and Anne Corden. 1996. *Low Income Self-Employment*. Aldershot: Avebury.

Elias, Peter. 2000. "Status in Employment: A World Survey of Practices and Problems." *Bulletin of Labour Statistics* 1.

Engblom, Samuel. 2001. "Equal Treatment of Employees and Self-Employed Workers." *International Journal of Comparative Labour Law and Industrial Relations* 17, no. 2.

England, Geoffrey, Innis Christie, and Merton Christie. 1998. *Employment Law in Canada*. Toronto: Butterworths.

Erickson, Christopher L., et al. 2002. "Justice for Janitors in Los Angeles: Lessons from Three Rounds of Negotiations." *British Journal of Industrial Relations* 40, no. 3.

Eustis, Nancy N., and Lucy Rose Rischer. 1991. "Relationships between Home Care Clients and Their Workers: Implications for Quality of Care." *Gerontologist* 31, no. 4.

Farkas, Lorraine. 1999. "Self-Employed Workers and Collective Bargaining." *Workplace Gazette* 2, no. 2.

Felstead, Alan. 1991. "The Social Organization of the Franchise: A Case of Controlled Self Employment." *Work, Employment and Society* 5, no. 1.

Fine, Janice. 1998. "Moving Innovation from the Margins to the Center." In *A New Labor Movement for a New Century*, edited by Gregory Mantsios. New York: Monthly Review Press.

Fink, Conrad C. 1988. *Strategic Newspaper Management*. Carbondale: Southern Illinois University Press.

Fitzgerald, Mark. 1995. "Beating the IRS in Independent Contractor Cases." *Editor and Publisher* 128, no. 40.

Flood, Colleen. 1999. *Unpacking the Shift to Home Care.* Halifax: Maritime Centre of Excellence for Women's Health.

Forrest, Anne. 1986. "Bargaining Units and Bargaining Power." *Relations industrielles/ Industrial Relations* 41, no. 4.

– 1995. "Securing the Male Breadwinner: A Feminist Interpretation of PC 1003." In *Labour Gains, Labour Pains: 50 Years of PC 1003*, edited by Cy Gonick, Paul Phillips, and Jesse Vorst. Winnipeg and Halifax: Fernwood Publishing.

Forsey, Eugene. 1982. *Trade Unions in Canada, 1812–1902.* Toronto: University of Toronto Press.

Fraser, Nancy, and Linda Gordon. 1997. "A Geneaology of Dependency: Tracing a Keyword of the U.S. Welfare State." In *Justus Interruptus: Critical Reflections on the Postsocialist Condition*, edited by Nancy Fraser. New York: Routledge.

Frenette, Marc. 2002. *Do the Falling Earnings of Immigrants Apply to Self-Employed Immigrants?* Ottawa: Statistics Canada, Analytical Studies Branch.

Fudge, Judy. 1993. "The Gendered Dimension of Labour Law: Why Women Need Inclusive Unionism and Broader-Based Bargaining." In *Women Challenging Unions: Feminism, Militancy and Democracy*, edited by Linda Briskin and Patricia McDermott. Toronto: University of Toronto Press.

– 1994. "Community Unionism: Coalition Fights to Clean Up the Garment Industry." *Canadian Dimension* 28, no. 2.

– 1997. "Little Victories and Big Defeats: The Rise and Fall of Collective Bargaining Rights for Domestic Workers in Ontario." In *Not One of the Family: Foreign Domestic Workers in Canada*, edited by Abigail Bakan and Daiva Stasiulis. Toronto: University of Toronto Press.

– 1999a. "The Commercialization of Canada Post: Postal Policy, Business Strategy and Labour Relations." In *Contract and Commitment: Employment Relations in the New Economy*, edited by Anil Verma and Richard P. Chaykowski. Kingston, ON: IRC Press.

– 1999b. "New Wine into Old Bottles? Updating Legal Forms to Reflect Changing Employment Norms." *University of British Columbia Law Review* 33, no. 1.

– 2000. "Lessons from Canada: The Impact of the Charter of Rights and Freedoms on Labour and Employment Law." In *Human Rights at Work*, edited by K.D. Ewing. London: Institute of Employment Rights.

Fudge, Judy, and Brenda Cossman. 2002. Introduction to *Privatization, Law and the Challenge of Feminism*, edited by Brenda Cossman and Judy Fudge. Toronto: University of Toronto Press.

Fudge, Judy, and Harry Glasbeek. 1995. "The Legacy of PC 1003." *Canadian Labour and Employment Law Journal* 3.
Fudge, Judy, and Eric Tucker. 2001. *Labour before the Law*. Toronto: Oxford University Press.
Fudge, Judy, and Leah Vosko. 2001a. "Gender, Segmentation and the Standard Employment Relationship in Canadian Labour Law, Legislation and Policy." *Economic and Industrial Democracy* 22, no. 2.
– 2001b. "By Whose Standards? Reregulating the Canadian Labour Market." *Economic and Industrial Democracy* 22, no. 3.
Galabuzi, Grace-Edward. 2001. "Canada's Creeping Economic Apartheid." Toronto: CJS Foundation for Research and Education.
García, Mario T. 1994. *Memories of Chicano History: The Life and Narrative of Bert Corona*. Berkeley: University of California Press.
Ghosh, Sabitri. 2003. "Left Out." *This Magazine*, January/February.
Gibson, Susan. "A Case Study: Rural Dignity, the Social Change Movement that Opposed the Privatization and Closure of Rural Post Offices," Carleton University School of Social Work, 1990.
Gilbert, Douglas G., et al. 1995. *A Guide to Workers' Compensation in Ontario*. 2d ed. Aurora, ON: Canada Law Book.
Glasbeek, Harry J. 1987. "Labour Relations Policy and Law As a Mechanism of Adjustment." *Osgoode Hall Law Journal* 25, no. 1.
Goldthorpe, John H. 1980. *Social Mobility and Class Structure in Modern Britain*. Oxford: Clarendon Press.
Gomm, Roger, Martyn Hammersley, and Peter Foster. 2000. *Case Study Method: Key Issues, Key Texts*. Sage: London.
Gordon, Colin. 1994. *New Deals: Business, Labor, and Politics in America, 1920–1935*. Cambridge: Cambridge University Press.
– 1999. "The Lost City of Solidarity: Metropolitan Unionism in Historical Perspective." *Politics and Society* 27, no. 4.
Grant, Michel. 2004. "De-regulating Industrial Relations in the Apparel Sector: The Case of the Decree System in Quebec." In *Challenging the Market: The Struggle to Regulate Work and Income*, edited by Jim Stanford and Leah F. Vosko. Montreal and Kingston. McGill-Queen's University Press.
Grusky, David B. 2001. *Social Stratification: Class, Race, and Gender in Sociological Perspective*. Boulder, CO: Westview Press.
Gulland, Sandra. 1999. "The Early Years." *Active Voice* 19, no. 2.
Gyles, Barbara Z. 1999. "Carrier 2000." *Presstime*, March.
Haiven, Larry. 1995. "Industrial Relations in Health Care: Regulation, Conflict and Transition to the 'Wellness Model.'" In *Public Sector Collective Bargaining in Canada: Beginning of the End or End of the Beginning?*, edited by

Gene Swimmer and Mark Thompson. Kingston, ON: Industrial Relations Centre, Queen's University.

Haiven, Larry, and Judy Haiven. 2002. *The Right to Strike and the Provision of Emergency Services in Canadian Health Care*. Ottawa: Canadian Centre for Policy Alternatives.

Hakim, Catherine. 1988. "New Recruits to Self-Employment in the 1980s." *Employment Gazette* 97.

Hannant, Joan. 1987. *The Impact of Privatization on Women in Canada*. Toronto: National Action Committee on the Status of Women.

Hardt, Hanno, and Bonnie Brenen, eds. 1995. *Newsworkers*. Minneapolis: University of Minnesota Press.

Hay, Douglas. 2000. "Master and Servant in England: Using the Law in the Eighteenth and Nineteenth Centuries." In *Social Inequality in the Industrial Age*, edited by Willibald Steinmetz. Oxford: Oxford University Press.

Hay, Douglas, and Nicholas Rogers. 1997. *Eighteenth-Century English Society: Shuttles and Swords*. Oxford: Oxford University Press.

Hébert, Gérard, ed. 1981. *Labor Relations in the Newspaper Industry*. Volume 5, Research Publications, Royal Commission on Newspapers. Ottawa: Minister of Supply and Services Canada.

Heckscher, Charles C. 1988. *The New Unionism: Employee Involvement in the Changing Corporation*. New York: Basic Books.

Hepple, B.A. 1995. "The Future of Labour Law." *Industrial Law Journal* 24.

Hernandez, Debra Gersh. 1996. "Watershed Moment." *Editor and Publisher* 129, no. 37.

Herod, Andrew. 1998. *Organizing the Landscape: Geographical Perspectives on Labor Unionism*. Ithaca: Cornell University Press.

Homel, David. 1999. "The Early Years." *Active Voice* 19, no. 2.

Hondagneu-Sotelo, Pierrette. 1994. "Regulating the Unregulated: Domestic Workers' Social Networks." *Social Problems* 41.

– 2000. *Domestica: Immigrant Workers Cleaning and Caring in the Shadows of Affluence*. Berkeley: University of California Press.

Hughes, Karen D. 1999. *Gender and Self-Employment in Canada: Assessing Trends and Policy Implications*. Changing Employment Relationships Series. Ottawa: Canadian Policy Research Networks.

– 2003. "Pushed or Pulled? Women's Entry into Self-Employment and Small Business Ownership." *Gender, Work and Organization* 10, no. 4.

Imrie, Rob. 1996. *Disability and the City: International Perspectives*. London: Paul Chapman Publishing.

Jackson, Andrew. 2002. "Is Work Working for People of Colour?" Research Paper no. 18. Ottawa: Canadian Labour of Congress.

Jalette, Patrice, and Peter Warrian. 2002. "Contracting-Out Provisions in Canadian Collective Agreements: A Moving Target." *Workplace Gazette* 5, no. 1.

Janzen, Russell, Jerry White, and Carla Lipseg-Mumme. 2001. "Junked Mail: The Politics and Consequences of Privatization." *Studies in Political Economy* 65.

Jurik, Nancy C. 1998. "Getting Away and Getting By: The Experiences of Self-Employed Homeworkers." *Work and Occupations* 25, no. 1.

Kates, Joanne, and Jane Springer. 1984. "Organizing Freelancers in the Arts." In *Women and Unions*, edited by Linda Briskin and Lynda Yanz. Toronto: The Women's Press.

Keigher, Sharon M. 1997. "Austria's New Attendance Allowance: A Consumer-Choice Model of Care for the Frail and Disabled." *International Journal of Health Services* 27, no. 4.

Labour Law Casebook Group. 1998. *Labour and Employment Law: Cases, Materials and Commentary*. 6th ed. Kingston, ON: IRC Press.

Lahey, Anita. 1999. "There's No Life like It: The Pay Is Erratic and Benefits Few, But Freelance Editors Enjoy Their Freedom." *Quill and Quire*, May.

Lamphere, Louise, et al. 1993. *Sunbelt Working Mothers: Reconciling Family and Factory*. Ithaca: Cornell University Press.

Langille, Brian A. 2002. "Labour Policy in Canada: New Platform, New Paradigm." *Canadian Public Policy* 28, no. 1.

Langille, Brian A., and Guy Davidov. 1999. "Beyond Employees and Independent Contractors: A View from Canada." *Comparative Labour Law and Policy Journal* 21, no. 1.

Langille, Brian A., and Patrick Macklem. 1988. "Beyond Belief: Labour Law's Duty to Bargain." *Queen's Law Journal* 13, no.1.

Leab, Daniel J. 1970. *A Union of Individuals: The Formation of the American Newspaper Guild, 1933–1936*. New York: Columbia University Press.

Leighton, Patricia, and Alan Felstead, eds. 1992. *The New Entrepreneurs: Self-Employment and Small Business in Europe*. London: Kogan Page.

Light, Ivan, and Edna Bonacich. 1988. *Immigrant Entrepreneurs: Koreans in Los Angeles, 1965–1982*. Berkeley. University of California Press.

Linder, Marc. 1989. *The Employment Relationship in Anglo-American Law: A Historical Perspective*. New York: Greenwood Press.

– 1990. "From Street Urchins to Little Merchants: The Juridical Transvaluation of Child Newspaper Carriers." *Temple Law Review* 63.

– 1997. "What's Black and White and Red All Over?: The Blood Tax on Newspapers; or, How Publishers Exclude Newscarriers from Workers' Compensation." *Loyola Poverty Law Journal* 3.

Lord, John, Peggy Hutchison, and D'Arcy Farlow. 1988. *Independence and Control: Today's Dream, Tomorrow's Reality: Review of Support Service Needs of Adults with Physical Disabilities in Ontario.* Toronto: Centre for Research and Education in Human Services.

Lorinc, John. 1995. *Opportunity Knocks: The Truth about Canada's Franchise Industry.* Scarborough, ON: Prentice Hall Canada.

Loutfi, M.F. 1991. "Self-Employment Patterns and Policy Issues in Europe." *International Labour Review* 130, no. 1.

Lowe, Graham, and Grant Schellenberg. 2001. *What's a Good Job? The Importance of Employment Relationships.* Ottawa: Canadian Policy Research Networks.

MacDonald, Diane. 1998. "Sectoral Certification: A Case Study of British Columbia." *Canadian Labour and Employment Law Journal* 5.

Macklem, Patrick. 1990. "Developments in Employment Law: The 1988–89 Term." *Supreme Court Law Review* 1 (2d).

MacPherson, Elizabeth. 1999. "Collective Bargaining for Independent Contractors: Is the *Status of the Artist Act* a Model for Other Industrial Sectors?" *Canadian Labour and Employment Law Journal* 7, no. 3.

Marjoribanks, Timothy. 2000. *News Corporation, Technology and the Workplace.* Cambridge: Cambridge University Press.

Malhotra, Ravi. 2001. "Tracy Latimer, Disability Rights and the Left." *Canadian Dimension* 35, no. 3.

McKenna, Barrie. 1998. "Union Coalition Targets Canada Post in Complaints over Rural Mail Carriers." *Globe and Mail*, 2 December.

Meager, Nigel. 1991. *Self-Employment in the United Kingdom.* Brighton: University of Sussex Institute of Manpower Studies.

Meager, Nigel, Gill Court, and Janet Moralee. 1996. "Self-Employment and the Distribution of Income." In *New Inequalities*, edited by John Hills. Cambridge: Cambridge University Press.

Meyer, Madonna Harrington, ed. 2000. *Care Work: Gender, Labor and the Welfare State.* New York and London: Routledge.

Middleton, Jennifer. 1996. "Contingent Workers in a Changing Economy: Endure, Adapt or Organize?" *New York University Review of Law and Social Change* 22.

Milkman, Ruth, ed. 2000. *Organizing Immigrants: The Challenge for Unions in Contemporary California.* Ithaca: Cornell University Press.

Minsky, Alan M. 2001. "Some Labour Relations Issues in the Construction Industry." *Construction Law Reports* (3d) 9.

Mitchell, J.C. 1983. "Case and Situation Analysis." *Sociological Review* 31, no. 2.

Morris, Jenny. 1993. *Independent Lives?: Community Care and Disabled People.* London: MacMillan.

Morris, Marika, et al. 1999. *The Changing Nature of Home Care and Its Impact on Women's Vulnerability to Poverty*. Ottawa: Canadian Research Institute for the Advancement of Women.

Muckenberger, Ulrich. 1989. "Non-standard Forms of Employment in the Federal Republic of Germany: The Role and Effectiveness of the State." In *Precarious Employment in Labour Market Regulation: The Growth of Atypical Employment in Western Europe*, edited by Gerry Rodgers and Janine Rodgers. Belgium: International Institute for Labour Studies.

Neysmith, Sheila M., ed. 2000. *Restructuring Caring Labour: Discourse, State Practice and Everyday Life*. Toronto: Oxford University Press.

Neysmith, Sheila M., and Jane Aronson. 1997. "Working Conditions in Home Care: Negotiating Race and Class Boundaries in Gendered Work." *International Journal of Health Services* 27, no. 3.

Novitz, Tonia. 2003. *International and European Protection of the Right to Strike: A Comparative Study of Standards Set by the International Labour Organization, the Council of Europe and the European Union*. Oxford: Oxford University Press.

O'Grady, John. 1992. "Beyond the Wagner Act, What Then?" In *Getting on Track: Social Democratic Strategies for Ontario*, edited by Daniel Drache. Montreal and Kingston: McGill-Queen's University Press.

– 1995. *Job Control Unionism vs. the New Human Resource Management Model*. Kingston, ON: IRC Press.

Ocran, Amanda Araba. 1997. "Across the Home/Work Divide: Homework in Garment Manufacture and the Future of Employment Regulation." In *Challenging the Public/Private Divide: Feminism, Law and Public Policy*, edited by Susan B. Boyd. Toronto: University of Toronto Press.

Orth, John V. 1991. *Combination and Conspiracy: A Legal History of Trade Unionism, 1721–1906*. Oxford: Oxford University Press.

Palmer, Bryan D. 1995. "Small Unions and Dissidents in the History of Canadian Unionism." In *Hard Lessons: The Mine Mill Union in the Canadian Labour Movement*, edited by Mercedes Steedman, Peter Suschnigg and Dieter. K. Buse. Toronto: Dundurn Press.

Parker, Eric, and Joel Rogers. 2001. "Building the High Road in Metro Areas: Sectoral Training and Employment Projects." In *Rekindling the Movement: Labor's Quest for Relevance in the Twenty-First Century*, edited by Lowell Turner, Harry C. Katz, and Richard W. Hurd. Ithaca: ILR Press.

Parker, Ian, et al. 2000. *Powershift: How Self-Managed, Direct Funded Attendant Services Came about in Ontario*. Toronto: Centre for Independent Living in Toronto.

Pearson, Carole. 1999. "Special Delivery: Mavis Wiebe and the RRMC." *Our Times*, May/June.

– 2000. "While the City Sleeps." *Our Times*, April/June.
Polins, Jim. 1987. "Post May Appeal Union Decision." *Hamilton Spectator*, 30 April.
Popaleni, Kathy. 1988. "Shouldering the Burden for Canada Post: Privatization's Impact on Rural Women." *Resources for Feminist Research* 17, no. 3.
Postol, Todd Alexander. 1997. "Creating the American Newspaper Boy: Middle-Class Route Service and Juvenile Salesmanship in the Great Depression." *Journal of Social History* 31.
Rainbird, Helen. 1991. "The Self-Employed: Small Entrepreneurs or Disguised Wage Labourers?" In *Farewell to Flexibility?*, edited by Anna Pollert. Oxford: Blackwell.
Rankin, W. Parkman. 1986. *The Practice of Newspaper Management*. New York: Praeger.
Roeher Institute. 1993. *Nothing Personal: The Need for Personal Supports in Canada*. North York, ON: Roeher Institute.
– 1997. *Self-Managed Attendant Services in Ontario: Direct Funding Pilot Project, Final Evaluation Report*. North York, ON: Roeher Institute.
– 2001. *Disability-Related Support Arrangements, Policy Options and Implications for Women's Equality*. North York, ON: Roeher Institute.
Sack, Jeffrey, Michael Mitchell, and Sandy Price. 1997. *Ontario Labour Relations Law and Practice*. 3rd ed. Markham, ON: Butterworths.
Schellenberg, Grant, and Christopher Clark. 1996. *Temporary Employment in Canada: Profiles, Patterns and Policy Considerations*. Ottawa: Canadian Council on Social Development.
Schiller, Jay. 2001. "Top Ten Ways Newspapers Mistreat Carriers." *Editor and Publisher* 131, no. 31.
Schneiderman, David. 1996. "NAFTA's Takings Rule: American Constitutionalism Comes to Canada." *University of Toronto Law Journal* 46.
Scholz, Roland W., and Olaf Tietje. 2002. *Embedded Case Study Methods: Integrating Quantitative and Qualitative Knowledge*. Thousand Oaks, CA: Sage.
Seamon, Marc. 2000. "How Demographic Variables Affect Newspaper Delivery." *Newspaper Research Journal* 21.
Sen, Amartya. 2000. "Work and Rights." *International Labor Review* 139, no. 2.
Simpson, Roger. 1992. "Seattle Newsboys: How Hustler Democracy Lost to the Power of Property." *Journalism History* 18, nos 1–2.
Smillie, Elizabeth. 1988. "Stamping out Rural Life." *Network of Saskatchewan Working Women*, March/April.
Springer, Jane. 1999. "The Early Years." *Active Voice* 19, no 2.

Stanger, Howard. 2000. "Labor Relations in the U.S. Daily Newspaper Industry, 1976–1998: Preliminary Findings and Emerging Issues." In *Proceedings of the 52nd Annual Meeting, Industrial Relations Research Association Series*, edited by Paula B. Voos. Boston: Industrial Relations Research Association.
– 2002. "Newspapers: Collective Bargaining Decline amidst Technological Change." In *Collective Bargaining in the Private Sector*, edited by Paul F. Clark, John T. Delaney, and Ann C. Frost. Champaign IL: Industrial Relations Research Association.
Stanworth, Celia, and John Stanworth. 1997. "Managing an Externalized Workforce: Freelance Labour Use in the UK Book Publishing Industry." *Industrial Relations Journal* 28, no. 1.
– 1995. "The Self-Employed without Employees: Autonomous or Atypical? *Industrial Relations Journal* 26, no. 3.
Svirsky, G. 1998. "The Division of Labour: An Example of Certification Requirements." *Osgoode Hall Law Journal* 36.
Swimmer, Gene, and Mark Thompson. 1995. "Collective Bargaining in the Public Sector: An Introduction." In *Public Sector Collective Bargaining in Canada: Beginning of the End or End of the Beginning?*, edited by Gene Swimmer and Mark Thompson. Kingston, ON: Industrial Relations Centre, Queen's University.
Thompson, Mark. 1994. *Rights and Responsibilities in a Changing Workplace: A Review of Employment Standards in British Columbia*. Victoria, BC: Ministry of Skills, Training and Labour.
Thorn, William J., and Mary Pat Pfeil. 1987. *Newspaper Circulation: Marketing the News*. New York: Longman.
Tomlins, Christopher L. 1985. *The State and the Unions*. Cambridge: Cambridge University Press.
Travers, Max. 2001. *Qualitative Research through Case Studies*. London: Sage.
Tsogas, George. 2001. *Labor Regulation in a Global Economy*. Armonk, NY: M.E. Sharpe.
Tucker, Eric. 1985. "The Gospel of Statutory Rules Requiring Liberal Interpretation According to *St. Peter's*." *University of Toronto Law Journal* 35.
– 1994. "The Faces of Coercion: The Legal Regulation of Labour Conflict in Ontario in the 1880s." *Law and History Review* 12.
– 1995. "And Defeat Goes On: An Assessment of Third-Wave Health and Safety Regulation." In *Corporate Crime: Contemporary Debates*, edited by Frank Pearce and Laureen Snider. Toronto: University of Toronto Press.
Tufts, Stephen. 1998. "Community Unionism in Canada and Labour's (Re)Organization of Space." *Antipode* 30, no. 3.

Ungerson, Clare. 1999. "Personal Assistants and Disabled People: An Examination of a Hybrid Form of Work and Care." *Work, Employment and Society* 13, no. 4.

Upton Reed, Claudette. 1999. "Recent Years (1994–1999)." *Active Voice* 19, no. 2.

Ursel, Jane. 1992. "Private Lives, Public Policy: 100 Years of State Intervention in the Family." Toronto: The Women's Press.

Valée, Guylaine, and Jean Charest. 2001. "Globalization and the Transformation of State Regulation of Labour: The Case of Recent Amendments to the Quebec *Collective Agreement Decrees Act*." *International Journal of Comparative Labour Law and Industrial Relations* 17.

Vosko, Leah F. 2000. *Temporary Work: The Gendered Rise of a Precarious Employment Relationship.* Toronto: University of Toronto Press.

– 2002. "Rethinking Feminization: Gendered Precariousness in the Canadian Labour Market and the Crisis in Social Reproduction." Annual Robarts Lecture, Robarts Centre for Canadian Studies, York University, Toronto, 11 April.

– 2003. "Gender Differentiation and the Standard/Non-standard Employment Distinction: A Genealogy of Policy Intervention in Canada." In *Social Differentiation: Patterns and Processes,* edited by Danielle Juteau. Toronto: University of Toronto Press.

Walters, Vivienne, and Margaret Denton. 1990. "Workers' Knowledge of Their Legal Rights and Resistance to Hazardous Work." *Relations industrielles/Industrial Relations* 45, no. 3.

White, Jerry, and Russell Janzen. 2000. "The Industrial Relations Implications of Privatization: The Case of Canada Post." *Relations industrielles/Industrial Relations* 55, no. 1.

Wial, H. 1993. "The Emerging Organizational Structure of Unionism in Low-Wage Services." *Rutgers Law Review* 45.

Williams, Allison, et al. 2000. *Women's Formal (Paid) Home Care Work in Transition: The Impact of Reform on Labour Process Change in Saskatoon, SK. Final Report.* Saskatoon: Department of Geography and College of Nursing, University of Saskatchewan.

Wilton, Robert, and Cynthia Cranford. 2002. "Toward an Understanding of the Spatiality of Social Movements: Labor Organizing at a Private University in Los Angeles." *Social Problems* 49, no. 3.

Woods, Harry Douglas, and the Task Force on Labour Relations. 1969. *Canadian Industrial Relations: The Report of the Prime Minister's Task Force on Labour Relations.* Ottawa: Queen's Printer.

Wright, Erik Olin. 1997. *Class Counts: Comparative Studies in Class Analysis*. Cambridge: Cambridge University Press.

Wright, Erik Olin, et al. 1982. "The American Class Structure." *American Sociological Review* 47.

Yin, Robert K. 1994. *Case Study Research: Design and Methods*. Thousand Oaks, CA: Sage.

Zerker, Sally F. 1982. *The Rise and Fall of the Toronto Typographical Union, 1832–1972: A Case Study of Foreign Domination*. Toronto: University of Toronto Press.

Index

Note: Page numbers followed by an *f* indicate a figure.
Page numbers followed by a *t* indicate a table.

Active Voice, 142
advertising mail delivery, 80
agencies: attendant employees of, 115–24; government as ghost at the bargaining table, 114; represented by CAW and SEIU, 116
agricultural workers, exclusion of from collective bargaining, 184
Ahn, Jenny, 117, 118, 121, 217n62
Ajax Pickering News Advertiser, and newspaper delivery drivers, 44
Algonquin Tavern, 44, 106–7, 215n35
Alliance of Canadian Cinema, Television and Radio Artists, 146
American Federation of Musicians of the United States and Canada, 146
Ancaster, meeting of couriers in, 63
Anfinson, Mark, 35–6
anti-combinations legislation, 15
anti-competition, artists as independent contractors and, 145
arbitration, 52; first-contract, 24, 50–1, 199n48
Archbold, Rick, 155

Arthurs, Harry, 18–19, 62, 68
artists, 187; collective bargaining legislation, 146; employment status of, 145; federal collective bargaining legislation, 145; as independent contractors, 145, 149; legal collective bargaining rights, 137
artists' associations, as combinations of employees, 149
Association of Rural Route Mail Carriers (ARRMC), 67, 80; on Canada Labour Relations Board decision, 70; Canada Post's response to, 63; request of that couriers be recognized as employees, 65
attendant care, concept of, 102; demand for, 98
Attendant Care Action Coalition, 99
attendant employees: definition of, 212n1; of non-profit agencies, 115–24
authors, editors as, 157, 160
authorship, expansive definition of, 161
average annual incomes, self-employed, 11–12

Bailey, Rhonda, 155
bargaining rights, 21–4
bargaining units, 173; bargaining structure, 48; Canadian Union of Postal Workers (CUPW), 79; combining, 49; determination of, 21–4; organizing appropriate, 47–50; scope of, 52
Belgrade Recommendation, 146
benefits: for freelance editors, 221n6; for part-time employees, 119
Blaikie, Bill, *Canada Post Corporation Act,* subsection 13(5), 92
Bloc Québécois, *Canada Post Corporation Act,* subsection 13(5), 84
Boudreau, Alice, 86, 88; and CPAA, 87; and rural couriers' demands, 84
bourgeoisie, 6
Bourque, Deborah, 76–7, 79; and CPAA, 87; as CUPW national president, 85–7; and ORRMC, 86; and rural couriers' demands, 84
British Columbia: bargaining units in, 49; definition of employee, 19; entitlement of newspaper carriers to minimum standards, 39; legislation in, 188; organizing carriers in, 44–6; unions at small enterprises, 189
British Columbia Employment Standards Act, student carriers and, 40
British Columbia *Labour Code,* 52
British Columbia Labour Relations Board, 45, 49–51
business unionism, 186

Calgary Herald, 40–1
California, public authorities, 191
Canada Industrial Relations Board (CIRB), 58, 144; CUPW application to, 89; unfair labour practice complaint of Canada Post, 89
Canada Labour Code, 19, 57, 61–2, 68–70, 137, 143–4, 147–8, 169; definition of dependent contractor, 137;

definition of employee, 137; exclusion of couriers from, 73, 89; union membership cards, 88
Canada Labour Relations Board: ARRMC standing, 66; employee status, 65; and exclusive representative of urban postal operations bargaining unit, 76; judicial review of decision of, 71; responses to decision on rural route mail couriers, 70–1; review of bargaining units at Canada Post, 57; and union-organizing campaigns, 67
Canada Post: amounts for rural route contractors, 63; business strategy of, 91; commercialization of, 57; contracting out, 179; control exercised by, 69; and CUPW collective agreements, 85, 92; judicial review of Canada Labour Relations Board's decision, 71; and NAFTA complaints, 90; plan of to revise rural route system, 64–5, 71–2; postal policy shift of, 76; public policy mandate of, 57; public tendering system, 60–2, 84–5; Radwanski recommendation, 80; response of to ARRMC, 64; review of postal bargaining units, 66; and right to organize of rural couriers, 88; and rival unions, 180–1; rural delivery service manual, 85; rural route mail couriers, 26; strike issues, 91; unfair labour practice complaint, 89
Canada Post Corporation Act, 57, 61, 66, 70; subsection 13(5), 74, 84, 90, 92, 201n3, 211n118
Canadian Actors' Equity, tribunal decision, 158
Canadian Actors' Equity Association, 146
Canadian Artists and Producers Professional Relations Tribunal (CAPPRT), 136, 148; certification of EAC/ACR, 160–1; composition of, 224n40;

on EAC/ACR application, 159; editors as joint authors, 138; intervener status before, 225n58; new collective bargaining regime, 150–2
Canadian Auto Workers (CAW), 99; merger with CTCU, 116
Canadian Auto Workers (CAW), Local 40, 97; employers organized by, 116; gender in, 104; health and safety issues, 121; personal-care workers, 115, 178; strike launched by, 118; tactics of dispute resolution, 182
Canadian Charter of Rights and Freedoms, 27, 66, 174; charter challenge on legislative exclusion for couriers, 73; charter challenge to *Canada Post Corporation Act*, 68; freedom of association, 79, 86, 89; and Local 1801, 73–4
Canadian Competition Tribunal, and Canadian Artists and Producers Professional Relations Tribunal, 149
Canadian Daily Newspaper Association, and the goods and services tax, 41
Canadian Labour Congress (CLC): *v. Algonquin Tavern*, see *Algonquin Tavern*; charter for rural couriers, 67; funding and support for, 23; jurisdictional dispute resolution process, 90; and rural route mail couriers, 62; support of CUPW's right to represent the rural couriers, 90
Canadian Postmasters and Assistants Association (CPAA), 59, 87; conflict over right to represent couriers, 78; and CUPW, 89–90, 209n90; and organizing drive of rural couriers, 66, 88
Canadian Textile and Chemical Union (CTCU), 116
Canadian Union of Postal Workers (CUPW), 79; advertising mail delivery, 80; and ARRMC, 79; and Canada Post collective agreements, 85, 92; and Crown corporations issue, 62; exclusive bargaining representative of RSMCs, 93; invoking of NAALC process, 81; political pressure of, 81; political process, 92; rural and suburban mail couriers, 86, 87, 92; rural route mail carriers, 182; rural route mail couriers, 75–94, 76–7, 80, 86–9, 178, 190–1; status of couriers as issue in negotiations, 91; strike mandate, 92; struggle between LCUC and, 66; temporary technical assistants (TTAs), 88, 209n95; training, 80; unionization of rural and suburban carriers, 57–8
Canadian Union of Public Employees (CUPE), 99, 117; organizing personal-care workers, 115
capitalism, 6, 179
CAPPRT. *See* Canadian Artists and Producers Professional Relations Tribunal
Caribbean, child-care workers from, 104
CCAC. *See* Community Care Access Centre
Centre for Independent Living in Toronto (CILT), 124, 125; administration of Self-Managed Care, 126; Direct Funding Pilot Program, 99; employees of, 124, 125–7; and the government, 125; on Self-Managed Care, 101; and self-managers, 128
CEP. *See* Communications, Energy and Paperworkers Union of Canada
certification, 159; as fixed-term renewable licenses, 152, 187; under the *SAA*, 142
Charter of Rights and Freedoms. *See Canadian Charter of Rights and Freedoms*
child-care workers, percentage unionized, 115

child labour, 32
Chrétien, Jean, review of Canada Post's mandate, 80
CILT. *See* Centre for Independent Living in Toronto
CIRB. *See* Canada Industrial Relations Board
class, and structure of societies, 6
CLC. *See* Canadian Labour Congress
Clement, Wallace, 7
client/consumer: control over, 189; demands made by, 117; discretion in hiring and firing, 191; impact of strike on, 117; and the legislation, 120; role of, 119; and scheduling flexibility, 122; term, 212–13n4; in the workplace, 115
client/self-employed contractor relationship, 131
clients, of freelance editors, 139
Cobble, Dorothy Sue, 113, 188
collective agreements: constraints on contracting out, 25; CUPW and Canada Post, 85, 92; first-contract, 24, 196n32; rural and suburban mail carriers (RSMCs), 92–3; rural and suburban mail couriers (RSMCs), 92; *Toronto Star*, 53–4
collective bargaining, 16, 20, 50, 172, 177–9; decentralized nature of, 180; exclusive bargaining agency, 180; freelance editors' rights under *SAA*, 153–67; independent professional artists, 148–9, 169; law, 15, 185; limitations, 177–83; professionals, 144–5; *Public Service Staff Relations Act*, 62; rights, 3–4; sector suitable for, 152; self-employed workers, 5, 183–6; Self-Managed Care: Direct Funding, 133; and self-managers, 129; service industries, 112; under *SAA*, 148; and workers, 55

collective representation: and bargaining, 4; history of, 140
combination, 15
Combines Act, 147
common law, 15, 18
Communications, Energy and Paperworkers Union of Canada (CEP): Local 87-M, 29; newspaper distribution workers, 29–30; and *Star* carriers, 44, 46, 178, 179
community-based services, 97–8
Community Care Access Centre (CCAC): on nursing service providers, 107–9; and OPSEU, 106
community unionism, 186, 190–2
Competition Act, 15, 145, 157, 168, 169–70, 176; combinations of employees, 148–9, 167; section 4(1)(a), 149–50; section 4(2), 149–50; self-employed artists under, 149
competition law, 20, 33
competition policy, 174
conflict of interest, 174, 175
Conservative government: commercialization of post office, 57; and direct funding, 99; and dispute resolution mechanism, 182; labour law reforms, 51; labour relations policy of, 76–7; post office as private-sector business, 76; repeal of NDP's labour law amendments, 49; restructuring of the rural network, 64; and the rural route mail couriers, 63
Conservative Party: *Canada Post Corporation Act,* subsection 13(5), 84
construction industry, 17, 187; multi-employer bargaining in, 185
construction unions, 188
contract of employment, 16
contracting out, 23, 24–5, 52; newspaper distribution, 34; *Star* home deliv-

ery, 30, 52, 53; as unfair labour practice, 51
contractors, 7
control: and employee status, 143; and self-managers, 128
Coopers and Lybrand, 51
copyright, and the Crown, 226n70, 229n101
Copyright Act, 147, 148, 153, 157, 169; authors of literary works, 161–2; definition of author, 154, 157, 164; editors as authors, 158, 161, 224n37; joint authorship, 161, 162, 164; section 6(2)(b)(i), 150; section 13(3), 150; self-employed artists under, 149
corporate capitalism, 15–16
Country Mail Association of Canada, 67
CPAA. *See* Canadian Postmasters and Assistants Association
craft unionism, 113, 187, 192; construction industry, 188
Crean, Susan, 229n103
Criminal Code of Canada, 20, 147; 1939 amendment, 173
Crown: and authorship, 228n88; and copyright, 226n70, 229n101
Crown corporation, Canada Post as, 57–61, 61–2
CTCU. *See* Canadian Textile and Chemical Union
CUPE. *See* Canadian Union of Public Employees
CUPW. *See* Canadian Union of Postal Workers

Dale, Angela, 6
dependent contractors, 20, 105, 132; under *Canada Labour Code*, 69, 143; and collective bargaining, 19, 178; definition of, 43, 62, 67–9, 137, 143–4
Dickens, Penny, 156–7

direct funding, 134; labour's critique of, 100; model, 178; neo-liberal ideology of, 101; of people with disabilities, 99; Pilot Program, 99; regulatory status of workers, 124–5
disability activists, 97–8, 212n4; definition of care, 102
dispute resolution, 181–3
Dolphin Delivery, 49
domestic workers, 127–30; and collective organization, 135; definition of, 212n1; employed in a private home, 21; under *ESA*, 219–20n101; exclusion of from collective bargaining, 184; exclusion of from *OLRA*, 109; personal-care workers, 97; for purposes of collective bargaining, 127; right to organize trade unions, 109
driver-salespeople, and collective bargaining, 19
Dunmore v. Ontario (AG), 88

EAC/ACR. *See* Editors' Association of Canada
economic dependence: under *Canada Labour Code*, 144; and the four-factors test, 42
economic realities test, 143
economic status. *See* socio-economic status
editing: authorship and, 156; as highly skilled work, 140
Editing Canadian English (EAC/ACR), 142
"The Editor as Merlin: A Case Study of the Editing Process for *Zigzag: A Life on the Move* by James Houston," 155
editors: as authors, 167; professional status of, 155; stresses of, 139; TWUC on, 156; undervaluation of, 140
Editors' Association of Canada (EAC/ACR), 153–67; arguments of and TWUC's response, 154–7; bargaining

agency role, 159; bylaw change requirement, 160; certification, 136, 138, 153, 161–6, 221n1; conception of authorship, 157; definitions of types of editing, 225–6n59; history, 137, 140–2; limited victory of, 165–7; membership, 142; opposition to, 136; SAA sections 6(2)(b)(i) and (ii), 156; scale agreements, 168, 183; self-identification of as a professional association, 170; transformed into a union, 190; tribunal's decision (numbers 33 and 36), 165; tribunal's decision (number 36), 164; voting membership, 221n13; on writer-editor relationship, 158. *See also* freelance editors
elites, and collective bargaining, 16
employee status, 65, 105; collective bargaining law, 20; for couriers, 73; rural and suburban mail contractors, 92; rural route mail couriers, 75, 95
employees, 177; under *Canada Labour Code*, 143; as category, 6; under collective bargaining legislation, 19; common-law definition, 195–6n27; concept of, 195n25; couriers as under *Canada Labour Code*, 69–70; definition of, 97, 105, 137; and dependent contractors, 196n31; full-time, 48; and independent contractors, 20, 36–41, 137; legal distinction between independent contractors and, 47; with multiple employers, 135; part-time, 102–3; of person with a disability, 127; postmasters, 59; self-employed as, 4; of a self-manager, 129; temporary, 102–3
employer of record, and the paymaster, 114
employers: Canada Post, 56–7; establishing an organization as, 109–12; and links with the client/consumer, 117; non-profit contractor as, 118;

under the OLRB, 132; resistance to change of, 172; restructuring by, 54; self-employed as, 13
employment, establishing status of, 105–9
employment contract, 15
employment insurance, qualifying for, 132
Employment Insurance Act, to qualify under, 220n110
employment security, craft unions and, 188
Employment Standards Act (ESA), 39, 51, 119; domestic workers, 129, 219n101; and newspaper carriers, 39; residential-care workers, 220n104
Employment Standards Branch (Ontario Ministry of Labour), 39
Employment Standards Tribunal, 40
employment status: establishing, 35–47; newspaper distribution workers, 38; personal-care workers, 179; Supreme Court of Canada, 73
entrepreneurs, 4, 5, 20, 176, 183; as category, 6; rural route mail couriers, 58, 61–3
ESA. See *Employment Standards Act*
ethic of invisibility, 140, 154, 155–6, 159, 221n12
ethnicity, of personal attendants working through Self-Managed Care, 104
Europe: collective bargaining regimes in, 23; juridical extension of labour relations and standards, 190
Evening News, 37–8
Eybel, Sue, 63, 64–5, 71, 78; and ARRMC, 80; Canada Labour Relations Board decision, 70–1; Local 1801, 67, 74; organizing campaign, 79; and ORRMC, 79–80; Standing Committee on Consumer and Corporate Affairs and Government Operations, 74; unfair labour practice complaint of, 72

fair labour standards, 97
Fair Labor Standards Act (US), exclusion of news-delivery workers from, 35
farm workers. *See* agricultural workers
Federal Court of Appeal, 41, 71, 73, 154; and Canada Post, 57
first collective agreements, 181
first-contract arbitration, 181; Quebec, 182–3
fisheries, 7
fishers, and collective bargaining law, 18
Floresco, George, election of as CUPW national vice-president, 87
four factors: employee or independent contractor, 38–9; *Montreal Locomotive*, 41
fourfold test, and employee status, 143
franchisees, 7
free competition, 175
Freedman, Bill, 156
freedom of association, 172, 174, 186, 230–1n5; components of, 172–7; for self-employed workers, 183–6
freedom of competition, 172
freelance artists, status of, 144–5
freelance editors, 3–4, 14, 26, 27, 176; agreements with federal producers, 136; as authors under SAA, 154; autonomy of, 139; collective bargaining and, 160, 178, 187, 190; functions performed by, 138; independent contractors, 20; as independent professional artists, 179; precarious status of, 136; professional association or union debate, 141; SAA section 6(2)(b)(iii), 153; self-employed, 179; socio-economic situation of, 137; status of as artists, 138. *See also* Editors' Association of Canada (EAC/ACR)
Freelance Editors' Association of Canada: expansion of, 141–2; name change of, 142

freelance journalists: and collective bargaining, 19; as employees, 222n18
freelance reviewers, as dependent contractors, 222n18
Frenette, Marc, 9–10
funding, individualized, 134

Garza, Irasema, 82
Gélinas, Gratien, 146
gender, personal-care workers and, 97, 103
geographical unionism: and occupational unionism, 189; United States, 189
Georgetti, Kenneth, 90
Globe and Mail, newspaper distribution shift to adult carriers, 34
good-faith bargaining, 52
goods and services tax (GST), 41
Great Depression, 15–16
Gulland, Sandra, 141

Harris government, 118
health and safety issues: heavy lifting, 217n72; personal-care workers, 119–21; training, 121
health care, regionalization of, 133–4
Hearst Publications Inc. v. National Labor Relations Board, 36–7
Holtman, Felix, 64
Holtman Committee, 64–5
home-care sector, 14, 134, 213n11; and collective bargaining, 19; competition for workers in, 100; dependent contractors, 106; people with disabilities and, 98
Homel, David, 141
homemakers, 106; Tax Court classification of, 107
home-support workers, percentage unionized, 115
hot shops, and CAW, Local 40, 117
House of Commons: patronage issues in, 59; petitions presented to from

rural couriers, 84; rural route mail couriers' campaign, 83
House of Commons Standing Committee on Communications and Culture, 148
House of Lords, common law on restraint of trade, 175
house parents, and collective bargaining, 19
Howland, W.H., 32
Hugessen, Judge, 71
Hughes, Karen, 12
Huntsville District Memorial Hospital, homemakers at, 107

ICMA. *See* International Circulation Managers Association
ILO. *See* International Labour Organization
immigrants, 176; barriers faced by, 14; and own-account self-employment, 10; paid workforce, 9–10; personal-care workers, 97, 103; shift to adult newspaper carriers, 34; type of self-employment by, 28
immigrants of colour, as personal-care workers, 101
income, definition of, 194n15
Independence and Control: Today's Dream, Tomorrow's Reality (Lord Report), 99
independent contractors, 33, 132, 135; collective bargaining regime for, 187; distinction between employees and, 36–41, 47, 137; freelance editors as, 138–9, 140; personal-care workers, 97; precarious status of, 184; and professionals, 143–5; rural route mail couriers, 58, 59; status of for tax purposes, 40; and workers' compensation, 42–3
Independent Living: The Time Is Now, 99

Independent Living Resource Centres (ILRCS), 125
industrial labour relations, 112–14
industrial relations model, 133
industrial unionism, 16, 25, 171, 192; and precarious workers, 133
institutional reform, 183–6
institutionalization, of employment relationship, 112
International Brotherhood of the Teamsters, 65
International Circulation Managers Association (ICMA), 33
International Labour Organization (ILO), 15; Convention 87, *Freedom of Association and Protection of the Right to Organize*, 173; Freedom of Association Committee, 177; workers rights and freedoms, 184
IRLCS. *See* Independent Living Resource Centres

job control unionism, 113
job security, 123, 124; and seniority, 113; with single employer, 188
John, Connie, 154–5, 156
joint authorship, 159, 227n87
Journal Le Droit, and newspaper delivery drivers, 43–4

Kates, Joanne, 141
Kingston Whig-Standard, 40
Kitchener-Waterloo Record, and newspaper delivery drivers, 44

labour and capital, 6
Labour Force Survey, 97
labour law, 30, 33, 186; accessing, 4; employment platform, 14–28; NDP amendments, 46; redesign of, 171; reform, 55; and worker collective action, 15

labour legislation, 105; and personal-care workers, 96, 119; and trade union structures, 113
labour market unionism, 186, 190, 192
labour markets, 16, 103
labour relations: boards, 18, 22; ICMA strategies, 33; legislative jurisdiction over, 17; post–World War II, 173; rights and freedoms, 173; statutes, 30
labour supply issues, 190
labour tribunals, 17; and bargaining unit policies, 24
LCUC. See Letter Carriers Union of Canada
Lebel, Mr Justice, 174
legal status: mail contractors, 62; rural and suburban mail carriers (RSMCs), 92; rural route mail couriers, 61–3, 95; of self-employed workers, 3–4
legislation: collective bargaining, 17–21, 43, 58; exclusion from collective bargaining, 202n9; social wage, 40, 42–3
letter carriers, working conditions of, 60
Letter Carriers Union of Canada (LCUC), 65; organizing drive for rural route mail contractors, 72; struggle between CUPW and, 66
Liberal government: *Canada Post Corporation Act*, subsection 13(5), 84; and direct funding, 99; public service with private enterprise, 76; and rural route mail couriers, 58
Local 1801. See Rural Route Mail Carriers of Canada, Local 1801
London, Ontario, newsboy unions in, 32–3
long-term care, definition of, 213n11
Lord Report (Ministry of Community and Social Services), 99
Los Angeles Newsboys Local Industrial Union Number 75, 36

Lyons, Jim, 156, 227n87

Maguire, Charles, 66; ARRMC and bargaining unit review, 65; death of, 74; poem, 200n1; Standing Committee on Consumer and Corporate Affairs and Government Operations, 74
mail contractors: definition of, 204–5n43, 205n48, 212n120; legal status of, 62
managed competition, 100
management personnel, exclusion of from collective bargaining, 174–5
Manitoba: organizing carriers in, 44–6; right to organize in, 177
Manitoba Labour Board: certification vote, 46; designated carriers as employees, 46
Manitoba Labour Relations Board, 40, 45
Manitoba New Democratic Party (NDP), labour law amendments, 46
manufacturing industries, collective bargaining and, 112
Martin, Pat, 84
Marx, Karl, 6
mass-circulation newspapers, 33
Meager, Nigel, 8
Meeting Editorial Standards (EAC/ACR), 142
men: agency-provided attendant care, 103; letter carriers, 60; newspaper delivery in rural areas, 32; and self-employment, 8; and social location, 12
Minister of National Revenue, ruling on WFP carriers, 40
Ministry of Community and Social Services Act, 99, 125
Minnesota Newspaper Association, 35
Montreal, newsboys unions in, 32–3
Montreal v. Montreal Locomotive Works Ltd, 38; four factors, 41

Moore, Christopher, 156
Mulroney, Brian, 64
multi-employer: agreements, 186, 189; bargaining, 185–6; scale agreements, 169
multi-ethnic workforces, and unions, 55
multiple employers, 189
musicians, and collective bargaining, 19

NAALC. *See* North American Agreement on Labour Cooperation
NAFTA. *See* North American Free Trade Agreement
National Administrative Office (NAO), 81–3
National Labor Relations Act (NLRA) (US), 33, 36; classification of carriers under, 37–8
National Labor Relations Board (NLRB), 36; classification of carriers under, 37–8
National Rural Letter Carriers' Association, 60
neo-liberalism, 172–3, 175
New Brunswick: discrimination by Canada Post in, 72; unfair labour practices complaints in, 72
New Democratic Party (NDP): Bill 101, 99; *Canada Post Corporation Act*, subsection 13(5), 84; direct funding, 99; funding for long-term-care programs, 125; labour law, 49; newspaper carriers and exemption from ESA, 39; and rural route mail couriers, 62
newsboys, home delivery in urban areas, 32
newspaper carriers: classification of, 35–47; as dependent contractors, 178; as employees, 40; and exemption from ESA, 39; and workers' compensation, 43
newspaper distribution workers, 52; collective bargaining and, 34; employment status, 38, 39; as independent contractors, 40
newspaper guild, bargaining units in, 47
newspapers, distribution of, 31–4
non-profit agencies, workers employed by, 97
North America, craft unionism, 192
North American Agreement on Labour Cooperation (NAALC), 81, 82, 173–4; public workshop, 83
North American Free Trade Agreement (NAFTA), 27; allegations by UPS of violations by Canada Post, 85; labour-side agreement, 81, 182; UPS and Canada Post, 91
Nova Scotia Board of Appeal, 18
Nucleus Housing Incorporated: represented by CAW, Local 40, 116–17; and SEIU, Local 204, 110
nurses, OLRB and status of, 108–9

Occupational Health and Safety Act (OHSA), 120, 219n99; health and safety issues, 121; and self-managers, 129
occupational unionism, 113–14, 188–9
OECD. *See* Organization for Economic Co-operation and Development
OHSA. *See* Occupational Health and Safety Act
OLRB. *See* Ontario Labour Relations Board
OMA. *See* Ontario Medical Association
Ontario: definition of employee, 19; dependent contractors in, 22; *Industrial Standards Act*, 151; legislation in, 188; privatization in, 25; *Re Telegram Publishing Co. Ltd and William Amm and Others*, 38; service-delivery model, 27
Ontario Advisory Council for Disabled Persons: attendant-care allowance, 98; *Independent Living: The Time Is Now*, 99

Ontario government: administration of Self-Managed Care, 126; client as direct employer, 179
Ontario *Human Rights Code*, 123–4; right to equal treatment, 219n97; and self-managers, 129
Ontario Labour Relations Act (OLRA), 21, 132; bargaining units and, 113; definition of dependent contractor, 105–6; definition of employee, 105; labour legislation, 96
Ontario Labour Relations Board (OLRB), 45, 49, 178; carriers as employees, 53; and certification of *Star* carriers, 29–30; criteria, 132–3; employee or independent contractor relationship, 106–7; employer for the purposes of the act, 132; jurisprudence, 132; and Nucleus Housing Incorporated, 126–7; Nucleus Housing Incorporated and SEIU, Local 204, 110; nurses as dependent contractors of the CACC, 108; *Star* carriers, 182; status of dependent contractors, 43; teamsters' union and *Toronto Sun*, 48
Ontario Medical Association (OMA), exclusive bargaining agent for doctors, 185
Ontario Ministry of Citizenship, 125
Ontario Ministry of Culture and Recreation, 125
Ontario Ministry of Health, 125
Ontario Ministry of Labour, Employment Standards Branch, 39
Ontario Public Service Employees Union (OPSEU), 99; and Community Care Access Centre (CCAC), 106; organizing personal-care workers, 115
OPSEU. *See* Ontario Public Service Employees Union
Organization for Economic Co-operation and Development (OECD), 5

Organization of Rural Mail Couriers (ORRMC), 58, 80; agreement to join CUPW, 86–7; dissolution of, 88; established, 78; first general members' meeting, 81
organized labour, disability activists, 99
organizing, 49–50; commitment of resources, 50; difficulties and successes with, 116–17; newspaper distribution workers, 49
ORRMC. *See* Organization of Rural Mail Couriers
Ottawa Citizen, and newspaper delivery drivers, 43–4
Ouellet, André, 62, 70, 95; appointment as president of Canada Post, 91; *Canada Post Corporation Act,* subsection 13(5), 84
Outreach Attendant Services (Outreach), 98, 116; CAW, Local 40, 115; compared to Self-Managed Care, 101; health and safety issues, 120; task flexibility, 122; work schedule of, 102
outsourcing plan: complaint before the OLRB, 53; strike action by carriers, 53–4
own-account self employed, 9, 14; freelance editors, 144; personal-care workers, 102
owner-drivers, and collective bargaining, 19
owner-operators, and collective bargaining, 19

Pacific Press, 45, 49, 51–2
Palmer, Bryan, 21
parity principle, 172, 183–6; principle of equal treatment, 184–5
part-time employees, 48
patronage, and rural contracts, 59
Patterson, Cynthia, 87; and rural couriers demands, 84; Rural Dignity, 83
pay equity, 119

people with disabilities, 26, 27, 133; definition of care, 102; dispute resolution, 182; home-care program, 98; inadequate funding for, 121–2; living options of, 97–8; and twenty-four-hour back-up services, 129; vulnerability of, 104
performers, 187
Periodical Writers' Association of Canada (PWAC), 162, 165
personal-care services, 96, 189; individualized funding impact, 114; multiple clients or multiple jobs of workers, 114; options, 98–9
personal-care workers, 20, 26, 27, 97, 176, 184, 192; and CAW, 178; and collective bargaining, 105–14; definition of, 212n1; direct funding threat, 181; dispute resolution, 181–2; employed by non-profit agencies, 178, 182; employment relationship and OLRA, 111; housekeeping tasks, 122–3; in private homes, 3–4; right to bargain, 181; small workplaces of, 112; vulnerablitity of, 179; work of, 101–2
persons of colour, 123–4; and systemic discrimination, 10
petit bourgeoisie, 6–7
Philippines, child-care workers from, 104
Playwrights' Union of Canada (PUC), 162, 163, 165
plurality of representational forms, 172, 186; principle of, 184–5
politics, and reforms, 172
Porter, Mr Justice, 40–2
postal employee, definition of, 61
Post Office Act, 61
postmasters: employee status of, 59; social status of, 59
power and authority, 6
precarious contract workers, employee status, 47
precarious employment, 14; freelance editing, 138–42; of personal-care work, 101; at risk, 54
precarious self-employed: and collective bargaining rights, 59; vulnerability of, 179
precarious status: artists, 148–53; of freelance editors, 136, 140
precarious workers, 21, 55; collective bargaining, 34, 133; evaluating the SAA model, 167; newspaper distribution, 31–4; risks and difficulties of organizing, 94
PricewaterhouseCoopers, report on distribution costs, 52
printing trades, unions in, 47
private sector: collective bargaining legislation, 22; labour relations, 31
privatization: Conservative government policy of, 100; impact on female paid workers and unpaid caregivers, 100; of personal care, 97–101
producers' associations, 152–3
professional artists, limits of collective bargaining rights, 165
professional employee: under *Canada Labour Code*, 144; excluded categories of, 145
professionals, 7; under *Canada Labour Code*, 143; definition of, 137; exclusion of from collective bargaining, 174–5
property rights, 24–5, 50–4
public policy, 173
public sector: contracting out in, 25; organizing in, 112; workers, 173
Public Service Staff Relations Act, 62, 148, 169
publishers, and contracting out, 179
PUC. See Playwrights' Union of Canada
PWAC. See Periodical Writers' Association of Canada

Quebec: *Collective Agreement Extension Act*, 147, 151; decree system, 190; labour legislation in, 182–3; legislation in, 188; rural route contractors in, 63–4; self-employed artists in, 168; status of the artist in, 147

race/ethnicity, 176; personal-care workers, 97, 103
racism, 123–4; and workers and clients/consumers, 121
Radwanski, George, 80; review of Canada Post's mandate, 80
Rainbird, Helen, 7
Raymond, Gilles, 64
Recommendation on the Status of the Artist, 146
Reform Party, 84
reforms, 32; and legislation, 183–6, 190
representivity issue, 160
residential-care workers, 129–30; under ESA, 220n104
restructuring, 50–4, 179; Canada Post, 57; employers and, 31, 54; of long-term care, 99; personal-care-service-delivery model, 27
retail industries, collective bargaining and, 112
Revenue Canada, and self-managers, 128
right of association, 173
Roltek Holdings Inc., 39
RSMCs. *See* rural and suburban mail carriers
Rural Dignity, 64, 74, 80, 83
Rural Mail Delivery Service in Canada (Canada Post), 68
rural route mail carriers, dispute resolution, 182
Rural Route Mail Carriers of Canada, Local 1801, 67, 71–4; application for certification, 71; motion to dismiss Local 1801, 73

rural route mail couriers, 3–4, 14, 24, 176; bargaining unit structure, 180–1; *Canada Labour Code*, 20; collective bargaining rights, 26; and CUPW, 178; as employees, 57–8, 67; employee status of, 68, 84; fight over right to represent, 66; legal status, 79, 95; negotiating issues of, 88–9; organizing of directly into CUPW, 87; right to bargain collectively, 208n81; right to organize, 88; second campaign, 75–94; status of prior to 2004, 56–7; temporary technical assistants (TTAs), 88; third campaign drive, 85–94
rural and suburban mail carriers (RSMCs): CUPW and Canada Post, 92–4; CUPW exclusive bargaining representative of, 93; immediate benefits, 93; justifications for excluding from labour protection, 94–5; new name of, 92; working conditions of, 60. *See also* rural route mail couriers
rural and suburban mail couriers (RSMCs), readiness to join CUPW, 86
Rutledge, Mr Justice, on legal definition of employee, 36
Ryerson University, publishing program, 163

Sabourin, Lynda, rural route mail courier, 201n6
St. Joseph (Missouri) News-Press, newspaper carriers as employees at, 38
SARTEC. *See* Société des auteurs de radio, télévision et cinéma
Saskatchewan: right to organize in, 177; self-employed artists in, 168
scale agreements, 148, 150, 151, 153, 168, 169; artists' associations, 152–3; producers' associations, 152–3
scheduling, OLRB's consideration of, 108

Schous, Leslie, 87
scientific management, and newspaper circulation, 33
Seattle, newsboys unions in, 32–3
SEIU. *See* Service Employees International Union
self-employed: artists, and collective bargaining legislation, 148; as category, 6; contractors, 124, 176, 187; defining characteristics, 7; distinguished from employees, 6; income differences among, 11
self-employed workers, 4, 171, 177; as employees, 177; entitlement of to collective bargaining, 171–2; exclusion of, 175; inequality, 177; legal support for, 172; small business, 187
self-employment, 13; changing nature of, 7; entrepreneurship, 176; growth of, 9; by immigrant status and sex, and visible minority status and sex, 28t; by immigrant status, visible minority status, and sex, 11f; range in, 5; renaissance of, 5; as share of total employment, own-account, and employers, 10f
self-insurance systems, 13
Self-Managed Care, 101; compared to SSLUs and Outreach, 101; Direct Funding, 96–7, 99, 104, 124–33; drawbacks of working under, 131
self-managers, 124, 127–30; functional flexibility of, 219n92
Semiahmoo Management: organizing drives of carriers, 49; unfair labour practice complaint against, 45
servant, under *Occupational Health and Safety Act*, 219n99
service-delivery model, 27
Service Employees International Union (SEIU), 99; Nucleus Housing Incorporated and, 110; organizing personal-care workers, 115

service industries: collective bargaining and, 112; workers in, 113
Shipton, Rosemary, 163
Siren, Paul, 146
Siren-Gélinas Task Force, 146–7, 148
Sisters of St. Joseph, 216n48; personal-care workers at, 111
Small Business Protection Act (US), 36
social inequality, 104
social justice groups, 172
social location, 8, 12
Social Security Act (US), exclusion of minors from, 35
Social Support Living Units (SSLUs), 98, 115–16; CAW, Local 40, 115; compared to Self-Managed Care, 101; health and safety issues, 120; and housekeeping, 123; task flexibility, 122
social wage legislation, 40, 42–3
Société des auteurs de radio, télévision et cinéma (SARTEC), 162, 165
socio-economic status: personal-care workers, 97, 101–4; professional artists, 146; rural route mail couriers, 58–61
sole proprietors, and workers' compensation, 42–3
Southern Ontario Newspaper Guild, 29
Speller, Bob, *Canada Post Corporation Act*, subsection 13(5), 74
Spinney, Barbara, rural route mail courier, 201n6
Springer, Jane, 141
SSLUs. *See* Social Support Living Units
Standing Committee on Communications and Culture, 148, 151
Standing Committee on Consumer and Corporate Affairs and Government Operations, 74
statistics, self-employment in Canada, 8–14
Statistics Canada: child-care and home-support workers data, 102; data on

self-employment, 5; definitions of self employed, 13
Status of the Artist Act (SAA), 27, 136, 138, 150, 153–67, 157, 179–80; bargaining model and scale agreements, 26; and *Canada Labour Code*, 143–5; and CAPPRT, 151; certifications, 187; collective bargaining rights, 137, 145–53; EAC/ACR and subsection 23(I), 157; and federal government collective bargaining, 168; freelance editors and, 180, 190; multi-employer bargaining, 184; origins of, 146–8; professional artists, 168; professional in, 137; profound limits of model, 167; renewable licenses, 187; representation without majority support, 184; royal assent, 148; scale agreements, 168, 183, 187; section 6(2)(b)(i), 157, 166; section 6(2)(b)(ii), 157, 158, 160, 161; section 6(2)(b)(iii), 161; section 9(2), 149; section 18(b), 155; section 23(I), certification prerequisites for, 151; shape of, 148–53
statutory exclusion, independent contractors, 38
strikes: dispute resolution and, 181–2; launched by Local 40, 118; wage increases and extended benefits from, 118
subcontracting, publishers, 221n9
Supreme Court of Canada: *Advance Cutting and Coring Ltd*, 230n5; agricultural workers, 202n9, 207n70; couriers appeal Federal Court of Appeal's decision, 71; *Dunmore v. Ontario (AG)*, 88; employment status and discrimination, 73; on freedom of association, 79, 86, 174

Taft-Hartley Amendments of 1947, 36–7
Task Force on Labour Relations, 19
Task Force on the Status of the Artist (1986), 146
Tax Court of Canada, 40; *Thomson Canada Ltd (Winnipeg Free Press) v. Canada (Minister of National Revenue)*, 40–2
taxicab drivers, and collective bargaining law, 18
Taylorism, 113
teamsters' union, and *Toronto Sun*, 48
Telegram (Toronto), 39
Telegram Publishing Co. Ltd and William Amm and Others, 38–9
Thompson, Mark, 39
Thomson Canada Ltd (Winnipeg Free Press) v. Canada (Minister of National Revenue), 40
Thomson newspaper chain, 46
Times Herald Record, 38
Tingley, Darryl, unionization of rural couriers, 78
Toronto: bargaining units in, 116; licensing of street vendors, 32; newsboy unions in, 32–3; precarious social location, 103
Toronto Star, 80; bargaining units in, 49; contracting out, 52, 53, 54, 179, 180; delivery of to homes, 3; distribution costs, 52–3; and its carriers, 43–4; newspaper distribution shift to adult carriers, 34; organizing drive at, 29–30; outsourcing, 53, 54; property rights of, 50–1
Toronto Star carriers, 20, 26, 176; CEP organizing, 46; contracting out, 25; dispute resolution, 181–2; newspaper carriers, 3; separate bargaining unit for, 180
Toronto Sun, and teamsters' union, 48
Trade Union Act (1872), 173
trade unions, 172
Treaty of Versailles, 1919, 15
truck drivers, and collective bargaining law, 18
TWUC. *See* Writers' Union of Canada

UNEQ. *See* Union des écrivaines et écrivains québécois
UNESCO, *Recommendation on the Status of the Artist*, 146
unfair labour practices, 21–4
Union des artistes, 146
Union des écrivaines et écrivains québécois (UNEQ), 162, 165
union organizers, access to workers, 50–1
unionism, 186; industrial model of, 16, 25
unionization, 104; of newsboys, 32–3; on-call workers, 119; part-time workers, 119; at periphery of public sector, 112–13; rural route mail couriers, 57–8, 63–75; shift workers, 119; of small workplaces, 112–13
unions: and access to workers, 22; and benefits for part-time employees, 119; and choice of individual workers, 123; in Europe, 23; exclusive bargaining rights of, 23; as obstacles to restructuring, 179
United Auto Workers (UAW), and motor-route carriers, 37–8
United Kingdom, self-employed in, 7, 11
United Parcel Service (UPS): allegations of NAFTA violations by Canada Post, 85; NAFTA complaint against Canada Post, 90–1
United States: collective bargaining in, 33; employment status in, 35; geographical unionism in, 189; rural route couriers unionized in, 78; union organizing in, 32–3; working conditions of letter carriers in, 60
United States National Administrative Office, refusal of to accept CUPW's submission, 82
United States Postal Service (USPS), 60
United States Supreme Court, 36; *Hearst Publications Inc. v. National Labor Relations Board*, 36, 39

USPS. *See* United States Postal Service

Vancouver, organizing newspaper carriers in, 34
Vancouver Province, 45, 49
Vancouver Sun, 45, 49
Villeneuve, André, 70
visible minorities, 10; average annual incomes, 12; and lack of power of personal-care workers, 103; type of self-employment by, 28t
voluntarist model, collective bargaining system, 50

wage rates: freelance editors, 139; increase in, 118; at periphery of public service, 114; personal-care workers, 103; range of, 119; Self-Managed Care, 125–6; self-managers, 128, 130–1
Wagner model of industrial relations, 146
waitresses, 113
Weber, Max, 6
WGC. *See* Writers' Guild of Canada
White, Robert, 83
Wiebe, Mavis, rural route mail courier, 201n6
Winnipeg, organizing newspaper carriers in, 34
Winnipeg Free Press (WFP), 40–1, 46; MRN ruling on carriers, 40; strike at, 50
women: as adult newspaper carriers, 34; care work, 103; and individualization of the care model, 104; own-account self-employment, 9, 10; part-time work, 197n7; as personal-care workers, 101; precarious employment of, 101; push-pull factors of self-employment, 12–13; as rural route mail couriers, 60; and self-employment, 8; and social location, 12
women of colour, personal-care workers, 103

workers: categories of in self-managed care, 131–3; and conflict with clients/consumers, 118; employees of agencies, 124; employment security of, 191; and people with disabilities, 134; reasons for organizing, 117; as self-employed contractors, 130–3
workers' associations, 191
workers' compensation, 42
Workers' Compensation Act, 129
working conditions: difficulties and successes with ensuring good, 117–24; work refusals, 217n73, 217–18n74
workplace: apartment as, 119; definition under OHSA, 120
Workplace Hazardous Materials Information System Act, 147
Workplace Safety and Insurance Act, 128
Workplace Safety and Insurance Board (WSIB), 108, 129; scope of employment, 43
writers, tensions between editors and, 140; who are authors, 167
Writers' Guild of Canada (WGC), 162, 163, 165
Writers' Union of Canada (TWUC), 136, 162–3, 165; application of for judicial review, 161, 224n37; intervener before tribunal, 156; opposition of to EAC/ACR certification, 154; opposition to EAC/ACR's application, 156
WSIB. *See* Workplace Safety and Insurance Board